بِسْمِ ٱللَّهِ ٱلرَّحْمَٰنِ ٱلرَّحِيمِ

*Also by Maulana Wahiduddin Khan*

The Prophet of Peace
*Tazkiyah:* The Purification of the Soul
What is Islam
Islam As It Is
Religion and Science
A Treasury of the Quran
Woman in Islamic Shari'ah
Islam and Modern Challenges
Islam: Creator of the Modern Age
Words of the Prophet Muhammad
Islam: The Voice of Human Nature
An Islamic Treasury of Virtues
Words of the Prophet Muhammad
Woman Between Islam and Western Society
Islam and the Modern Man
Muhammad: A Prophet for All Humanity
Islam and Peace
Principles of Islam
The Call of the Quran
The Quran An Abiding Wonder
No End to Possibilities
The Good Life
The Way to Find God
The Teachings of Islam
The Garden of Paradise
The Fire of Hell
Indian Muslims
Tabligh Movement

# GOD ARISES

Evidence of God
in Nature and in Science

**Maulana Wahiduddin Khan**
Translated by Farida Khanam

Malay version: *Islam Menjawab Tantagan Zaman*
Malayalam version: *Islam Velluvilikkunnu*
Sindhi version: *Jadid Ilm Jo Challenge*
Turkish version: *Islam Meydan Okuyor!*
Arabic version: *Al-Islam Yatahadda*
Urdu version: *Mazhab aur Jadid Challenge*

First published 1985
Reprinted 2016
© Goodword Books 2016

Goodword Books
A-21, Sector 4, NOIDA-201301, India
Tel. +91-8588822675, +91120-4314871
email: info@goodwordbooks.com
www.goodwordbooks.com

Chennai
Mob. +91-9790853944, 9600105558

Hyderabad
Mob. +91-7032641415

Printed in India

# Contents

Preface • 7

Challenge of Modern Knowledge • 9

Review • 21

The Method of Argument • 49

Nature and Science Speak about God • 69

Argument for the Life Hereafter • 113

Affirmation of Prophethood • 151

The Challenge of The Quran • 171

Religion and Society • 231

The Life We Seek • 257

A Final Word • 277

Index • 281

# Preface

The title of this book was inspired by a verse from the Bible:

> Let God arise, let His enemies be scattered:
> Let them also that hate Him flee before Him.
> As smoke is driven away, so drive them away:
> As wax melteth before the fire, so let
> the wicked perish at the presence of God.
> But let the righteous be glad; let them rejoice
> before God: yea, let them exceedingly rejoice.
>
> Psalms 68:1-3

This is one of those passages in the Bible which prophesy the revolution that was to be brought about by the Prophet Muhammad, upon whom be peace. Before his time, pantheism and polytheism had held sway all over the world. From Noah to Jesus, prophets and reformers had been sent by God to the world where they appealed to the people to renounce their evil practices and in particular, to reject polytheism and to worship only one God. But it was never more than a tiny minority which responded to the call of God's messengers, and that is why a civilization with its roots in ploytheism continued to dominate throughout the known world of the time.

It was then that God sent His final messenger, Muhammad, upon whom be peace, with exactly the same message as had been brought by his predecessors. As he was to be the last in the chain of prophets, God decreed that he should not only bring revelation to mankind, but should, with divine assistance, be successful in extirpating the practice of polytheism once and for all.

This event did indeed take place through the instrumentality of the Prophet, and it is to this that the above mentioned biblical quotation alludes.

This monotheistic revolution continued to predominate for one thousand years. Then history witnessed a new age—the age of atheism. It was in the 18th and 19th centuries that it reached its culminating point. During this epoch, it was asserted, on the strength of scientific findings, that modern research had destroyed the foundations of religion quite definitively. It is this claim which has thus been expressed by a certain atheist: "Science has shown religion to be history's cruelest and wickedest hoax."

But today, that very same weapon—science—which was supposed to have brought religion to an ignominious end, has at last, been turned against the scoffers and atheists and we are, at the moment, witnessing the same momentous revolution in thinking as took place in the seventh century with the advent of the Prophet of Islam. God Himself has razed the walls of atheism to the ground and science stands ready to bear out His word.

This book is an attempt to describe and explain this new revolution. It strives, moreover, to demonstrate how 20th century research has, on academic grounds, totally demolished the atheistic claims put forward in the 18th and 19th centuries.

In the seventh century, God had opened up new possibilities which were at once availed of by the Prophet of Islam and his companions. As a result, monotheism attained intellectual dominance and the polytheism of that civilization was banished forever. In a like manner, through a modern scientific revolution, God has once again created new opportunities. If alerted to these trends, people of a religious bent of mind can quickly seize these opportunities, and can certainly turn the tide against atheism and set up monotheism in its place. In so doing, they will ultimately be setting history upon one of the finest courses of our human era.

The Islamic Centre,  
New Delhi.

Wahiduddin Khan  
July 12, 1987

# Challenge of Modern Knowledge

With the splitting of the atom, all of man's conceptions of matter have been drastically altered. In fact, the advance of science in the past century has culminated in a knowledge explosion, the like of which has never before been experienced in human history, and in the wake of which all ancient ideas about God and religion have had to be re-examined. This, as Julian Huxley puts it, is the challenge of modern knowledge. In the following pages, I propose to answer this challenge, for I am convinced that, far from having a damaging effect on religion, modern knowledge has served to clarify and consolidate its truths. Many modern discoveries support Islamic claims made 1400 years ago that what is laid down in the Quran is the ultimate truth, and that this will be borne out by all future knowledge.

> **We still show them Our signs in all the regions of the earth and in their own souls, until they clearly see that this is the truth.**[1]

Modern atheistic thinkers dismiss religion as being unfounded in fact. They maintain that it springs from man's desire to find meaning in the universe. While the urge to find an explanation is not in itself wrong, they hold that the inadequacy of our predecessors' knowledge led them to wrong conclusions, namely, the existence of a God or Gods, the notions that creation and destruction were a function of the godhead, that man's fate was of concern to God, that there was a life after death in heaven or hell, as warranted by the morality of man's life on earth, and that all thinking on these matters must necessarily be regulated by religion. They feel that, in the light of advanced learning, man is now in a position to make a re-appraisal of traditional ways of thinking and to rectify errors of interpretation, just as in secular matters he has already exploded myths and overturned false hypotheses whenever facts and experience have forced the truth upon him.

According to Auguste Comte, a well-known French philosopher of the first half of the nineteenth century, the history of man's intellectual development can be divided into three stages—*the theological stage*, when events of the universe are explained in terms of divine powers, the *metaphysical stage*, in which we find no mention of specific gods (although external factors are still referred to in order to explain events) and the *stage of positivism*, where events are explained in terms of common laws deduced from observation and calculation without having recourse to spirit, God or absolute power. We are now passing through the third intellectual stage which, in philosophical terms, is known as *Logical Positivism*.

## Logical Positivism

Scientific empiricism, or logical positivism, became a regular movement in the second quarter of the 20th century, but as a trend of thought, it had already – long before – taken hold of people's minds. From Hume and Mill up to the time of Bertrand Russell, many philosophers have been its proponents, and it has now become the most important contemporary trend of thought, buttressed as it is by numerous centres of research and propagation all over the world. A dictionary of philosophy published in New York gives the following definition of logical positivism:

> All knowledge that is factual is connected with experiences, in such a way that verification or direct or indirect confirmation is possible (p. 285).

Anti-religionists feel, therefore, that man's recent mental evolution is the very antithesis of religious thinking. Modern, advanced knowledge has it that reality is only that which can stand up to the tests of observation and experience, whereas religion is based on a concept of reality which cannot in this way be subjected to analysis and scientifically proved: it follows then that it has no basis in actuality. In other words, religion gives an unrealistic account of real events. Since man's knowledge was limited in ancient times, the correct explanations of natural phenomena were bound to elude him. This being so, the suppositions he made which hinged on religion were distinctly far-fetched and, at best, tangential. But, thanks to the universal law of evolution, man has at last emerged from the darkness in which he was engulfed, and now, in the light of modern knowledge, it is possible for him to discard odd, conjectural beliefs and arrive at the true nature of things by purely empirical methods. T.R. Miles writes:

> It might be said that metaphysicians of the past have done something comparable to writing a cheque without adequate funds in the bank. They have used words without proper 'cash' to back them; they have been unable to give their words 'cash-value' in terms of states of affairs.
>
> 'The Absolute is incapable of evolution and progress' is a grammatically correct sentence; but the words are like a dud cheque, and cannot be 'cashed'.[2]

All those things, which were formerly attributed to supernatural forces, are now wholly explainable in terms of natural causes, modern thinking having it that the "discovery" of God was a mere assumption arising from ignorance. With the spread of knowledge, this belief has automatically disappeared. Julian Huxley writes:

> Newton showed that God did not control the movements of the planets. Laplace in a famous aphorism affirmed that

astronomy had no need of the god hypothesis; Darwin and Pasteur between them did the same for biology; and in our own century, the rise of scientific psychology and the extension of historical knowledge have removed gods to a position where they are no longer of value in interpreting human behaviour and cannot be supposed to control human history or interfere with human affairs.[3]

Physics, psychology and history have proved conclusively that all those events which man explained in terms of the existence of a God or gods, or some abstract 'Power' had entirely different causes, but that man, steeped in ignorance, continued to speak of them in terms of religious mystery.

In the world of physics, Newton is the hero of this revolution. It was he who put forward the theory that the universe is bound by certain unchangeable principles, there being certain laws according to which all celestial bodies revolve. Later, many other scholars carried this research forward to the point where all events on earth and in the heavens allegedly took place according to the immutable "Law of Nature."

After this discovery, it was but natural that the concept of an active and omnipotent God as the power, which made things

move appeared meaningless. At the most this discovery allowed for a God who had initially set the universe in motion. Therefore, Newton himself, along with other like-minded scientists, believed in God as the Prime Mover. Voltaire for his part said that God had created the universe in just the same way as a watch-maker made a watch, assembling the parts, arranging them in a particular order, but afterwards having

12 • *God Arises*

nothing to do with it. Hume subsequently abolished this "inactive and worthless God" by advancing the argument that we had seen watches being made, but that since we had not seen the world in the process of creation, it was not possible for us to believe in God.

Atheists maintain that the progress of science and the expansion of knowledge had enabled man to observe that which was beyond his observation in the past. Being in the dark about chains of events, we had not been in a position to understand isolated events. Now, equipped with knowledge, we no longer stood in awe of natural phenomena. For instance, the rising and setting of the sun are now understood as matters of common knowledge. But in early times these events seemed inexplicable, and man supposed that there must be a God who was responsible for them. This led to the acceptance of there being a supernatural power: he described whatever was beyond man's knowledge as a miracle wrought by that power. But now that we know the rising and setting of the sun is the result of the earth's revolving upon its axis, where is the need to believe that there is a God who makes the sun rise and set? Similarly, the functioning of all other things, which had been attributed to some invisible power, purported, according to modern studies, to result from the action and interaction of the natural forces now known to us. That is, after the revelation of natural causes, the need to posit, and to believe in the existence of God, or a supernatural force, vanished of itself. If the rainbow is merely a reflection of sunlight in minute droplets of water in the air, it is not in any way a sign placed in the sky by God. If the plague is inevitably an outbreak of this disease it can no longer be looked on as a sign of divine wrath. If animals and plants have slowly evolved over hundreds of millions of years, there is no room for a 'creator' of animals and plants, except in a metaphorical sense quite different from that in which the word was originally and is now normally used. If hysteria and insanity are external symptoms of disordered minds, there is no place left in them for possession by devils. Citing such events in support of his argument, Julian Huxley

observes with great conviction: "If events are due to natural causes, they are not due to supernatural causes."[4]

He holds that their ascription to Supernatural Beings is merely due to man's ignorance combined which his passion for some sort of explanation. Subsequent research carried out in the field of psychology further strengthened this point of view, as it revealed that religion is the creation of man's subconscious self rather than the discovery of some external reality. In the words of a western scholar: "God is nothing but a projection of man on a cosmic screen." The concept of another world was nothing but "a beautiful idealisation of human wishes." Divine inspiration and revelation were merely an "extraordinary expression of the childhood repressions."

All these ideas are based on the premise that there is something called the subconscious. Modern research has revealed that the human mind is divided into two major parts, one being termed the conscious mind, the centre of those of our ideas, which take shape in a state of consciousness. The other part is the subconscious. In this part of the mind, ideas are not usually alive in the memory, but exist below the surface and find expression either in abnormal circumstances, or in sleep, in the form of dreams. Most human thoughts are buried in this subconscious cell, the conscious part of the mind being the smaller part. The subconscious is like the eight-ninths of the iceberg, which remain below water, while only one ninth, the conscious part is visible. After extensive research in psychology, Freud discovered that, during childhood, certain happenings and ideas are repressed in our unconscious minds, which can later result in the irrational behaviour of adults. The same applies to the religious concepts of the hereafter, heaven, hell, etc., which are but echoes of those very wishes which were born in the child's mind but never fulfilled, circumstances being unfavourable, and consequently, repressed in the subconscious. Later, the subconscious, for its own satisfaction, supposed the existence of a dream world in which its unfulfilled wishes would be realized, just as, deep in sleep, one dreams of wishes coming miraculously true. When childhood fancies, which had been thoroughly repressed, suddenly burst through to the surface, producing a state of frenzy or hysteria, or other abnormal behaviour, people mistakenly attributed this to supernatural forces which had found expression in human language. Similarly, the generation gap and the 'Father complex' in a family gave rise to the concept of God and slave. Thus what was simply a social malaise was carried to the cosmic scale in order to forge a theory. In the words of Ralph Linton:

> The Hebrew picture of an all-powerful deity who could only be placated by complete submission and protestations of devotion, no matter how unjust his acts might appear, was a direct outgrowth of this general Semitic family situation. Another product of the exaggerated superego to which it gave rise was the elaborate system of taboos relating to every aspect of behaviour. One system of this sort has been recorded and confided in the Laws of Moses. All Semitic tribes had similar series of regulation differing only in content. Such codes provided those who kept them with a sense of security, comparable to that of the good child who is able to remember everything that his father ever told him not to do and carefully abstains from doing it. The Hebrew Yahveh was a portrait of the Semitic father with his patriarchal authoritarian qualities abstracted and exaggerated. Such a judicial concept which

believes in God being a political authority has occupied a central place not only in Judaism, but is also incorporated in the religious concepts of Christianity and Islam as well.[5]

The third argument against the reality of religion is provided by history. Anti-religionists maintain that it was the particular historical circumstances in which man found himself which gave birth to religious concepts. In ancient times, before the discoveries of modern science, man had no means of saving himself from natural calamities, such as floods, storms and epidemics. Frequently finding himself in insecure positions, he pictured to himself extraordinary forces which could be invoked in times of need, which could be trusted to come to his rescue in the face of disaster and which would act as a panacea of all ills. In order that society might be well-integrated and its members firmly focussed around one central point, a cohesive force was needed. Deities of one sort or the other fulfilled these needs and man then began to worship such gods as were considered superior to all human beings and whose favours had to be sought as a matter of religious duty by all individuals. The *Encyclopaedia of Social Science* has this to say:

> Political and civic forces also permanently influence the development of religion. The attributes and the names bestowed upon the gods automatically change in accordance with the form of the State. The God as King is merely a transposition of the human as king, the divine kingdom merely a transposition of the earthly kingdom. Moreover, since the prince or king is supreme judge, the deity is likewise clothed with the judicial function and vested with the final decision as to human guilt or innocence (7, p.233).

Thus the condition of a particular historical

period and the interaction of the human mind with prevailing circumstances have given birth to concepts which are collectively known as religion. Religion is a product of the human mind resulting from ignorance and a sense of helplessness in the face of external forces. Julian Huxley sums it up thus: "Religion is the product of a certain type of interaction between man and his environment."[6]

Since that particular environment which was responsible for bringing about this interaction has either disappeared or is disappearing, there is no further justification for the perpetuation of religion. To this Huxley adds:

> The concept of God has reached the limits of its usefulness: it cannot evolve further. Man to carry the burden of religion created supernatural powers. From diffuse magic *mana* to personal spirits; from spirits to gods; from gods to God— so crudely speaking, the evolution has gone. The particular phase of that evolution which concerns us is that of God. In

one period of our Western civilization the gods were necessary fictions, useful hypotheses by which to live.[7]

The Communist philosophy too holds religion to be a historical hoax. Since Communism studies history exclusively in the light of economics, to it, all historical factors were offshoots of the economic situation. It holds that it was the feudal and capitalistic systems prevailing in the past that had led to the birth of religion. Now that these outdated systems are dying a natural death, religions should also be treated as dead along with it. As Engels puts it, moral concepts, in the last analysis, are the product of contemporary economic conditions. Human history is the history of class wars, in which the ruling classes have been exploiting the backward classes, and religion and morals were invented to provide an ideological basis for safeguarding the interests of the ruling class. According to the Communist Manifesto, laws, morals, and religion—all are the fraudulent innovations of the Bourgeoisie under the cloak of which most of its vested interests are hidden.

Addressing the third All-Russia Congress (October, 1920) Lenin had said that of course, they did not believe in God. They knew very well that the church authorities, landlords and bourgeois who spoke with reference to God, were simply interested in safeguarding their own interests as exploiters... They denied all such moral laws, as had been borrowed from a Super-human power, or were not based on the concept of class. They called this a hoax, an illusion, the befogging of the minds of farmers and labourers in order to serve the interests of landlords and capitalists. They asserted that their moral code was subject to the class struggle of the Proletariat alone, the source of their moral principle being the interest of the class-struggle of the Proletariat.[8]

This is the case put forward by the antagonists of religion, on the basis of which a large number of people in our modern age have rejected religion. An American professor of psychology sums it up thus: "Science has shown religion to be history's cruelest and wickedest hoax."[9]

# Notes

1. Quran, 41:53.
2. *Religion and the Scientific Outlook*, George Allen & Unwin Ltd., p. 20.
3. *Religion without Revelation*, New York, 1958, p.58.
4. *Ibid*, pp.18-19.
5. Ralph Linton, *The Tree of Culture*, 1956, p. 288.
6. Julian Huxley, *Man in the Modern World*, p. 130.
7. Ibid, *Man in the Modern World*, p. 134.
8. Lenin, *Selected Works*, Moscow, 1947, Vol.II. p. 662.
9. C.A. Coulson, *Science and Christian Belief*, p. 4.

# Review

An account has been given in the preceding pages of those anti-religionist arguments which are generally put forward in order to prove that modernity leaves no room for religion.

Let us first examine the argument which is based on research carried out in the field of the physical sciences, i.e. that studies of the universe have shown that whatever events take place, do so in accordance with specific laws of nature. This argument would have it that there is no necessity to assume the existence of an unknown God in order to explain these events, since known laws already exist to explain them. The best answer to this argument is the one given by a Christian theologian: 'Nature is a fact, not an explanation.'

Physicists, of course, are right in saying that they have discovered the laws of nature, but what they have discovered is not, in essence, the answer to the problems for whose solution religion has come into existence. It is religion which points towards the real causes of the creation of the universe, whereas the findings of physicists are confined to determining the outward structure of this universe as it appears to exist before us. What modern science tells us is only an elaboration upon, rather than an explanation of reality. The entire body of modern scientific enquiry is concerned only with the question: 'What is it that exists?' The question: 'Why does it exist?' is far beyond its purview. Yet it is upon this second issue that we should be seeking enlightenment.

To illustrate this point, let us consider how a chick comes into this world. The embryo develops inside the smooth, hard shell of an egg, then the chick emerges when the shell breaks up. How does it come about that the shell breaks up at the right moment and the fledgling, which is no more than a small lump of flesh find its way into the outer world? In the past, the obvious answer was: 'It is the hand of God.' But now, microscopic studies have shown that on the completion of twenty-one days, when the chick is ready to emerge, there appears on its beak a small hard horn with which this 'lump of flesh' is able to break through the walls of its shell. The horn, having done its job, falls off a few days later. This observation, from the point of view of the anti-religionists, contradicts the old concept that it is God who brings the chick out of the shell, because the microscope has clearly shown that a 21-day law exists which is responsible for creating conditions which make it possible for the chick to emerge from the shell. This is a mere fallacy. What modern observation has done is to add a few more links to the chain of factors which lead up to an event. It does not tell us the real cause of the occurrence. It has just shifted the problem of the breaking up of the shell to the development of the horn. The breaking of the shell by the chick is simply an intermediate stage in the occurrence rather than its cause. Will the cause of the event be understood only when we learn what made the horn appear on the chick's beak? In other words, when we have traced the event back to its primary cause, the cause which 'knew' that the chick required some hard instrument to break through the shell and, therefore, in exactly twenty-one days, compelled a hard substance to appear on the beak in the form of a horn and to fall off after having discharged its function?

'How does the shell break?' was the question that faced man previously. Now, in the light of recent observations, instead of an answer, we have another question: 'How does the horn develop?'

In the context of perceived phenomena there is no difference in the nature of these two questions. At the most, questions of the type that lead us from one link to another in the chain of cause and effect, demand an extension of the observation of facts, if they are to be answered at all. On this basis, they do not elicit any valid explanation. The American biologist, Cecil Boyce Hamann, has this to say:

> Where the mysteries of digestion and assimilation were seen as evidence of Divine intervention, they now are explained in terms of chemical reactions, each reaction under the control of an enzyme. But does it rule God out of His universe? Who determined that these reactions should take place, and that they should be so exactly controlled by the enzymes? One glance at a present-day chart of the various cyclic reactions and their interaction with each other rules out the possibility that this was just a chance relationship that happened to work. Perhaps here, more than any place else, man is learning that God works by principles that He established with the creation of life.[1]

From this, one can understand the actual value of modern discoveries. Science and technology having vastly increased the practicability and precision of human observation, it has been possible to deduce the natural laws that bind the universe and according to which it functions to perfection. For instance, in ancient times, man simply knew that drops of water fell out of the clouds on to the earth. But now the whole process of rainfall is widely understood, from the evaporation of sea-water to the precipitation of rain and the final journeying of the fresh water back to the sea. But the kind of understanding brought by these discoveries is nothing but the possession of more highly detailed information, which does not tell us ultimately why these physical processes take place. Science does not tell us how or why the laws of nature came into being, how or why they continue to exist or why they cause the earth and the heavens to function with such unfailing precision that, simply by observing of them, it was possible to establish immutable scientific laws. The claim that by learning the laws of nature one could arrive at an explanation of the universe was a mere delusion. It provided an answer to the question, but it was an irrelevant one in that it accepted the intermediary physical links in the chain as primary causes. As Cecil Boyce Hamann so aptly says, 'Nature does not explain, she is herself in need of an explanation.'

'Why is blood red in colour?' If you were to ask a doctor the reason, he would answer, 'Because your blood contains millions of little red discs (5 millions to each cubic centimeter), each some seven thousandths of an inch in diameter, called the red corpuscles.'

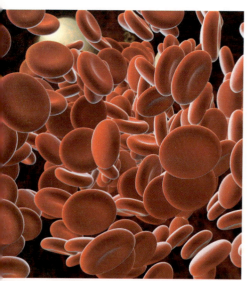

'Yes, but why are these discs red?'

'Because they contain a substance called haemoglobin, which, when it absorbs oxygen from the lungs, becomes bright red. That is why the blood in the arteries is scarlet. As it flows through the body, the blood gives up its oxygen to the organs of the body and the haemoglobin becomes brownish—this is the dark blood of the veins.'

'Yes. But where do the red corpuscles with their haemoglobin come from?'

'They are made in the spleen.'

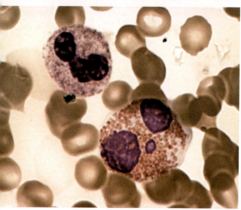

'That's marvellous, Doctor. But tell me, how is it that the blood, the red corpuscles, the spleen, and the thousand other things are so organised into one coherent whole, work together so perfectly that I can breathe, run, speak, live?'

'Ah! That is nature.'

'Nature!'

'When I say "nature," I mean the interplay of blind physical and chemical forces.'

'But, Doctor, why do these blind forces always act as if they were pursuing a definite end? How do they manage to coordinate their activities so as to produce a bird which flies, a fish which swims, and me.... who ask questions?'

'My dear friend, I, a scientist, can tell you how these things happen. Do not ask me why they are like that.'

While there is no gainsaying the fact that science has set up for us a vast storehouse of knowledge, this dialogue clearly shows that it has its limits. There is a point beyond which it can offer no further explanations. Its discoveries then fall very far short of giving us the kind of answers provided by religion. Even if the quantum of scientific discoveries were increased by billions, the necessity for religion would in no way be obviated, for such discoveries throw light only on what is concrete and observable. They tell us what is happening. They do not provide answers to the question, 'Why is it happening?' and 'What is the primary cause?' All such discoveries are of an intermediate, subsidiary and non-absolute nature.

If science is to replace religion, it shall have to discover the ultimate and absolute explanation. Let us take the example of a machine which is functioning without our being able to see how it works, because it is enclosed in a metallic casing. When we remove this casing, we can see how the various cogwheels move in conjunction with a number of other parts of the mechanism. Does this mean that, in discovering the mechanics of the thing, we have truly understood the cause of its motion? Have we really grasped its secrets? And does the possession of knowledge about the functioning of a machine give us proof that it is self-manufacturing, self-replicating and works automatically? If the answer to this is 'No,' then how do a few glances at the mechanism of the universe prove that this entire system came into existence unaided and of its own accord, and is continuing to function independently? Criticizing Darwinism, A. Harris made a similar remark: 'Natural Selection may explain the survival of the fittest but cannot explain the arrival of the fittest.'[2]

Now take the psychological argument, which holds that far from being a reality, the concept of God and the life hereafter is a myth, a mere fiction, a stretching of the human personality and human wishes to the cosmic scale. I fail to understand what possible basis there can be for this claim. Moreover, if I were indeed to claim that human personality and human wishes did, in fact, exist on a cosmic plane, I doubt if my antagonists would have sufficient factual data to refute my claim.

If we are to talk of scales, let us see what is happening at the atomic level, where we are dealing with infinitesimally small distances. According to the Bohr theory, an invisible atom possesses an internal structure similar to our solar system, with electrons revolving around a nucleus in the same way that planets revolve around the sun. How vastly different the scales,

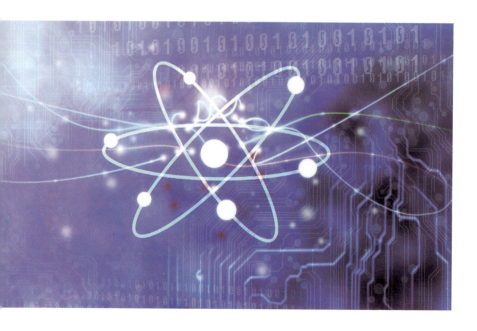

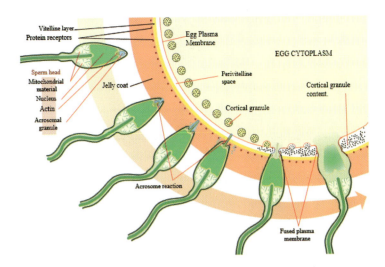

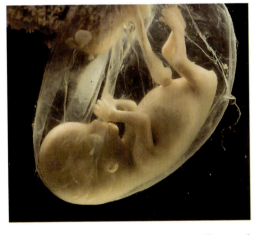

for in the solar system, distances are measured in millions of miles. Yet, in spite of the scales being so different as to boggle the imagination, the systems are exactly the same. Would it be any wonder then if the consciousness, which we as human beings experience existed on a cosmic scale but in a totally perfect form? As an intellectual exercise, it is no more difficult to accept this, than to accept the notion that genes, although only microscopic elements in the human embryo, control the growth and development of a six-foot-tall man. Might not the human and natural desire for a world immeasurably vaster than our own be an echo—spiritual and other-worldly—of a world already existing in this universe in a form invisible to human eyes?

Psychologists are right in holding that sometimes ideas are repressed in our minds during childhood, which erupt at a later stage in an extra-ordinary form. But to infer that it is this very

characteristic in humans which has given birth to religion is to jump to wrong conclusions. It is a misinterpretation, if not an actual distortion of a perfectly ordinary fact. It is as if observing a potter designing an image of clay, I deduce that it must be he who has created human beings. Image-making and the creation of the human body differ from each other in so qualitative a fashion that to draw any parallels with God's creativity would be utterly preposterous. It is only minds which see fit to make such analogies which look upon religion as a result of the inchoate ramblings of mentally deranged individuals.

It is a general weakness of modern thought that it jumps to extraordinary conclusions on the basis of facts which carry no weight from the logical point of view. An emotionally disturbed individual may babble abnormally under the influence of thoughts repressed in the unconscious, but how does this prove that the knowledge of the universe revealed to the prophets is also a 'babbling' of the same nature—a 'miracle' of the unconscious? It is possible to accept incoherence in sleeping and in waking as the result of mental disturbance, but to assert that this is the true source of divine revelation is to descend to illogical and unscientific argument. It merely shows that those who reason in this way are hard put to find any other criterion by which to judge the extraordinary words of the prophets. It does not follow that because agnostics possess only one yardstick by which to measure reality, there exists, de facto, one and only one such yardstick.

Let us suppose that a group of creatures who possessed the faculty of hearing, but not that of speech, landed on earth from a distant planet. On hearing the conversation and discourses of human beings they started to investigate sound. What was it, and where did it come from? In the course of their research, they came across a tree whose branches, being interlocked, produced grating, squeaking noises because of the friction accidentally created by sudden, squally winds. As soon as the wind stopped blowing, the noise stopped too. This phenomenon was repeated with each gust of wind. Now an 'expert' from amongst them, on careful observation of this phenomenon, conveyed telepathically that the secret of human speech had been discovered, namely, that the teeth in the upper and lower jaws in the human mouth were responsible for producing sound. When the upper and lower teeth came close together – causing friction – a sound was produced called human speech. The friction between two objects does, in fact, produce sound, but just as it is incorrect to explain the origin of human speech by referring to this friction, it is likewise ludicrous to explain prophetic words as garbled utterances welling up from a deeply troubled unconscious.

The thoughts suppressed in the unconscious mind are mostly those reprehensible wishes which could not be realized for fear of social and familial castigation. For instance, if someone felt a desire to have incestuous relations with his sister or his daughter, he should repress such feelings, lest their expression should bring down upon him the full weight of social censure. Similarly, if anyone felt inclined to commit murder, the fear he would have of being put behind bars and the ensuing feelings of frustration would very likely cause him to repress his initial impulses.

In other words, the wishes suppressed in the unconscious are mostly such evil designs as could not be realized for fear of punishment and or social ostracism. Now, if the subconscious part of the mind of a mentally disturbed person begins to find an outlet, what is likely to come gushing out of it? Obviously the afflicted person will talk incoherently while attempting to give expression to those same hostile feelings and evil desires which had remained suppressed in his subconscious. And, if we are to think of him as a prophet, it will be as a prophet of evil, certainly not of good. Religious thoughts expressed in prophetic diction are, by comparison, virtue and purity par excellence. The true prophet is himself the epitome of virtue and his purity in thought, word and deed has no parallel. His ideas, moreover, exercise such a powerful influence upon people that the very society from which at one time the prophet had initially to conceal his ideas—out of fear—is now so greatly attracted towards them, that even after a lapse of centuries together, it still steadfastly adheres to them.

From the psychological point of view, the unconscious mind is actually a vacuum. In it, nothing initially exists. It receives all impressions through the conscious part of the mind. This implies that the unconscious stores only those experiences to which people have been exposed at one time or the other. The unconscious can never become a repository for facts which have not been experienced. But surprisingly, religion as proclaimed by the prophets, contains truths which were previously unknown to them and for that matter, to the entire human race. It was only with the advent of the prophets that certain facts could be propagated. Had the unconscious been the repository on which they drew, they could not have become the purveyors of great, but unknown truths which they were.

The religion proclaimed by the prophets contain a great body of knowledge, touching in one way or the other all branches of learning, such as astronomy, physics, biology, psychology, history, civilization, politics and sociology. No individual, however gifted, whether drawing on the conscious or subconscious minds, has ever been able to produce such an all-embracing discourse, free from erroneous decisions, vain conjectures, unreal statements, miscalculations and unsound logic. But religious scriptures are admirably and miraculously free of such deficiencies. In their approach, reasoning and decisions, they encompass all of the human sciences. Over the centuries, succeeding generations have sifted through the finding of their predecessors, examined them, considered them from all angles, and often disproved and rejected what their forebears had considered truths as firm as rocks. But the truths which are enshrined in religion remain unchallenged to this day. So far, it has not been possible to point out a single error, or even discrepancy in them worth the name. Those who have ventured to attack the bastions of religion have eventually been forced to fall back without scaling its battlements, for they themselves have finally been proved to be in the wrong.

At this point, I think it would be pertinent to give the gist of an article in which James Henry Breasted, an astronomer, has claimed, beyond all question of doubt, to have discovered a technical error in the Quran. He points out that, among the West Asian nations, age-old custom and the dominance of Islam in particular, gave currency to the lunar calendar, and that Muhammad (peace be on him) carried the difference between the solar and lunar years to the furthest extreme of absurdity. Breasted claims that he was so ignorant of the nature of the problems of a calendar that, in the Quran, he categorically prohibited the addition of intercalary months. The so-called lunar year of three hundred and fifty four days lags behind the solar year by eleven days. This being so, during the course of each of its cycles, it exceeds the solar year by one year in every 33 years, and by three years in every century. If a religious practice such as fasting, (in the month of Ramadan) falls at this time in June, then after six years it will fall in April. Now (in 1935 A.D.) 1313 years have elapsed since the migration which initiated the Hijri era. Each century of ours consists of 103 years according to the Lunar year of the Muslims. After 1313 years of the Solar Calendar, the Muslim Calendar records approximately 41 years more. In this way, the Hijri era of Muslims, at the time of this writing has reached upto 1354, i.e., according to the solar scale, there is an addition of 41 years in 1313 years. The Jewish church of the oriental countries have done away with this type of absurdity, and have adopted the practice of intercalation, thus bringing its lunar calendar in line with the solar year. Because of this disparity, the entire West Asia has to suffer from this most antiquated practice of using the lunar calendar.[3]

I shall not at this point go into the intricacies of the solar and lunar calendars. I would merely point out that the charge of 'extremely absurd ignorance' levelled against the Prophet of Islam is based upon a misunderstanding of the Quran, and is, therefore, without foundation. It is not 'intercalation' which is prohibited by the Quran, but the practice of *nasa'* (9:37). *Nasa'* in Arabic, means delay, i.e. to postpone, or place in a different order. For example, if an animal is drinking at a fountain and you take it away and put your own animal on its place so that it may drink first, this would amount to an unwarrantable seizure of a privilege. In Arabic, this act of placing animals in different order or replacing animals would be termed: نَسَاءُ الدابة

This interpretation of the expression has a direct bearing on the ordering of the Islamic calendar, with special reference to the four months out of the twelve designated as sacred by the Prophet Abraham (blessings on him). These months were known as Zu'l-Qa'dah, Zu'l-Hijjah, Muharram and Rajab, during which fighting and bloodshed were totally prohibited. People could then travel about freely, knowing that they could carry on their trading in complete safety. They could also go on the Hajj pilgrimage without fear of brigandage.

However, at a later period, when rebellious tendencies were

beginning to make themselves felt among the Arab tribes, the latter devised the custom of postponement in order to evade this law. Whenever any powerful Arab tribe was determined to do battle during the month of Muharram – which was a sacred month – the tribal chief would declare that they had deleted Muharram from the list of sacred months and had replaced it with the month of Safar, which was now to be regarded as sacred. This practice of tampering with the sacred months was called *nasa'* and it is this practice which the Quran has called 'an act more ignoble than infidelity,' for it gave tamperers an undue advantage over others, who would obviously hesitate to fight during the sacred months.

Certain scholars have written that it was the general practice among Arabs to regard particular years as consisting of fourteen months instead of twelve. A commentator of the Quran, Abdullah Yusuf Ali, points out that: The intercalation of a month after every three years as practised by some nations in order to make an adjustment in the calculation of months does not come under the heading of *nasa'*, which is prohibited.

'It also upsets the security of the Month of Pilgrimage. In the verse 9:36 this arbitrary and selfish conduct of the pagan Arabs which abolished a wholesome check on unregulated warfare which is condemned.'

Another commentator, George Sale remarks:

**This was an invention or innovation of the idolatrous Arabs, whereby they avoided keeping a sacred month, when is suited not their convenience, by keeping a profane month in its stead;**

transferring, for example, the observance of Muharram to the succeeding month, Safar.

This clearly shows that, even in an age of ignorance, the Prophet of God said nothing that 'smacked of ignorance.' Had his words emanated from his unconscious mind, he would inevitably have uttered such words as would have revealed such ignorance.

Scholars who study religion in the context of history or the social sciences suffer from the fundamental drawback of not looking at religion in the correct perspective. In doing so, their views become thoroughly distorted. They are like people who stand in a crooked position in order to look at a square, and, viewing it from an acute angle, decide it is rectangular. The square is still a square, it is just that the viewers' standpoint is wrong, or merely irrelevant.

It was from just such a skewed angle that T.R. Miles asserted that 'the religion is the product of a certain type of interaction between man and his environment.' The basic mistake these scholars make is to study religion as an objective issue (Julian Huxley, *Man in the Modern World*, p. 129). That is, they collect indiscriminately all the historical material that goes under the name of religion, and then form an opinion about religion in the light of whatever material has come their way. Thus they take up a wrong position at the very outset.

Miles' summing up is that 'religion' like any other subject, can be treated as an objective problem, and studied by the method of science. The first step is to make a list of the ideas and practices associated with different religions—gods and demons, sacrifice, prayer, belief in a future life, taboos and moral rules in life. It is like making a collection of animals and plants. Science always begins in this way, but it cannot stop at this level; it inevitably seeks to penetrate deeper to make an analysis.

This analysis may take two directions. It may seek a further understanding of religion as it now exists, or it may adopt the historical method and search for an explanation of the present in the past.

With regard to the historical approach, it is clear that religion like other social activities evolves. Further, its evolution is determined by momentum, its inner logic and the influence of the material and social conditions of the period. As an example of the first, take the tendency from polytheism towards monotheism: granted the theistic premise, this tendency seems almost inevitably to declare itself in the course of time.[4]

Religion consequently comes to be regarded as a mere social process, rather than as a revelation of reality. That which is a revelation of reality is an ideal in itself, and its history with all its manifestations has to be studied in this light. On the other hand, that which is only a social process has no inherent ideal. The response of society alone determines its position. Anything which enjoys the status of a social norm or social tradition can retain its position so long as society gives it a de facto status. If society discards it and adopts any other practice in its place, then its historical interest only can survive and its importance as a social tradition falls into oblivion.

But the case of religion is vastly different from this. As the eminent physician, Fred Hoyle puts it, "This moral or religious impulse, whatever we choose to call it, is extraordinarily strong. When faced by opposition, and even by powerful political attempts at suppression, it obstinately refuses to lie down and die. One often comes on statements that religion is a primitive superstition that modern man can well do without. Yet if the impulse were truly primitive in a biological sense (as for instance patriotic loyalty to the group in which one happens to live is primitive) we would surely expect to see it in other animals. As far as I know, no one has advanced any evidence for this idea. The religious impulse appears to be unique to man, and indeed to have become stronger in pre-history the more advanced man became in his intellectual attainments. Admittedly, the trend has reversed over the recent past, but the change over the past two centuries may well prove to be impermanent… Stripped of the many fanciful adornments with which religion has become surrounded, does it not amount to an instruction within us that expressed rather simply might read as follows: You are derived from something "out there" in the sky. Seek it and you will find much more than you expect."[5]

We cannot, therefore, study religion in the same fashion as we take stock of our household goods, modes of conveyance, clothing, housing, etc. This is because religion is an entity in itself, which is either accepted, rejected or accepted in a partial or distorted form by society of its own freewill. As a result, religion remains the same in its essence while assuming a diversity of forms which evolve according to the practices of particular societies. It is wrong, therefore, to classify all the different forms of religion prevalent in different societies under the common heading of "religion." We shall illustrate this with reference of democracy.

Democracy is a system of government by the people, directly or by representation, and a country may be said to be truly democratic only when its political organization abides by this criterion. Now if an approach to the understanding of democracy is made by examining all those countries who call their governments democratic, and then trying by a process of induction to form a clear picture of it on the basis of whatever common denominators present themselves, the image which will emerge, rather than being crystal clear, will be like muddied water stirred up by some floundering animal. Democracy, as a term, will then be meaningless. Consider the democracies of Britain, America, China and Egypt. Do they really have anything in common? In what way is the democracy of India similar to the democracy of Pakistan? The term democracy becomes even more confusing if all the varieties of democracy in the world today are placed within an evolutionary framework. A study of the development of democracy in France—its very birthplace—will show that at a later stage of its evolution, it was synonymous with the military dictatorship of General de Gaulle (1890-1970).

Such a study of religion, in which the process of induction is unlikely to yield correct results, might well bring one to the conclusion that the idea of God can be dispensed with, because the history of religion presents the example of Buddhism—a religion without a God. Today, the idea is widely advocated that religion should be studied, but that God, as a possibility, should be excluded. Advocates of this course tend to argue that even if religion is necessary for the inculcation of discipline, belief in God should not be regarded as compulsory. They feel that a godless religion serves the same purpose. Citing Buddhism, they maintain that, in the present advanced age, such a form of religious structure is more suitable to the needs of society. To such thinkers, society, along with its political and economic objectives is itself the God of the modern age. 'Parliament is the Prophet of this God, through which He informs mankind of His will, and dams and factories rather than mosques and churches are His places of worship.'[6]

The study of religion by the evolutionary method holds it to be progressing from belief in God to denial of God (e.g. Buddhism). Scholars who adhere to this view first collect all the material which has been attributed over the ages to religion, then, independently of those whose approach is essentially an internal one, they arrange this material in an evolutionary sequence, intentionally omitting any details which might cast doubt on its validity.

For instance, after extensive research, anthropologists and sociologists 'discovered' that the concept of God began with polytheism and, progressing gradually, was developed into monotheism. But, according to them, this cycle of evolution has turned in the reverse direction, turning the concept of monotheism into contradiction. The concept of a 'multiplicity of gods,' according to them, at least had a certain intrinsic value in that, while putting their faith in 'different gods,' people could live in harmony, acknowledge the existence of the gods of other communities. But the doctrine of 'one God' has naturally negated all other gods and their believers, thus giving birth to the concept of a 'Higher Religion' which, in turn, gave rise to unending wars among the various groups and nations. Thus the concept of God, having evolved in the wrong direction, has dug its own grave in accordance with the law of evolution.[7]

The fact that the concept of God started with monotheism has been totally omitted in this evolutionary sequence. According to known history, Noah (blessings on him) was the first prophet who, it has been established, exhorted people to believe in one God. Moreover, 'Polytheism' does not mean a multiplicity in the absolute sense, as is commonly understood. No nation has ever been 'polytheist' in the sense that it believed in many gods of the same order. In fact, polytheism implies a hierarchy with one 'Supreme God' at the top and his entourage of demi-gods spreading downwards from Him on the rungs of the divine ladder. Polytheism has always carried with it the concept of a 'God of gods'. This shows how baseless are the claims of this so-called evolutionary religion.

The Marxist approach to history is even more bereft of meaning, being based on the hypothesis that it is economic conditions alone which are the real factors which shape man. According to Marx, religion came into existence in an age of feudalism and capitalism. Since these systems were tyrannical and fostered exploitation, the moral and religious concepts which evolved under them had, of necessity, reflected their environment. They were no more than doctrines which condoned and upheld exploitation. But this theory does not, academically, carry any weight. Nor does experience testify to it. This theory, based on a total denial of the human will, regards man simply as a product of economic conditions. Like the soap-cakes manufactured in a factory, man is moulded in the factory of environment. He does not act with an independent mind, but simply conforms to

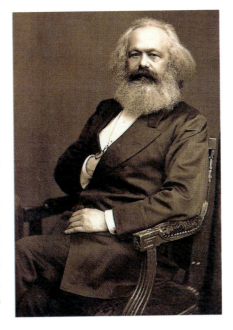

*Review* • 39

whatever conditioning he has been subjected to. If this were an incontrovertible fact, how could it have been possible for Marx himself the product of a 'capitalist society,' to revolt against the economic conditions prevailing in his time? If the contemporary economic system gave birth to religion, why not believe then, according to the same logic, that Marxism too is the product of the same conditions? If the stand taken by Marxism on religion is correct, why should this not be applicable to Marxism itself? It follows that this theory is absurd. There is no scientific and rational proof to support it.

Experience too has exposed the false premises of this theory. The example of the U.S.S.R., where this ideology has been predominant for the last sixty-five years, will serve to illustrate our point.

It has been claimed for a long time now that material conditions in the Soviet Union have changed. The system of production, exchange and distribution have all become non-capitalistic. But after the death of Stalin, it was admitted by the Russian leaders themselves that Stalin's regime was one of tyranny and coercion, and that the masses had been exploited in the same manner as in capitalist countries. It should be borne in mind that it was absolute control of the press by the government which made it possible for Stalin to project his tyranny and exploitation as justice and fair play to the rest of the world. As the press is still under complete government control, we must infer that the same drama, which was staged with such success in Stalin's times, is still going on today under the cloak of blatantly misleading propaganda. The 20th Congress (February 1956) of the Russian Communist Party exposed the tyrannical acts of Stalin. It will not be surprising if the 40th Congress of the party brings to light the barbarity of his successors. This half-a-century old experience clearly shows that the systems of production and exchange have nothing to do with the shaping of ideas. Had the human mind been subservient to the system of production, and had ideas taken shape in accordance with it, a communist state like Russia ought, strictly speaking, to have curbed the tendencies to oppress and exploit. Thus the whole argument of the modern age is nothing short of sophistry in the garb of scientific reasoning—a patchwork, a hotchpotch of discordant elements. Of course, the 'Scientific Method' has been adopted to study these 'facts,' but this, by itself, cannot arrive at the correct results. Other essential factors must be taken into account. That is to say, that, if the scientific method is applied, but applied only to half-truths and one-sided data, in spite of its ostensible bona fides from the intellectual standpoint, it is bound to yield results which are far from being accurate.

Here is an apt illustration of this point. In the first week of January, 1964, an International Congress of Orientalists held in New Delhi, was attended by 1200 participants. On this occasion, one of the orientalists read a paper in which it was claimed that several of the Muslim monuments of India had actually been built by the Hindu Rajas and not by the Muslim rulers. The paper claimed that the Qutb Minar, a tower, known to have been built by Sultan Qutbuddin Abek, was originally 'Vishnu Dhwaj', a symbol of Lord Vishnu built by Samudra Gupta 2300 years ago. 'Qutb Minar' was a misnomer, the brainchild of Muslim historians of a later period. The main argument in support of the claim was that the stones used in the construction of the Qutb Minar were very ancient and that their carvings had been done centuries before the period of Qutbuddin Abek. Prima facie, the argument is scientific in that such ancient stones are to be found in the structure of the Qutb Minar. But the study of the Qutb Minar with reference only to its stones cannot give support to any truly scientific argument. Over and above this, several other aspects of the question have to be borne in mind, the most important one being that old stones from the ruins of ancient buildings were often used in new structures by subsequent builders, including the Muslims. This, together with the Qutb Minar's architectural design, the technique of placing the stones in position, the incomplete mosque in the vicinity of the tower, the remaining traces of the parallel tower, plus other pieces of similar historical evidence, points to Sultan Qutbuddin as being the actual builder, and shows the orientalist's contentions to be totally fallacious. The theories of the anti-religionists are no better. Just as in the above example, an attempt has been made to make a show of 'scientific' reasoning by a willful misinterpretation of the presence of certain ancient stones, similarly, by presenting certain half-truths and a large number of irrelevant facts viewed from a distorted angle, the enemies of religion claim that their so-called scientific method of study has actually done away with religion. On the contrary, if the factual data on the subject is studied in its entirety and from the correct angle, an entirely opposite conclusion will most certainly be arrived at.

Indeed, the veracity of religion is proved by the fact that even the most intelligent of thinkers begin to talk nonsense when they refuse to make any reference to religion. Do away with religion and you do away with the essential framework within which your problems may be discussed and solved. Most of the scholars whose names figure on the list of anti-religionists are very intelligent and learned persons. These geniuses have

entered the arena of religious debate, equipped with the most valuable of contemporary sciences. But judging from the poor performance of these 'intelligent' people, one wonders what had so blighted their minds that they should have committed such absurdities on paper. Their outpourings are notorious for their waverings, contradictions, tacit admissions of ignorance and 'reasoning' which is, to say the least of it, haphazard. They make tall claims on flimsy grounds with an almost total disregard for facts. Their case must unquestionably fall to the ground, because it could only be a false case which is 'supported' by such erroneous statements and patently flawed arguments. A case which had the slightest merit would never be beset by such serious shortcomings.

The picture of life and the universe which takes shape in our minds on accepting religion is a very beautiful and gladdening one. This in itself establishes the truth of religion and the falsity of anti-religious theories. It conforms to the noble ideas of man in the very same way as the material universe is echoed in

mathematical formulae. On the contrary the picture of reality which forms in consonance with an anti-religious philosophy is completely out of step with the human mind. On this point, J.W.N. Sullivan has made a very pertinent quotation from Bertrand Russell:

> That man is the product of such causes which had no prevision of the end they were achieving; that his origin, his growth, his hopes and fears, his loves and beliefs, are but the outcome of accidental collocations of atoms; that no fire, no heroism, no intensity of thought and feeling can preserve an individual life beyond the grave; that all labours of the ages, all the devotion, all the inspiration, all the noon-day brightness of human genius, are destined to extinction in the vast death of the solar system. And that the whole temple of man's achievement must inevitably be buried beneath the debris of a universe in ruins. All these things, if not quite beyond dispute, are yet so nearly certain that no philosophy which rejects them can hope to stand.[8]

This extract sums up the irreligious, materialistic school of thought. According to such thinking, our prospects in life are darkened by gloom and despair. The materialistic interpretation of life also dispenses with any definite criterion for the judgement of good and evil. It justifies the dropping of bombs on human beings, the use of flame-throwers and chemical warfare, to name but a few of the scourges of modern times. This is not considered outrageous, tyrannical or bestially aggressive. After all, human beings have to die one way or another. Religious thought, by contrast, affords a glowing ray of hope, giving to both life and death a joyous and meaningful radiance. In this way it fulfills our psychological needs. When a scientist propounds a theory, which is found to conform to mathematical formula, he is convinced that what he has discovered is a reality. Similarly, when religious concepts find a harmonious echo in the human psyche, this is a proof that this was the reality which human nature was in search of. It gives us such a sense of fulfillment that we are left with no real grounds for denying its truth. To quote the words of Earl Chester Rex, an American mathematician:

> I use the accepted principle in science which governs the choice between two or more conflicting theories. According to this principle, the theory which explains all the pertinent facts in the simplest way is adopted. This same principle was used, long ago, to decide between the Ptolemaic, or earth-centered theory and the Copernican theory which claims that the sun is the center of the solar system. The Ptolemaic theory was so involved and so much more complicated than the Copernican that the earth-centered idea was discarded.[9]

I admit that this argument would not be regarded as foolproof by many. The concept of God and religion will never fit into the narrow frame of their materialistic minds. Yet their dissatisfaction is not really due to any lack of sound reasoning behind religion—of that I am satisfied. No, the actual reason for their disaffection is that their prejudiced minds are not prepared to accept religious reasoning. Sir James Jeans, at the end of his book, *The Mysterious Universe* correctly remarked: 'Our modern minds have a sort of bias in favour of the materialistic explanation of the facts' (p. 189).

In his book, *Witness*, Whittacker Chambers tells of how he was watching his little daughter one day, when he found that he had unconsciously become aware of the shape of her ear. He thought to himself how impossible it was that such delicate convolutions could have come about by chance. They could have been created only by premeditated design. But he pushed this thought out of his agnostic mind, because he realized that the next step in logical sequence would have to be: design presupposes God—a thesis he was not yet ready to accept. With reference to this incident, Thomas David Park, a research chemist, formerly Chairman of the Department of Chemistry, Stanford Research Institute, writes: 'I have known many scientists among my professors and research colleagues who have similar thoughts about observed facts in chemistry and physics.'[10]

'Scientists' of the 'Modern' age are agreed upon the theory of evolution. This concept is becoming dominant in all scientific fields. An enchanting idol of spontaneous evolution has been set up in place of God. If the truth were told, the very dogma of organic evolution, from which all of the evolutionary concepts have been borrowed, is nothing but a hypothesis without any evidence. But this is not all. Some scientists have openly confessed that if they believe in the concept of evolution, it is simply because they can find no other alternative.

Sir Arthur Keith[11] (1866-1955) said in 1953 that evolution was unproved and unprovable and that we believed in it only because the only alternative was special creation and that was unthinkable.[12]

Scientists are thus agreed upon the validity of the evolution theory simply because, if they discard it, they will be left with no option but to believe in the concept of God.

I confess that it is beyond my power to satisfy those scholars whose bias in favour of materialistic reasoning is so strong that they are unable to keep their minds open to self-evident facts. There is a particular reason for the bias, about which George Herbert Blount, an American physicist has this to say:

> **Conviction of the reasonableness of theism and the tenuousness of atheism usually in itself does not cause a man to accept practical theism. There seems to be an almost innate suspicion that the recognition of Deity will somehow rob one of freedom. To the Scholar, who cherishes intellectual liberty, any thought of abridged freedom is especially dreadful.**[13]

In much the same vein, the concept of prophethood has been described by Julian Huxley as an 'intolerable demonstration of superiority.' That is, the acceptance of someone as a prophet implies his elevation to such a high status that his word becomes the word of God, giving him, in consequence, the right to impose his will on the people, the right to make people accept his word as law. But then that is what it means to be a prophet, and when man is the creature and not the Creator, he is in the position of being the humble slave of God, and not God, how can this situation be changed or avoided simply on the basis of concepts which are the result of ignorance or wishful thinking?

Cressy Morrison asks with reason in his book, *Man Does not Stand Alone*, 'How much must man advance before he fully realises the existence of a Supreme Intelligence, grasps His goodness that we exist, assumes his full part in destiny and strives to live up to the highest code he is capable of understanding without attempting to analyse God's motive, or describe His attributes?'

Things are as they are. We cannot change the hard reality: we simply have to acknowledge it, accept it, bow to it. Now, if we are not to adopt an ostrich-like attitude, our best course is to believe in actuality, rather than deny it. By denying the truth, it is man who loses. His denial of the truth in no way alters, harms, or diminishes it. The truth is the truth.

## Notes

1. *The Evidence of God in an Expanding Universe*, p. 221.
2. A. Lunn, *Revolt Against Reason*, p 133.
3. *Time And Its Mysteries*, New York, 1962, p. 56.
4. T.R. Miles, *Religion and the Scientific Outlook*.
5. Fred Hoyle, *The Intelligent Universe*, p. 233.
6. Julian Huxley, *Religion without Revelation*.
7. Julian Huxley, *Man in the Modern World*, p. 112.
8. J.W.N. Sullivan, *Limitations of Science*, p. 175.
9. *The Evidence of God*, p. 179.
10. *The Evidence of God in an Expanding Universe*, edited by John Clover Monsma, (New York, 1958), pp. 73-74
11. Anatomist and physical anthropologist who specialized in the study of fossil man. A doctor of medicine, science, and law, Keith became a professor at the Royal College of Surgeons of England, London (1908), was professor of physiology at the Royal Institution, London (1918-23), and was rector of the University of Aberdeen (1930-33).
12. *Islamic Thoughts*, December 1961.
13. *The Evidence of God*, p. 130.

# The Method of Argument

## The Line of Argument

The modern age versus religion is basically a case of reasoned argument versus the acceptance of revelation. Modernity has it that religious beliefs and dogmas do not pass muster when subjected to tests devised by the most advanced methods of scientific reasoning. Today's apprehension of reality is through observation and experiment, but since religious beliefs concern the supra-rational sphere of existence, they are thus considered unverifiable. Arguments in their favour are based entirely on assumption and inference: this being so, they are declared to have no acceptable scientific basis. In his book *Religion and the Scientific Outlook*, T.R. Miles writes:

> It might be said that metaphysicians of the past have done something comparable to writing a cheque without adequate funds in the bank. They have used words without proper 'cash' to back them; they have been unable to give their words 'cash-value' in terms of state of affairs, 'The Absolute is incapable of evolution and progress' is a grammatically correct sentence; but the words are like a dud cheque, and cannot be 'cashed.'

This statement purports to show that the claims of religion are unfounded as they are neither based on any valid argument, nor scientifically demonstrable; religion belongs strictly to the domain of faith, and reality is considered verifiable as such only when it is external to this domain.

But this case against religion has itself no basis in fact. It should not be forgotten that the modern method of reasoning does not insist that only those things which can come under direct observation have a real existence. A scientific supposition which is based on direct observation can also be as much a fact as the result of scientific experiment. We cannot, however, say that a scientific experiment is always right simply because it is an experiment, just as we cannot take it that a scientific supposition is wrong, simply because it is a supposition. Either has the possibility of being right or wrong.

The distinguished physicist, Robert Morris Page, makes the important point that the "test of a hypothesis involves the establishment of conditions consistent with the hypothesis to produce results predicted by the hypothesis *on the assumption that the hypothesis is true.*" He then goes on to narrate an incident which clearly bears this out:

> When ships were built of wood because it was commonly believed that in order to float they had to be built of materials lighter than water, the proposition was made that ships could be built of iron and still float. A certain blacksmith stated that ships built of iron could not float because iron would not float, and he proved his point by tossing a horseshoe into a tub of water. His assumption that the hypothesis was untrue foreclosed the possibility of his devising an experiment consistent with the hypothesis, which might have produced the result, predicted by the hypothesis. Had he assumed the hypothesis to be true, he would have tossed an iron wash basin into the tub of water instead of an iron horseshoe.[1]

To all intents and purpose, the blacksmith had conducted an experiment and had arrived at the truth. We must obviously be extremely wary of activities which are said to be experiments and which are, therefore, supposed to produce correct results.

We must also be wary of incomplete or inadequate observation. In the days before high-powered telescopes had been developed, ordinary telescopes revealed distant clusters of heavenly bodies as masses of diffused light. On the basis of such observation, a theory was advanced that those heavenly bodies were actually gaseous clouds undergoing a formative process, which could turn them into stars. But when these bodies were observed later through more powerful telescopes, it was noticed that what had initially appeared as luminous clouds was, in fact, a whole galaxy of completely formed stars which had obviously only appeared gaseous in composition because of its enormous distance form the earth.

It may not be possible to prove the existence of God by observing Him through a telescope, but it should be remembered that we do base our arguments for His existence on the meaningfulness and design of the visible universe. Claude M. Hathaway, the designer of the "electric brain" for the U.S. National Advisory Committee on Aeronautics at Langley Field writes in an essay entitled "The Great Designer" of what he thinks of the rational bases of his belief in a supernatural God. He states, most pertinently that "design requires a designer." As an engineer he had learned to appraise order and to appreciate the difficulties associated with design which brings together the forces, materials and laws of Nature in such a way as to accomplish a desired objective. He had, in short, learned to appreciate the problem of design by being faced with the problems of design.

> It was my job several years ago to design an electric computer that would rapidly solve some complicated equations encountered in two-dimensional stress theory. This problem was solved by an assembly of hundreds of vacuum tubes, electro-mechanical devices, and complicated circuitry, and the completed "brain," in a cabinet about the size of three large pianos, is still in use by the National Advisory Committee on Aeronautics at Langley Field. After working on this computer for a year or two and after facing and solving the many design problems which it presented, it is completely irrational to me to think that such a device could come into being in any other way than through the agency of an intelligent designer.

Now the world around us is a vast assembly of design or order, independent but interrelated, vastly more complex in every small detail than my "electronic brain." If my computer required a designer, how much more so did that complex physio-chemical-biological machine which is my human body—which in turn is but an extremely minute part of the well-nigh infinite cosmos?[2]

It is the perfection of the functioning and intricacy of design of the universe, which brings us to the conclusion that it must be the creation of some divine mind.

Our reasoning does not directly prove the existence of God, but it certainly establishes a credible framework within which one is, of necessity, induced to believe in God. The point must be made that observation and experiment are not absolute sources of knowledge in themselves. Moreover, it must also be accepted that our direct experience and observation alone rarely yield complete knowledge. For instance, if it is claimed that water harbours micro-organisms, this appears to be a very queer assertion. But the moment we look at water through a microscope, it is seen to be true. Similarly, the claim that the earth is round — an inference — must be backed up, not by unaided human observation, but by pictures taken by telescopic cameras from spacecraft.

The modern age had undoubtedly seen the invention of a number of sophisticated instruments, which enable us to experiment and make observations on a much wider and more detailed scale than was hitherto possible. But the things that such devices are able to bring under our observation and within our experience are in themselves superficial and relatively unimportant. What is important is the theory, which is based on them. All the theories later formulated on the basis of these observations and experiments relate to the invisible and, as such, the unobservable. Looked at as a matter of theorizing, the whole of science boils down to an explanation of certain observations. Although theories themselves do not come under observation, the process of observation and experiment compel scientists to believe that such and such facts may be accepted as established.

But the antagonists of religion deny believers the right to affirm the truths by the same scientific methods by which they imagine they have rejected religion. They should then find themselves obliged to concede that religion is a rational matter. It is rather like having an efficient lawyer for the prosecution, but disallowing a lawyer of similar calibre for the defendant just in case the latter should benefit from the legal system! Then suppose we accepted the definition of reality as something which we could directly observe and experience, the claims of the anti-religionists that there is no God, no divine power at the helm of things, would be justifiable only if they could prove that every single thing which was observable in the universe had been observed by them, and that neither God, angels, heaven, nor hell had been discovered. Obviously, they are not in a position to do so. Then what method, or procedure, has provided them with the basis for an argument against religion? Whatever it is, it is not based on the direct observation of religion, but on an explanation of certain observations. For instance, the discovery of gravitation led them to believe that there was no God sustaining the universe, since the law of gravitation was there to explain this phenomenon. It is clear that the observation on which this theory is based is not of the non-existence of God. That is, no telescope has quite finally given us the news that this universe is free from any signs of God. His non-existence had rather been inferred from the observation of quite other events.

I maintain that the method of argument, which is based on inference and has been considered in modern times sufficiently valid to reject religion, can—it would appear paradoxically—provide the soundest proofs of the veracity of religion. The fault does not lie in the principle of the argument used, but in its application. When correctly applied, the result will confound the anti-religionists.

Scientists and materialists should stop and think that they cannot move forward by so much as an inch without using terms like force, energy, nature, laws of nature, etc. But do any of them know what force is, or what nature is? The maximum that scientists have managed to contribute is an interpretative vocabulary by which the invisible causes—unknown and unknowable—of certain known occurrences and manifestations may be referred to. For instance, the electron is unobservable. It is so tiny that neither can a microscope show it, nor a weighing scale weigh it. Yet, in the world of science, the existence of the electron is considered a reality. This is because, although the electron itself is not visible, some of its effects repeatedly come within our experience, and no explanation can be found for them other than the existence of a system like that of the electron. The electron is a supposition, but since the basis of this supposition is indirect observation, science must concede that it exists.

Yet a scientist is unable to offer any explanation of its inner reality, in the same way that a religious man cannot explain God. Both of them in their respective fields harbour a blind faith in an unknowable cause of the universe. According to Dr. Alexis Carrel, "The mathematical universe is a magnificent network of calculations and hypotheses in which there exists nothing but unutterable abstractions consisting only of equations of symbols."[3]

Science does not, and cannot claim that reality is limited only to what enters directly into our experience through the senses. We can see with our own eyes that water is a liquid, but the fact that each molecule of water consists of two atoms of hydrogen and one of oxygen is something which escapes us, because these atoms are not visible. But perceived facts are far from being the only facts we can know. There are facts which we can know of, rather than know. The way to arrive at them is by inference. For instance, we apprehend water by direct perception of its appearance. If I examine a drop of water through a microscope, I can have a better understanding of it. But it is only by inference, and not by direct observation that I can grasp the fact that each molecule of water is composed of two atoms of hydrogen and one of oxygen.

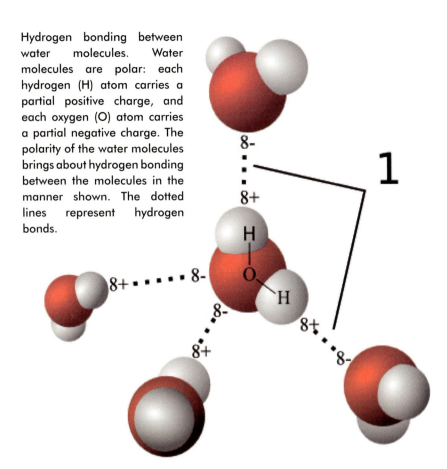

Hydrogen bonding between water molecules. Water molecules are polar: each hydrogen (H) atom carries a partial positive charge, and each oxygen (O) atom carries a partial negative charge. The polarity of the water molecules brings about hydrogen bonding between the molecules in the manner shown. The dotted lines represent hydrogen bonds.

A.E. Mander, in his book *Clearer Thinking*, observes with great pertinence:

> It is useful to reflect that, if we were equipped with different senses, all that we now perceive would be unknowable to us by direct perception. For example, if our eyes were as powerful as a microscope, we should be able to see bacteria. But we could not then perceive elephants. We should be obliged to infer their existence.
>
> Similarly, we now perceive the phenomena, which, being of wavelengths lying within certain limits, are registered by our sense of sight. There are millions of facts we see. Yet if our eyes were differently constructed so that they were turned to

The Method of Argument • 55

long wave-lengths instead of very short ones, then we should have direct sense-perceptions of wireless waves, which now we know only by inference, but we should then have no direct perception of all that part of the universe which is now visible to our eyes. We could only infer it (p. 48).

Later, he goes on to remark:

Of all the facts in the universe of fact, we can know some, relatively few, by sense-perception. But how can we come to know of others? By inference, or reasoning. Inference or reasoning is a mode of thinking by which, staring from something known, we end by forming a belief that there exists a certain fact hitherto unknown.

How can we be sure that there is any validity in this thought-process that we call 'reasoning'? How can we be sure that the belief which we form by reasoning is true?

The answer to this is that we do begin by simply assuming that our methods of reasoning are reliable, that they lead us to conclusions, which correspond with facts. Starting from facts known by sense-perception, we may reason to the conclusion that some other fact, though not yet perceived, exists. We may thus be as sure of an inferred fact as we are of any perceived fact, provided that our original data are perceived facts.

The same method of reasoning leads us to thousands of different conclusions. They are now so highly probable that we can regard them as approximate certainties (p. 49).

This basic principle may be summed up in a single sentence: The reasoning process is valid because the universe of fact is rational (p.50).

The universe of fact is a harmonious whole. All facts are consistent with one another with an astonishing organization and regularity. Therefore, any method of study, which does not bring the harmony and balance among facts into bold relief, cannot be valid. Emphasising this point, Mander observes:

> The perceived facts are only isolated fragments of the universe of fact, only patches of fact. All that we know by sense-perception is partial and patchy, meaningless when regarded by itself. It is only when we come to know more facts—many more than we can directly perceive— that we begin to discover among them the first signs or order, regularity and system.

He makes his point with a very simple example.

> We may perceive a bird, after striking a telephone wire, fall dead to the earth. We perceive that some muscular effort is required to raise a stone form the ground. We perceive the moon passing across the sky. We perceive that it is more tiring to walk uphill than downhill. A thousand perceptions all probably unrelated. Then an inference is made—the law of gravitation. Immediately all these perceived facts, together with this inferred fact, fit together; and so we are able to recognize order, regularity, system, among them all. The perceived facts, regarded by themselves, are irregular, unrelated, and chaotic. But the perceived facts and the inferred facts together make up a definite pattern.
>
> A fact is said to be 'explained' when we are able to show how it fits into a system of facts; when we are able to recognize it as part of a regular, orderly, inter-related whole (p. 51).

Further to this he says:

> Another way of saying that we have explained a fact is to say that we have discovered its meaning. Or we may say we explain it by discovering the cause and conditions of its existence. All this comes to the same thing: we have fitted that fact into a definite pattern of facts; we have recognized its necessary relationship to other facts; and we have ascertained that this particular fact is only an instance of some universal law, or part of the universal order (p. 52).

In the above examples, the law of gravitation, in spite of being an accepted scientific fact, is in no way observable. What

Isaac Newton

scientists have observed with their own eyes, experienced as a matter of sensory perception or measured by scientific instruments is not gravity itself, but certain regularly occuring phenomena caused by gravity which compel them to believe that some force does exist which may be interpreted in terms of a law of gravitation.

It was Newton who first deduced the law of gravitation, and today it is accepted as a scientific fact throughout the world. Newton, in a letter to Bentely, comments on its nature from a purely empirical point of view:

> **It is incomprehensible that inanimate and insensitive matter can exert a force of attraction on another without any (visible) contact, without any medium between them.**[4]

Something which is incomprehensible, because invisible, is today accepted without question as a scientific fact. Why should this be so? The answer is simply that, if we accept it, we can explain some of our otherwise unfathomable observations. It follows that a fact may be accepted as such without its actually having been subjected to observation and experiment. An invisible concept that co-ordinates various observations in our mind and throws further light on known facts is itself a fact of the same degree and quality. Mander comments:

> **To say that we have discovered a fact is to say, in other words, that we have discovered its meaningfulness. Or to put it another way, we explain a thing by knowing the cause of its existence and its conditions. Most of our beliefs are of this nature. In fact they are statements of observation (p.53).**

Mander then broaches the problem of observed facts.

> **When we speak of an observation, therefore, we always mean something more than pure sense-perception. It is sense-perception plus recognition and some degree of interpretation (p.56).**

As John Stuart Mill says: 'We may fancy that we see or hear what in reality we only infer. For instance there is nothing of which we feel more directly conscious than the fact of the distance of an object from us. Yet what is perceived by the eye is nothing more than an object of a certain size and a certain shade of colour.'

Mill further remarks, 'It is too much even to say, "I saw my brother," unless we recognize that such a statement, as statement of observation, includes something more than pure sense-perception. For all that we perceive, strictly, is some object of a certain shape and colouring.

We compare this with memories of the appearance of our brother, then it is only by comparison and inference that we interpret this new sense-perception and judge that we are looking at our brother.

All reasoning is concerned with postulation and testing of theories. Every accepted theory is a statement of a fact about other facts. Whatever we arrive at by inference is a theory. If it can be shown to correspond with actual facts, it is true, and if not, it is false. The theory must fit all the known facts to which it refers, and only then can one proceed to deduce from it hitherto unknown facts.'

According to Mander, 'We may say that finding a theory is like discovering the pattern into which a number of particular facts and the general laws which govern them will fit. It is like putting together the pieces of a jigsaw puzzle from which one or more pieces are missing. When we have fitted together all the pieces available (the known facts), we can see what the missing pieces must be like to enable them to fit into the gaps' (p.123).

On the basis of this very principle, scientists have agreed upon the truth of organic evolution. To Mander, this doctrine has so many arguments in its favour that it may be regarded as an 'approximate certainty.'[5]

The authors of *Science of Life* assert that "no one now denies the truth of organic evolution except for those who are ignorant, or biased or superstitious." New York's Modern Pocket Library has published a series of books entitled *Man and the Universe*, the fifth of which series hails Darwin's *The Origin of Species* as an epoch-making work, and points out that of all theories of genealogy, this one has at one and the same time received the maximum religious opposition and the maximum scientific acclaim.[6]

G.G. Simpson contends that 'the theory of evolution is a fact proved finally and conclusively, and is no more simply a conjecture or alternative hypothesis adopted just for the sake of scientific research.' *The Encyclopaedia Britannica* (1958) accepts organic evolution as a truth and says that after Darwin, this theory has received a general acceptance among scientists and scholars. R.S. Lull writes:

> Since Darwin's day, evolution has been more and more generally accepted, until now in the minds of informed, thinking men there is no doubt that it is the only logical way whereby creation can be interpreted and understood. We are not so sure, however, as to the modus operandi, but we may rest assured that the process has been in accordance with great natural laws, some of which are as yet, unknown, perhaps unknowable.[7]

One can estimate the popularity of this theory by the fact that, in his 700-page book, Lull has summarily dismissed the concept of the special creation of life in just one page and a few lines, whereas the whole of the rest of the book is devoted to the concept of organic evolution. Similarly, the *Encyclopaedia Britannica* (1958) devotes less than a quarter of a page to the concept of creationism, while fourteen pages have been devoted to the concept of organic evolution. Here too, the evolution of life is treated as a fact and it is stated that after Darwin, this concept gained general acceptance among scientists and the intelligentsia.

Now we come to the question of whether this theory, which still receives general acceptance, has been observed by its upholder's own eyes, or its validity demonstrated by experiment. It must be conceded that, todate, this has not been done, nor will it ever be possible to do so. The reasons put forward for this are that the supposed process of organic evolution took place in too distant a past and that, in any case, it is too complicated to be subjected to observation or experiment. This is a 'logical method'—to quote Lull—of explaining the phenomenon of creation.

Then what are those arguments in favour of organic evolution, which have led scholars of this modern age to proclaim the 'truth' of this concept? Here I shall deal with some of their basic aspects.

1. The study of animal life shows that there are inferior and superior species. These range from single-cell life-forms to those with billions of cells. They differ too qualitatively, in terms of their abilities.
2. When this initial observation is correlated with the fossils preserved in the various layers of the earth's crust, it becomes apparent that an evolutionary order exists which correspond to the point in time at which they appeared on earth. The fossils of life-forms that inhabited the earth millions of years ago, although buried in the earth, are still traceable. These reveal that in far distant ages, the animal species living on earth were very simple, but gradually evolved into more complex and developed forms. This means that all of the present forms of life did not come into existence at one point of time; the simpler forms came first and the more developed forms came later.
3. Another feature of the evolutionary process is that, in spite of the difference in species, life-forms are marked by many resemblances in their biological systems. For instance, a fish resembles a bird, a horse skeleton resembles a man's and so on. It follows from this that all the living species have descended from the same family having one common ancestor.
4. How did one species follow another? Did some transmutation take place? It becomes clear when we

think of how an animal gives birth to many offspring, not all of which are uniform in their features, many actually being quite different from each other. These differences develop in the next generation and go on developing according to the process of natural selection. After hundreds of thousands of generations, this difference is increased to the extent that a small-necked sheep turns into a long-necked giraffe. This concept is considered so important that Haldane and Huxley, the editors of *Animal Biology*, have coined the term 'Selection of Mutation' of evolutionary changes.

It is this fourth criterion which is cited to prove the concept of evolution. That is, the supposition, or its effects, need not have come within our direct experience, but such observations have been made as help us to make a logical inference of the truth of the supposition, or, in other words, to verify the truth of the hypothesis.

The advocates of the theory of evolution have not yet, however, carried out any observation of, or experiments on the material basis of this theory. For instance, they cannot show in a laboratory how inanimate matter can give birth to life. The only basis they have for their claim is that the physical record shows that inanimate matter existed before life came into the universe. From this they infer that life came out of inanimate matter, just as a baby emerges from its mother's womb. Similarly, the change of one species into another had not been experienced or observed. Experiments cannot be set up in a zoo to show how the mutation of a goat into a giraffe takes place. The inference that the species did not come into existence separately has been made purely on the basis of the similarities between species and the differences that exist between siblings.

The belief, too, that intelligence has developed out of instinct, implies that man has also evolved from animals. But, in actual fact, instinct has never been seen to develop into intelligence. This is also purely an inference based on geological research which demonstrates that fossils of animals endowed with instincts are found in the lower strata, while those endowed with intelligence are to be found in the upper strata.

In all such arguments, the link between supposition and truth is only one of inference and not one of experiment or observation. Yet, on the basis of such inferential arguments, the concept of evolution in modern times has been considered a scientific fact. That is, to the modern mind, the sphere of academic facts is not limited only to those events which are known by direct experience. Rather, what *logically follows* from experiments and observations can be just as well accepted as established scientific facts as those facts, which come directly or indirectly under our observation.

The statement is, nevertheless, debatable. Sir Arthur Keith, who is himself a staunch supporter of organic evolution, did not regard the theory of evolution either as an empirical or inferential fact, but as 'a basic dogma of rationalism'.[8]

A reputed Encyclopaedia on Science describes Darwinism as a theory based on 'explanation without demonstration.'

Why is it then that an unobservable, and non-demonstrable process is accepted as a scientific fact? Mander writes that it is because:
a) it is consistent with all known facts;
b) it enables scientists to explain vast multitudes of facts which are otherwise inexplicable.
c) it is the only theory devised which is consistent with the facts (p.112).

If this line of reasoning is considered valid enough to bear out organic evolution as a fact, the same formula could well be used to establish religion as a fact. The parallel being evident, it seems paradoxical that scientists should accept organic evolution as a fact, while rejecting religion as having no basis in fact. It is evident that their findings relate, not to the method or argument, but to the conclusion. If something of a purely physical nature is proved by the method of logical positivism, it is immediately accepted by scientists. But if anything of a spiritual nature is so proved it is rejected out of hand, for no better reason than that this conclusion throws them into a state of mental disarray. It does not fit in with their preconceived ideas! The case of the modern age versus religion is, strictly speaking that of predisposition, and not that of particular scientific reasoning.

From the above discussion, it becomes quite clear that it is not proper to regard religion, on the one hand, as being based on faith in the unseen, and treat science, on the other hand, as being based on observation. It must be admitted that science, no less than religion, is ultimately a matter of having faith in the unseen. Scientific findings based on observation are tenable only so long as as they deal with the initial and external manifestations of nature, but when it comes to defining ultimate realities answering the question 'Why'? and not the question 'How?' science must yield pride of place to religion, for it fails to answer this momentous question; it has to fall back upon faith in the unseen, something for which religion in latter times has been much criticized.

Sir Arthur Eddington's view that the table at which the scientists of today are working is, in fact, a set of two different tables, is illuminating.

> I have drawn up my chairs to my two tables. Two tables! Yes; there are duplicates of every object—one of these tables has been familiar to me from my earliest years. It is a commonplace object of that environment which I call the world. How shall I describe it? It has extension; it is comparatively permanent; it is coloured; above all it is substantial, it does not collapse when I lean upon it; it is a thing.

> Table No.2 is my scientific table. My scientific table is mostly emptiness. Sparsely scattered in that emptiness are numerous electric charges rushing about with great speed, but their combined bulk amounts to less than a billionth of the bulk of the table itself.[9]

Similarly, everything has an invisible aspect, which cannot be observed even through a microscope or a telescope. It becomes comprehensible only in terms coined by physicists to fit their

own particular theories. Science does, of course, by means of advanced technology, observe the outward form of things in far greater detail than the naked eye is capable of, but it can never claim to be able to observe the *inner* form of things. Science observes external manifestations, and accordingly forms an opinion about them. So far as discovering the ultimate reality is concerned, science can only learn about unknown facts through facts which are already known.

When a scientist attempts to correlate observed facts in the process of producing a working hypothesis, he resorts primarily to instinctive, belief-like concepts in order to explain, organise and relate his findings. If the hypothesis which emerges from this stringing together of observed facts offers a reasonably satisfactory explanation for all of them, it is regarded as being 'scientific' and, therefore, as credible as an observed fact. It must also be borne in mind that an invisible reality is often regarded as a fact, simply for lack of other hypothesis, which will offer a cogent explanation for it. When a scientist says electricity is a flow of electrons, he does not mean that he has seen electrons flowing through an electric wire by means of a microscope. He merely explains an observed event in terms of the movement of the switch that makes the bulb light, the fans move and the factories run. What has come within our experience is simply an external phenomenon and not, by any means, the event that is being inferred. A scientist, in short, believes in the existence of an invisible fact, after having noted its instrumentality, or impact upon observable phenomena. But we should never forget that every fact that we believe in is always, in the beginning, a simple assumption. It is our making of an inference, which connects the switch and the bulb with one another. Therefore, even after admitting this observed relationship between the switch and the bulb, the fact of whether or not the scientific hypothesis regarding this connection is real or unreal, will still remain in doubt.

It is only later, as further information emerges to support this assumption, that its truth becomes more and more evident, until we feel that our belief has finally been confirmed. If the facts discovered do not support the original hypothesis, we feel justified in discarding it.

An atom provides an irrefutable example of scientists' faith in the unseen. An atom has never physically been observed. Yet it is the greatest established truth accepted by modern science. A scholar has rightly defined scientific theories as 'mental pictures that explain known laws.' In the field of science, the body of so-called 'observed' facts are not so in the strictest sense of the word: they are simply *interpretations* of certain observations. Human observation, even when aided by the most sophisticated devices, can never be assumed to be absolutely perfect. All interpretations based on human observation are, therefore, relative, and may change with an improvement in the technique of observation. J.W.N. Sullivan points out in his book, *The Limitations of Science*, that:

> It is evident, even from this brief survey of scientific ideas, that a true scientific theory merely means a successful working hypothesis. It is highly probable that all scientific theories are wrong. Those that we accept are verifiable within our present limits of observation. Truth, then, in science, is a pragmatic affair (p.158).

This notwithstanding, a scientist regards a hypothesis which provides a reasonable explanation for his observed facts as being in no way inferior to other academic facts based on observation. His contention is that his hypothesis is as much a matter of science as observed facts are. This, ultimately, is tantamount to a belief in the unseen. Belief in the unseen is not qualitatively different, as an intellectual activity, from belief in observed facts. It is not the same thing as 'blind faith.' It is rather the most appropriate explanation of the observed facts. Just as the corpuscular theory of light propounded by Newton was rejected by twentieth-century scientists because its explanation of the phenomenon of light was found unsatisfactory, we likewise reject the materialistic theory of the universe, because it does not offer a satisfactory explanation for the phenomenon of life and the universe.

The source of our belief in an all-powerful Divinity is exactly the same as that which a scientist takes recourse for his scientific theories. It is only after making a thorough study of observed facts that we have reached the conclusion that the explanations offered by religion are the ultimate truth—truth of such an order that, since time immemorial, it has remained unaltered. In the light of new observations and experiments, all man-made theories, which were formulated within the last few hundred years are being rescrutinised, and many, in the process, are being discarded. Religion on the other land, presents a truth which is becoming more and more clearly manifest with every advance in the field of scientific research. It is supported and testified to by innumerable significant discoveries.

In the next chapters, we shall study the fundamental concepts of religion from this standpoint.

## Notes

1. *The Evidence of God.* p. 26.
2. *The Evidence of God in an Expanding Universe*, Edited by John Clover Monsma, pp. 144-45.
3. *Man the Unknown*, p. 15.
4. *Works of Bentley*, Vol. III. p. 221.
5. *Clearer Thinking*, pp. 112-13.
6. *Philosophers of Science*, p. 244.
7. *Organic Evolution*, p. 15.
8. *Revolt Against Reason*, p. 112.
9. A.S. Eddington, *The Nature of the Physical World*, (Cambridge, The University Press 1948), p. 261.

# Nature and Science Speak about God

The greatest evidence of God before us is His creation. Nature itself and our study of nature, both proclaim the fact that there is one God who, in the infinity of His Wisdom, has created and continues to sustain this universe. By ignoring or rejecting this truth, we plunge ourselves into an abyss of murky incomprehension and its attendant evils.

The very existence of the universe, with its superb organisation and immeasurable meaningfulness, is inexplicable except as having been brought into existence by a Creator—a Being with an infinite intelligence—rather than by blind force.

Among the philosophers of our time, there is a group, perhaps fortunately a small one, which doubts the very existence of every thing, no matter what it may be. It asserts that there exists neither man nor universe. In its nihilism, it likewise rejects the existence of God, even as a remote possibility.

As far as this particular brand of agnosticism is concerned, this may be a philosophical point worth considering purely as an abstract exercise in logic, but it is in no way connected with reality. When we think, the very act of thinking gives evidence of our existence. The great French philosopher and mathematician Descartes (1596-1660), founded his philosophy on the precept: "I think, therefore, I am."[1] And from this point, he went on to deduce the existence of God. Our sensory perceptions too give clear indications of the external existence of material things. If for example while walking along the road we are hit by a stone, we feel the pain. This experience establishes that, apart from us and outside of us, there exists a world having its own separate identity.

In fact, our minds, through our senses, perceive innumerable objects and register countless sensations and impressions every moment of our waking existence. These acts of cognition are personal experiences which continually reinforce the concept of the world having its own existence. Now, if the philosophical inclinations of a particular individual make him sceptical about the existence of the universe, this is an exceptional case, bearing no relation to the experiences of millions of human beings. It is simply that such an individual is so engrossed in his own private predilections that he has became deaf and blind to common realities. For the sake of argument, he would have us concede his point, but this would in no way imply that God did not exist. The absurdity of arguments against the existence of commonly accepted things is so patent as to be hardly worth a comment. And quite apart from being incomprehensible to the common man, they could never gain credence in the world of learning.

Outside the nihilist group, the existence of the universe is accepted as a reality: the moment we admit its existence, we find belief in God inescapable, because the notion of creation having arisen spontaneously out of nothing is quite inconceivable. When everything big or small, has a cause, how can it be believed that such a vast universe has come into existence on its own, and

that it has no Creator? In his autobiography, John Stuart Mill, observed that his father had impressed upon him from the first, that the manner in which the world came into existence was a subject on which nothing was known: that the question "Who made me?" cannot be answered, because we have no experience or authentic information from which to answer it, and that any answer only throws the difficulty a step further back, since the question immediately presents itself, "who made God?"[2]

This is an old argument much relied upon by atheists, its implication being that if we do accept that there is a Creator of the universe, we shall be compelled to accept this Creator as being eternal. And when God has to be regarded as eternal, why should not the universe itself be regarded as eternal instead? Although such a conclusion is absolutely meaningless,—because no such attribute of the universe has come to light so far to justify the conclusion that the universe has come into existence of its own accord—up till the nineteenth century, this misleading argument of the atheists was regarded as the most attractive one. But now, with the discovery of the second law of the thermodynamics, this argument has lost its validity. Thermodynamics is a branch of science, which deals with energy transformation. In particular, it shows the quantitative relations between heat and other forms of energy. The importance of conservation in relation to energy, is expressed in the first law of the thermodynamics.

The law of Entropy is the second law of thermodynamics. To understand it, let us take the example of a metallic bar, which has been heated at one end but left cold at the other. Heat will instantly begin to flow from the hot end along the length of the bar to the cold end, and will continue to do so until the temperature of the whole bar becomes uniform. The flow of heat will always be in one direction, i.e. from warmer to colder bodies and this flow will never pass spontaneously in the opposite direction, or even haphazardly in just any direction. Other examples of such uniform and non-reversible processes abound in the physical world. For instance, gas always flows towards a vacuum or moves from a point of higher pressure towards that of a lower pressure till its pressure becomes uniform. It is impossible for any gas to flow in the reverse direction. Such observations provide the basis for the second law of thermodynamics. This law may be stated as follows.

All natural or spontaneous processes occurring without the intervention of an external agency are irreversible. The process of one-way movement goes on till a state of equilibrium is reached. On the relevance of these laws to creation, Edward Luther Kessel, an American zoologist, writes:

Science clearly shows that the universe could not have existed from all eternity. The law of entropy states that there is a continuous flow of heat from warmer to colder bodies, and that this flow cannot be reversed to pass spontaneously in the opposite direction. Entropy is the ratio of unavailable to available energy, so that it may be said that the entropy of the universe is always increasing. Therefore the universe is headed for a time when the temperature will be universally uniform and there will be no more useful energy.

Consequently there will be no more chemical and physical processes and life itself will cease to exist. But because life is still going on, and chemical and physical processes are still in progress, it is evident that our universe could not have existed from eternity, else it would have long since run out of useful energy and ground to a halt. Therefore, quite unintentionally, science proves that our universe had a beginning. And in doing so it proves the reality of God, for whatever had a beginning did not begin of itself but demands a Prime Mover, a Creator, a God.[3]

James Jeans has expressed the same view thus:

The more orthodox scientific view is that the entropy of the universe must forever increase to its final maximum value. It has not yet reached this; we should not be thinking about it if it had. It is still increasing rapidly, and so must have had a beginning; and there must have been what we may describe as a 'creation' at a time not infinitely remote.[4]

There is much physical evidence of this type to prove that the universe has not always existed. On the contrary, its life span is limited. According to astronomy, the universe is in a state of continuous expansion outwards from the centre of its origin. All of the galaxies and celestial bodies are observably moving away from one another at enormous speeds. This phenomenon can be satisfactorily explained if we presume an initial point of time when all these constituents were an integrated whole, and the release of energy and the process of movement were subsequent developments.

On the basis of different observations of a similar type, it is generally held that the universe originated about 5 billion years ago. In theory, the entire universe was formed by an extraordinary explosion from a state of high density and high temperature. This has come to be known as the 'big-bang' theory. To accept

that the universe has a limited life-span, and at the same time to deny its having an originator is like accepting that the Taj Mahal has not existed for all eternity (it having been built some time in the middle of seventeenth century), while denying the existence of an architect or builder, and asserting, on the contrary, that it simply mushroomed all by itself on a particular date.

Studies in astronomy show that the number of stars in the sky is as numerous as all of the sand grains on all the sea-shores of our planet, many of the stars being vastly greater in size than our earth, some even being of such enormous girth that they could accommodate hundreds of thousands of earths inside them and still have room to spare. A few of them are even big enough to contain millions and millions of earths. The universe is so vast that an aeroplane flying at the greatest speed imaginable, i.e. at the speed of light (186,282 miles per second), would take about ten billion years to complete just a single trip around the whole universe. Even with such a huge circumference, this universe is not static, but is expanding every moment in all directions. So rapid is this expansion that, according to an estimate by Eddington[5], every 1300 million years, all the distances in this universe are doubled. This means that even our imaginary aeroplane travelling at the speed of light would not ever be able to fly all the way around the universe, because it would never be able to catch up with this unending expansion. This estimation of the vastness of the universe is based on Einstein's theory of relativity. But this is just a mathematician's guess. To tell the truth, man has yet to comprehend the vastness of the universe.

In a clear sky which is free of dust, five thousand stars can be seen with the naked eye. With the help of an ordinary telescope this figure is increased to 2 million and through a great 200-inch telescope on Mount Palomar in America, billions of stars are visible. But even this figure is small as compared with the actual figure. The universe is an infinitely vast space in which innumerable stars are continuously moving at extraordinary speeds. Some stars are moving singly, some in groups of two or more, while innumerable stars are grouped in constellations.

You may have noticed myriads of dust particles swirling around in the rays of light penetrating a room through some aperture. If you can visualize this same scene on a colossal scale, you will have a rough idea of the revolutions of the stars throughout the universe. The only difference is that dust  particles can collide and move in combination whereas the stars, notwithstanding their enormous numbers are at immeasurable distances from each other and follow their respective courses, like ships sailing hundreds of miles apart in the vastness of the oceans. The whole universe is made of countless constellations, or galaxies, all of which are in perpetual motion.

The nearest example of such motion is the moon's circling of the earth at a distance of 240,000 miles. It completes each revolution in 29½ days. Similarly, our earth, at a distance of 95 million miles from sun, rotates on its axis at a thousand miles an hour, and takes one full year to go around the sun. Besides the earth, there are in the solar system eight other planets, all of which are continuously revolving around the sun. Pluto is the farthest away of all, with an orbit of 75 million miles. All these planets move on their individual paths with thirty one moons in orbit around their respective planets simultaneously. In addition to these nine planets and thirty one moons, a group of thirty thousand asteroids, thousands of comets and innumerable meteors also remain perpetually in orbit. The central place among them is, of course, occupied by our Sun, which is also a star. Its diameter is 865,000 miles. That is, it is twelve hundred thousand times larger than the earth. The sun itself is not stationary, but is revolving along with all its planets and asteroids at a speed of 600,000 miles per hour. Within a vast galactic system, there are thousands of such mobile systems which combine to form a galaxy. A galaxy is like a huge plate upon which countless stars are in continuous revolution, singly as well as in groups, just like so many spinning tops. These galaxies themselves are, in turn, in continuous motion. The nearest galaxy, in which our solar system is situated, is rotating on its own axis in such a way that it concludes a single rotation within a period of 200 million years.

Astronomers estimate that the universe consists of five hundred million galaxies. Each galaxy contains about 100,000 stars. The nearest galaxy, the Milky way, which is partially visible at night, has an area of 100,000 light years. And we, the inhabitants of the earth, are thirty thousand light years away from the centre of this galaxy. This galaxy in turn forms part of an even larger super-galaxy within which seventeen galaxies similar to our own are in perpetual motion. The diameter of this entire cluster is 2 million light years.

Over and above all these revolutions, another kind of movement is going on, i.e. the whole universe is expanding in all directions just like a balloon. Rotating with an incredible rapidity, at a speed of 12 miles per second, our own Sun is continuously whirling away towards the outer margin of its galaxy, carrying all the members of the solar system with it. Similarly, in perpetual rotation, all the stars are moving away in one direction or the other at tremendous speeds—some at eight, some at 33 and some at 84 miles per second.

The amazing part is that all of this motion is going on with a remarkable organization and regularity. Neither do the stars collide, nor does their speed alter. The rotation of our earth around the sun is a model of regularity. Likewise, its rotation on its own axis is so precise in timing that there has not been a discrepancy of even a second over the centuries. The moon, the earth's satellite, similarly hardly strays from its orbit by so much as a hair's breadth, there being only a minuscule deviation in its course which is repeated with clock-work precision every eighteen and a half years. The other celestial bodies spread throughout the universe function with a similar degree of precision.

According to astronomical calculations, it has frequently happened that entire galactic systems consisting of millions and millions of moving stars have entered other galactic systems and have passed right through them without any collisions having taken place. In the face of such astonishing organization, the human intellect is left with no option but to accept that this is no self-organized system. On the contrary, there must be some unique Power that has set up, and is maintaining such a boundless and infinitely varied system.

This very organization and discipline that is found among the macrosystems is also extant in microsystems. According to the latest research, an atom is the smallest of all the known 'worlds,' being too small to be observed even by the most powerful of microscopes. (A recently developed one is capable of magnifying an object one hundred thousand times). As far as the optical range of a human being is concerned, an atom is non-existent. But astonishingly, within such an infinitesimal particle, there exists (according to the Bohr Theory) a revolving system just like our solar system. This consists of a positively-charged central core, the nucleus, surrounded by one or more negatively-charged planetary electrons. Between these there are surprisingly huge gaps. Even in a substance of great density, like a piece of lead, in which one might expect the atomic particles to be rigidly compressed, the electrically-charged particles occupy barely one out of a thousand million parts of the volume and the remaining portion is vacant. The revolution of the electrons around the nucleus is so swift as to be undetectable at any given point. On the contrary, they appear to be omnipresent in their orbit, making, as they do, a thousand billion rounds within a single second.

If science can suppose the existence of a barely comprehensible and totally unobservable organization simply because, without such a supposition, the mechanism of an atom cannot be explained, why should not the same logic apply to the supposition

that there is an organizer without whom no organization is possible within the atom?

Now let us turn to human biology to see how the different parts of the human body perform vital and highly complex functions in perfect co-ordination with one another.

**The Brain** is the central office which controls, directs and co-ordinates the varied activities of all the innumerable organs of the body. It receives messages from each of the senses, interprets them, sends the proper replies to the organs concerned so that the body reacts appropriately (jumps out of the way of approaching car, for instance), and registers all the information received in the archives of the memory. Think of a huge telephone exchange in continual contact with every man, woman and child on earth, sending and receiving messages to and from each one every few seconds—and you have a faint idea of the incredibly complex organization of the brain.

In the white and grey matter of the brain there are nearly a thousand million nerve cells, each of which is, by turns, an electric battery and a small telegraph transmitter. Each cell branches out into a number of fine conducting threads, the nerve fibres, which extend to all parts of the body. A large number of them run down the hollow back-bone, twisted together into a thick cable, the spinal cord, admirably protected by the bony and well-cushioned walls of the spine. Through these tiny threads, each of which is covered with an insulating sheath, current flows at the speed of about 70 m.p.h, carrying messages to and from the brain, with marvellous speed and accuracy. There is an elaborate system of relays, condensers, switches, etc., which permits the transmission of the most unexpected messages between the brain and each of millions of cells it controls, without the least confusion or delay.

The most complicated radio station, the most up-to-date telephone exchange is like a tin of sardines compared to the incredibly elaborate maze of the nerve system of the brain.

**The Ear:** Long before man discovered wireless, the ear knew all that was to be known about the reception of sound waves. The human ear consists of a funnel beautifully adapted to pick up sounds and equipped with fleshy folds, which enable it to perceive the direction from which the sounds come. Inside the ear, fine hairs and a sticky wax prevent harmful insects, dust, etc. from getting in. Across the inner end of the funnel there is a tightly stretched membrane, the ear-drum, which vibrates like the skin of a tambourine when sound waves strike it. The vibrations are passed on and amplified by three bones (called the hammer, the stirrup and the anvil) whose relative sizes are precisely adjusted to produce just the needed amplification. Indeed these bones never grow: they are of exactly the same size in the infant and in the adult.

The amplified vibrations are carried by the bones to another membrane just beyond which lies the wonderful organ of hearing, the inner ear. This is a small tube (the cochlea) coiled up like the shell of a snail, and filled with a liquid, in which a harp of 6,000 strings ranging in length from 1/20th to ½ mm., hangs suspended. Each string vibrates to a particular frequency of sound so that the ear can hear all possible combinations of 6,000 different sounds. The vibrations of the strings are transmitted to 18,000 nerve cells whose fibres communicate with the brain.

**The Eye** is the world's most efficient television station: it takes flawless pictures in colour and transmits them without the least blurring to the brain. It takes a photographer to appreciate fully the working of the eye. Like any camera it is a small dark box, with an aperture in front fitted with a transparent pane. In front of the pane there is a shutter of variable speed (the iris), with an adjustable slit and automatic release. Behind this, there is the crystalline lens whose curvature is continually adjusted by automatic muscles so that whatever is looked at is always sharply in focus. Six large powerful muscles control the movements of the eye and point it in any desired direction.

The delicate parts of this precision instrument are kept clean by the eyelids, which are window-wipers and use a cleaning fluid secreted by a gland at the corner of the eye and poured in through a siphon. A constant temperature is maintained, as in any laboratory with highly sensitive apparatus, by means of a heat regulating membrane, the choroid. The photographic plate of the eye is a small screen at the back, the retina, on to which the images of the things we see are focussed. The retina can take 10 direct pictures each second or 800,000 pictures a day, wiping itself clean after each. It is so 'fast' that 30,000 separate points of light can be recorded by a single square millimetre (the size of a nail head) of its surface. All the pictures are in vivid colour, with sharp outlines, and delicate shading; they are, besides, movies and in 3-dimensions, thanks to the stereoscopic focus of the two eyes.

**The Heart** is a small organ, about the size of the fist, (4 inches long and 2 ½ inches broad), weighing not much more than eight ounces, yet this small pump can work prodigiously. It keeps on pumping day and night for a whole lifetime without the least pause, rating some 100,000 strokes a day and sending about a gallon of blood circulating through the body, once every 13 seconds. In a single day the heart pumps enough blood to fill a good-sized oil truck; in a single year it could fill a train of 65 large oil wagons.

The heart is specially built for the immense job it has to do. Its walls are made up of very tough muscular fibres, and it is surrounded by a double membrane (the pericardium) containing a fluid that lubricates its continual movement. The beat of the heart takes place in two steps, as first the upper and then the lower half contracts. This enables each half of the heart to rest while the other is beating. Inside, the heart is divided into 4 chambers, two upper chambers called the auricles and two lower chambers called the ventricles. Blood always flows from the auricles to the ventricles, and this one-way traffic is maintained by umbrella-shaped valves which guard the openings between the two sets of chambers.

**Digestion:** The digestive system can be looked upon as a factory where food is tasted by the tongue, then crushed by the teeth, moistened with saliva and finally,—after elaborate precautions to avoid shunting mistakes,— is pushed through the gullet into the stomach, a chemical plant where the most astonishing changes occur. Here millions of cells, too small to be seen, produce a dozen highly complex chemicals which break up the food we have eaten, whether it be meat, spinach, rice, or cheese, into simpler substances which can be absorbed by the cells of our body and built up into our flesh and bones. The chemical changes that take place are truly marvellous—well beyond the capacity of the best equipped of our laboratories. And there are five million of these little chemical units in the stomach, some forty million in the intestines, and more than three and a half billion in the liver. They produce, not only the chemicals needed to digest our food, where and when required, but also effective remedies against diseases like cholera and dysentery.

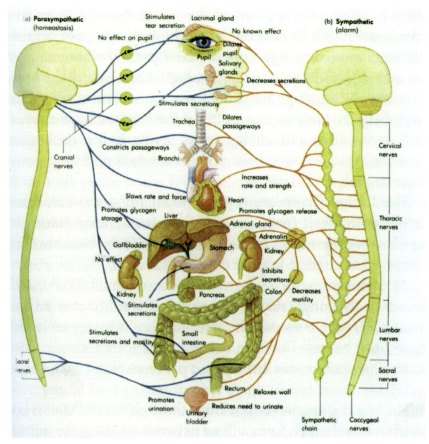

The fibers of (a) the parasympathetic and sympathetic divisions of the ANS are not identically distributed. Parasympathetic fibers come from four of the cranial nerves. The vagus nerve distributes about 80 percent of the parasympathetic fibers and is the only cranial nerve that sends fibers to the organs of the thoracic and abdominal cavities. The lower portion of the parasympathetic division exits the CNS from the sacral plexus in the pelvic cavity. (b) Sympathetic fibers leave the CNS via two chains of ganglia that parallel the spinal cord. Many organs of the body receive fibers from both ANS divisions, which generally oppose each other's actions. In general, parasympathetic fibers encourage a physiologic quieting of the body's systems. Sympathetic fibers activate changes that prepare the systems to cope with real or imagined threats.

At the same time, the liver manufactures substances which help the body to burn some of the food we have eaten, to provide the heat and energy every living being needs. The digestive system is not only a chemical factory, but a power house as well.

*Nature and Science Speak about God* • 83

**The Lungs:** These are organs which bring the blood into contact with clean fresh air—for they knew, long before we ourselves were aware of the fact, that to purify the blood nothing is better than a good bath of oxygen.

At each breath, air is drawn into more than 1,500,000 little air-sacs in the lungs, which if spread out would cover an area of some 200 square yards—the size of a nice little vegetable plot. These little balloon-like sacs are made of a thin elastic tissue which allows air to pass through but prevents blood from oozing in.

The blood is carried to the lungs through 50,000,000,000 tiny hair-thin tubes which form a close network all along the outside of the little bailoons of the lungs. Each day they bring in some 10,000 litres of blood. Oxygen is sucked in by the red blood cells, while waste products of the body like carbon dioxide and water are given up by the blood, pass into the little air sacs, and are breathed out.

As long as a child is in the womb of its mother its lungs do not function, and the flow of blood is turned away from the lungs by means of a special little door in the heart. As soon as it is born, the baby, who is on the verge of suffocation, utters a loud cry. The cry produces a whole series of wonderful changes. The great bags of the lungs open and air rushes in to fill them. A great flow of blood is drawn into the lungs which like a violent draught of air slams shut the little door inside the heart which had hitherto turned the blood away.

**The Skin,** with its vast network of sensitive fibres spread over the body's surface is equally fascinating. The moment a hot object comes in contact with our skin, or even comes close to it, about thirty thousand "hot cells" feel it, and instantly report it to the brain. Similarly, there are 250,000 "cold cells" within our skin which crowd the brain with messages as soon as contact is made with a cold object. The body then begins to shiver and veins in the skin become dilated in order to make up for the loss of warmth in the body. When intense heat is "reported" to the brain, three million perspiratory glands are activated to release the cool fluid we recognise as perspiration. The nervous system is divided into different parts, one of them being the autonomic branch, which deals with reflex functions that are performed within our body, such as digestion, respiration, heart beat and so on. This autonomic branch is further subdivided into two systems: the sympathetic system, which causes activity and the parasympathetic system, which serves as a brake. If our body were under the exclusive control of the sympathetic system, the heart would beat so rapidly that death would result. And if our body were left to the mercy of the parasympathetic system, the beating of our heart would be totally arrested. Both these systems function in perfect co-ordination with each other. Whenever our body is exposed to excessive stress and strain, causing a sudden need for extra strength to withstand it, the sympathetic system dominates, making the lungs function more rapidly, and pumping adrenaline into the system from which the body may derive extra energy. But while we are asleep, the parasympathetic system has the upper hand, anaesthetizing all our bodily activities.

Throughout the universe, there are countless examples of such superb organization, far surpassing even the most advanced systems of man-made machines. The imitation of nature has lately begun to be treated as a regular object of scientific enquiry. Until very recently the scope of science was confined to the discovery of unknown forces in nature, and their practical applications. But now the study of various organic systems of nature is receiving special attention in scientific spheres. This branch of science is called bionics. It seeks to understand how nature functions, transmitting nature's patterns into mechanical form, in order to solve the myriad problems, which arise in the field of engineering.

Such imitations of natural systems in the field of technology is well illustrated by the camera, which is in fact, a mechanical reproduction of the function of the eye. The lens, the diaphragm and the photosensitive film correspond respectively to the outer layer of the eyeball, the iris and the retina. No one in his right mind would claim that a camera had come into existence accidentally, but there are a good number of intellectuals in this world who believe that an eye came into existence by the merest chance.

At the Moscow University, a device has been developed for the detection and measurement of infrasonic vibrations. It is five times more powerful than conventional apparatus, being able to detect and report the approach of a storm twelve to fifteen hours in advance. What was it, which provided the pattern? Credit must go to the humble jellyfish whose organs are highly sensitive to infrasonic vibrations. Engineers simply imitated them. Similarly, the radar, a device of prime importance in defence technology, is a mechanical copy of the bat's use of sonic waves to compensate for its blindness.

These are but a few of the many examples. Physical science and technology have, in fact, received hints from nature on innumerable occasions for the development of novel concepts; so many problems that still remain an enigma to scientists have often been solved by nature long before. Yet, but for the human mind, the camera and the teleprinter system could not have come into existence.

It is even more unthinkable that the formidably complicated system of the universe could have come into existence without there having been a creative intelligence behind it. There is something quite irrational in refusing to believe in an Organizer of an organized universe. The human mind has, indeed, no rational grounds for denying the existence of God.

The universe is not just a heap of garbage. Quite the contrary. It is invested with a profound significance. This fact explicitly shows that some Mind is at work behind the creation and sustenance of the universe. It is impossible for anything to be as meaningful as the universe is without an intellectual planning behind it. A universe coming into existence by a blind, materialistic process could never evince such sequence, order and meaningfulness. The universe is such a wonderfully balanced organization that it is quite inconceivable that the order and balance could have come about accidentally. In his book *Man Does Not Stand Alone,* A. Cressy Morrison points out that:

> So many essential conditions are necessary for life to exist on our earth that it is mathematically impossible that all of them could exist in proper relationship by chance on any one earth at one time. Therefore, there must be in nature some form of intelligent direction. If this be true, then there must be a purpose.

In support of this view, we reproduce below a paper on this subject written by Frank Allen, a prominent biophysicist whose specializations are colour vision, physiological optics, liquid oil production and glandular mutations.

> It has often been made to appear that the material universe has not needed a Creator. It is undeniable, however, that the universe exists. Four solutions of its origin may be proposed: first, that it is an illusion—contrary to the preceding statement; second, that it spontaneously arose out of nothing; third, that it had no origin but has existed eternally; and fourth, that it was created.
>
> The first proposed solution asserts that there is no problem to solve except the metaphysical one of human consciousness, which has occasionally itself been considered an illusion! The hypothesis of illusion has been lately revived in physical science by Sir James Jeans who states that from the concepts of modern physics 'the universe cannot admit of material representation, and the reason, I think, is that it has become a mere mental concept.'[6] Accordingly, one may say that illusory trains apparently filled with imaginary passengers cross unreal rivers on immaterial bridges formed of mental concepts.
>
> The second concept, that the world of matter and energy arose of itself out of nothing, is likewise too absurd a supposition for any consideration.
>
> The third concept, that the universe existed eternally, has

one element in common with the concept of creation; either inanimate matter with its incorporated energy, or a Personal Creator, is eternal. No greater intellectual difficulty exists in the one concept than in the other. But the laws of thermodynamics (heat) indicate that the universe is running down to a condition when all bodies will be at the same extremely low temperature and no energy will be available. Life would then be impossible. In infinite time, this state of entropy would already have happened. The hot sun and stars, the earth with its wealth of life, are complete evidence that the origin of the universe has occurred in time, at a fixed point of time, and therefore the universe must have been created. A great First Cause, an eternal, all-knowing and all-powerful Creator must exist, and the universe is His handiwork.

The adjustments of the earth to life are far too numerous to be accounted for by chance. Firstly the earth is a sphere freely poised in space in perpetual rotation on its polar axis, giving the alternation of day and night, and in yearly revolution around the sun. "These motions give stability to its orientation in space, and, 'the 23.5 degree axial of orbit, or ecliptic, about the sun results in long winter nights and long summer days

alternating between both polar regions and causing seasonal variations in climate'.[7]

The habitable area of the earth is thus doubled and our Earth sustains a greater diversity of plant life than would be possible on a stationary globe.

Secondly, the atmosphere of life-supporting gases is sufficiently high (about 500 miles) and dense to blanket the earth against the deadly impact of twenty million meteors that daily enter it at speeds of about thirty miles per second. Among many other functions, the atmosphere also maintains the temperature within safe limits for life; and carries the vital supply of fresh water vapor far inland from the oceans to irrigate the earth, without which it would become a lifeless desert. Thus the oceans, with the atmosphere, are the balancing wheel of Nature.

Four remarkable properties of water,—its power of absorbing vast quantities of oxygen at low temperatures, its maximum density at 4 degrees C above freezing point whereby lakes and rivers remain liquid, the lesser density of ice than water so that it remains on the surface, and the power of releasing great quantities of heat as it freezes,—preserve life in oceans, lakes and rivers throughout the long winters.

The dry land is a stable platform for much terrestrial life. The soil provides the minerals which plant life assimilates and transforms into needful foods for animals. The presence of metals near the surface renders the arts of civilisation possible. Surely Prophet Isaiah is right (45:18 R.S.V.) in saying of God: 'He did not make it chaos: He formed it to be inhabited.'

The diminutive size of the earth compared with the immensity of space is sometimes disparagingly referred to. If the earth were as small as the moon, i.e. one-fourth of its present diameter, the force of gravity (one sixth that of the earth) would fail to hold both atmosphere and water, and temperatures would be fatally extreme. If double its present diameter, the enlarged earth would have four times its present surface and twice its force of gravity, the atmosphere would be dangerously reduced in height, and its pressure would be increased from 15 to 30 pounds per square inch, with serious repercussions upon life. The winter areas would be greatly increased and the regions of habitability would be seriously diminished. Communities of people would be isolated, travel and communication rendered difficult or almost impossible.

If our earth were of the size of the sun, but retaining its density, gravity would be 150 times as great, the atmosphere diminished to about four miles in height, evaporation of water rendered impossible and pressure increased to over a ton per square inch. A one-pound animal would weigh 150 pounds, and human beings would be reduced in size to that of, say, a squirrel. Intellectual life would be impossible to such creatures.

If the earth were removed to double its present distance from

the sun, the heat received would be reduced to one fourth its present amount, the orbital velocity would be only one-half, the winter season would be doubled in length and life would be frozen out. If its solar distance were halved, the heat received would be four times as great, the orbital velocity would be doubled, seasons would be halved in length, if changes could even be effected, and the planet would be too parched to sustain life. In size and distance from the sun, and in orbital velocity, the earth is able to sustain life, so that mankind can enjoy physical, intellectual and spiritual life as it now prevails.

If in the origin of life there was no design, then living matter must have arisen by chance. Now chance or probability as it is termed, is a highly developed mathematical theory which applies to that vast range of objects of knowledge that are beyond absolute certainty. This theory puts us in possession of the soundest principles on which to discriminate truth from error, and to calculate the likelihood of the occurrence of any particular form of an event (pp.19-23).

A tendency to take human existence too much for granted is easily corrected by considering for a moment the proposition that since the earth is moving continuously at a velocity of one thousand miles per hour (and although our feet are in contact with the ground, we are all of us hanging with our heads down in space) we ought to be cast off centrifugally into outer space, just like so many grains of sand flying off a rotating bicycle wheel. An alarming idea, isn't it! But, of course, nothing of the sort happens, because, fortunately for us, the gravitational force of the earth and the atmospheric pressure together hold our bodies safely in position on the earth's surface. This bilateral action keeps us clinging to the earth's surface no matter in which hemisphere we happen to be. The pressure which the atmosphere exerts upon the human body is the rather surprising figure of 15½ lbs (about 8 kilograms) per square inch. But we do not feel the effect of such intense pressure, because the blood in our bodies exerts an equal pressure in the opposite direction.

On the basis of his own observation and studies, Newton came to the conclusion that all bodies exert a mutual attraction. But he had no answer to the question, 'Why do bodies attract one another?' He himself confessed to having failed to offer any explanation for this. On this point, A.N. Whitehead, the noted American mathematician and philosopher, says:

> By admitting this fact, Newton has expressed a great philosophical truth, that is, if nature is inanimate, it can give no explanation to us, just as a dead man cannot narrate any incident. All rational and logical explanations are ultimately the expression of a purpose, whereas no ontology can be ascribed to a dead universe.'[8]

To the words of Whitehead, we might well add the query that if the universe is not under the supervision of any intelligent mind, how is it then invested with such profound meaningfulness? The earth completes one rotation on its axis in twenty-four hours. In other words, it is rotating on its axis at a speed of one thousand miles per hour. Suppose its speed were reduced to two hundred miles per hour—which is quite possible, our days and nights would then be prolonged to ten times their present duration. The heat of the summer would become scorching and would reduce the entire vegetation of the planet to ashes during the day time, and whatever survived the heat would be shrivelled up by the severe cold during the excessively long nights. Just one change in one set of conditions would bring total devastation

in its wake. Other changes could do the same. The sun, which is now our source of life, could become the most terrible scourge if, for example, the distance between the earth and the sun—approximately 95 million miles—were reduced by half; then its 12 thousand degrees Fahrenheit surface temperature would cause this paper to burst into flames.
Conversely, if the distance were doubled, the earth's surface would become too cold to allow any life to survive. A star ten thousand times bigger than the sun would keep the entire earth roasting hot, like an oven. The earth's inclination in space at an angle of 23.5 degrees is one of the greatest of marvels to man, because that is what causes the seasons, making the greater part of the earth habitable and providing a greater diversity of plant life. Had the earth's axis been perpendicular, there would have been perpetual darkness at the North and South Poles, the oceanic vapours would have travelled northwards and the earth's surface would have been covered in either glaciers or deserts—to describe but a few of the adverse effects. This would have rendered the survival of life on earth impossible. One can go on endlessly imagining different sets of physical circumstances which could have precluded or destroyed human existence. It is unthinkable then that the perfect conditions for man to come into existence on earth were simply self-generating and had no origin in divine inspiration.

If we think of what conditions were like at the time of the formation of the earth, it seems all the more miraculous that life could come into being at all. Isaac Asimov has painted a fearsome picture of the beginning of things. Correcting the earlier hypothesis in favour at the beginning of this century, he writes:

**Currently, scientists are convinced the earth and the other planets did not form from the sun, but were formed of particles**

coming together at the same time that the sun itself was being formed. The earth was never at sun temperature, but it did grow quite warm through the energies of collision of all the particles that formed it. It grew warm enough so that its relatively small mass could not hold an atmosphere or water vapor to begin with.

The solid body of the newly formed earth had, in other words, neither atmosphere nor ocean. Where then did they come from?

There existed water (and gases) in loose combination with the rocky substances making up the solid portion of the globe. As that solid portion packed together more and more tightly under the pull of gravity, its interior grew hotter and hotter. Water vapor and gas were forced out of combination with the rock, and came fizzing out from its substance.

The gaseous bubbles, forming and collecting, racked the baby earth with enormous quakes: escaping heat produced violent volcanic eruptions. For unnumbered years, liquid water did not fall from the sky; rather, water vapor whistled out of the crust and then condensed. The oceans formed from below, not from above.

What geologists mainly dispute now is the rate at which the oceans formed. Did the water vapor all fizz out within a billion years or less, so that the ocean has been its present size ever since life began? Or has the process been so slow that the ocean has been growing all through geologic time and is still growing?

Those who maintain the ocean formed early in the game and has been steady in size for a long time, point out that the continents seem to be a permanent feature of the earth. They do not appear to have been much larger in the past, when the ocean was supposedly, much smaller.

On the other hand, those who maintain the ocean has been

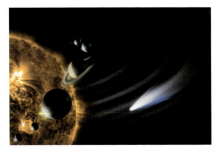
growing steadily point out that volcanic eruptions even today pour quantities of water vapour into the air; water vapor derived from deep-lying rocks, not from the ocean. Also, there are sea mounts under the Pacific with flat tops that may have once been at ocean level but are now hundreds of feet below.⁹

Be that as it may, if the oceans had been deeper by just a few feet more, they would have absorbed all available carbon dioxide and oxygen, and no vegetation of any kind could have survived upon the earth's surface. If the air in the atmosphere had been less dense than it is at present, the twenty million meteors that daily enter it at speeds of about thirty miles per second, would be crashing down all over the earth, burning up all combustible matter and perforating the whole of the earth's surface. The heat alone of a meteor travelling 90 times faster than a bullet would be enough to annihilate so vulnerable a creature as man. It is thanks to this atmospheric layer being of an appropriate density that mankind is safeguarded against these fiery showers of celestial debris. This density is also exactly right for solar actinic rays to reach the earth in such proportions as will promote the growth of vegetation, destroy harmful bacteria, and make vitamins available which may be absorbed directly from the sunlight through the skin, or indirectly from edible matter through the digestive system. How wonderful it is to have all these benefits in exact proportion to our requirements.

Take oxygen, for example. It is the source of life and is not obtainable from any source other than the atmosphere. But had it formed 50% of the atmosphere or more, instead of the present 21%, combustibility of all matter on the earth's surface would have been so high that even if just a single tree caught fire, whole forests would at once explode. Similarly, had the proportion of oxygen in the atmosphere been as low as 10%, life might conceivably have adjusted to this over the centuries, but it is unlikely that human civilization would have taken its present form. And if all of the free oxygen instead of only a part, had been absorbed by the matter present on the earth's surface, no animal life would have been possible at all.

Along with oxygen, hydrogen, carbon dioxide and carbon gases in their free form as well as in the form of different compounds are the most important ingredients of life; the very foundations, in fact, on which our life rests. There being not even one chance in a hundred million that all these elements should have assembled in such favourable proportions on any other planet at any one given time, we have to ask ourselves how it came about that such freely moving gases formed themselves into a compound and remained suspended in the atmosphere in exactly the right proportions to sustain life. As the noted physicist Morton White puts it, 'Science has no explanation to offer for the facts, and to say it is accidental is to defy mathematics'.[10]

We have to concede that there is a formidable array of facts in this world and the universe, which cannot be explained unless we admit the intervention of a superior mind. For instance, the density of ice is less than that of water, because as it freezes, its volume increases in relation to its mass. It is because of this that ice floats instead of sinking to the bottom of lakes and rivers and gradually forming a solid mass. On the surface of the water, it forms a layer of insulation to maintain the water below at a temperature above freezing point. Fish and other forms of marine life are thus permitted to survive throughout the winter, and, when spring comes, the ice melts rapidly. If water did not behave in this way, all of us in general, and people in cold countries in particular, would face severe calamities. Clearly this property of water is tremendously important to life.

In the world of arboriculture there are also numerous examples of nature aiding man. In the first two decades of the century, a chestnut blight, caused by the pathogen Endothia, spread rapidly across the forested regions of the U.S.A. It was widely felt that the holes it made in the forest canopy would never again be filled. This was highly regrettable because of the large number of useful things the chestnut tree yielded: high-grade, rot-resistant timber, wood pulp, tannin, and nuts—not to speak of its shade. It also had the special advantage of being able to grow on mountain ridges with scanty soil as well as in rich fertile valleys. The unique position occupied by the American chestnut was unsurpassed by any other species and, until the arrival of *Endothia* from Asia around 1900, it had truly been king of the forest. Now it is almost extinct. But the holes in the forest canopy were eventually filled. Tulip-trees were already there, waiting for just such openings as would provide sufficient light for that shade-intolerant species to develop. Up till then, these trees had been minor denizens of the forest, only occasionally developing into valuable timber trees. Now, chestnut trees are hardly missed where dense groves of tulip trees have become established, these often growing as much as one inch in diameter and six feet in height per year; as well as their growth being rapid, their wood is of superior quality. Can we in all conscience say that the master plan of nature is merely a set of accidental circumstances?

In the present century too, a crisis of a different but more alarming nature developed in Australia when a certain species of cactus was grown on an extensive scale to provide fencing for the fields. Cressy Morrison writes:

> The cactus had not insect enemies in Australia and soon began a prodigious growth. The march of the cactus persisted until it had covered an area approximately as great as England, crowded the inhabitants out of the towns and villages, and destroyed their farms, making cultivation impossible. No device which the people discovered could stop its spread. Australia was in danger of being overwhelmed by a silent, uncontrollable, advancing army of vegetation. The entomologists scoured the world

and finally found an insect which lived exclusively on cactus, would eat nothing else, would breed freely, and which had no enemies in Australia. Here the animal conquered the vegetation and today the cactus pest has retreated, and with it all but a small protective residue of the insects, enough to hold the cactus in check forever.[11]

Can such a great scheme of checks and balances as is found in Nature develop without any deliberate planning?

Consider the marvellous mathematical exactitude which is to be found in the universe. The behaviour of even inanimate matter is not in any way haphazard: on the contrary, it "obeys" definite "natural laws." No matter in which corner of the world, at any given time, the word "water" will invariably mean "a compound consisting of 11.1 percent of hydrogen and 88.8 percent of oxygen." Whenever a scientist in his laboratory heats a beaker filled with pure water until it boils, he knows, without using a thermometer, that the temperature of the boiling water is 100 degrees centigrade as long as the atmospheric pressure is 760 mm of mercury. If the pressure is less than 760 mm, less energy will have to be applied in the form of heat to produce vapour or steam, so the boiling point will be correspondingly less than 100 degrees. Conversely, if the pressure is greater than 760 mm, the boiling point will be greater than 100 degrees. No matter how often this experiment is performed, by ascertaining the pressure, we can, with certainty, predict the boiling point of the water on each occasion. If there were no system and organization inherent in the working of water and energy, there would be no basis for scientific research and invention. Life in the laboratory, in the absence of immutable natural laws, would be a succession of quandaries; it would be a life fraught with uncertainty and doubt, rendering all scientific enquiry futile. Thomas Parks, a research chemist, writes:

> One of the first things a freshman chemistry student learns is the periodicity or order found in the elements. This order has been variously described and classified, but we usually

credit Mendeleev, the Russian chemist of the last century with our periodic table. Not only did this arrangement provide a means of studying the known elements and their compounds, but it also gave impetus to the search for those elements which had not yet been discovered. Their very existence was postulated by vacant spaces in the orderly arrangement of the table.

Chemists today still use the periodic table to aid them in their study of reactions and to predict properties of unknown or new compounds. That they have been successful is sound testimony to the fact that a beautiful order exists in the inorganic world.

But the order we see around us is not a relentless omnipotence. It is tempered with beneficence—a testimony to the fact that the good and pleasure are as much a concern of Divine Intelligence as the immutable laws of Nature. Look around you at the exceptions and deviations that do, in fact, defy the laws of cold rationality.

Take, for example, water. From its formula weight of 18, one would predict it would be a gas at ordinary temperatures and pressures. Ammonia—with a formula weight of 17—is a gas at temperatures as low as minus 33°C at atmospheric pressure. Hydrogen sulphide, closely related to water by position in the periodic table and with a formula weight of 34, is a gas at temperatures down to minus 59°C. The fact that water exists as a liquid at all, at ordinary temperatures, is something to make one stop and think.[12]

"On August 11, 1999, there will be a solar eclipse that will be completely visible at Cornwall."

This is not a prediction based simply on conjecture. We know from calculations based on our observations of the solar system's functioning that this eclipse is bound to occur. We tend to take

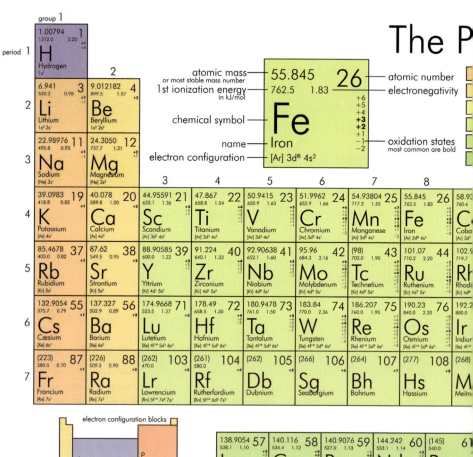

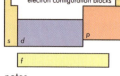

notes
- as of yet, elements 113-118 have no official name designated by the IUPAC.
- 1 kJ/mol ≈ 96.485 eV.
- all elements are implied to have an oxidation state of zero.

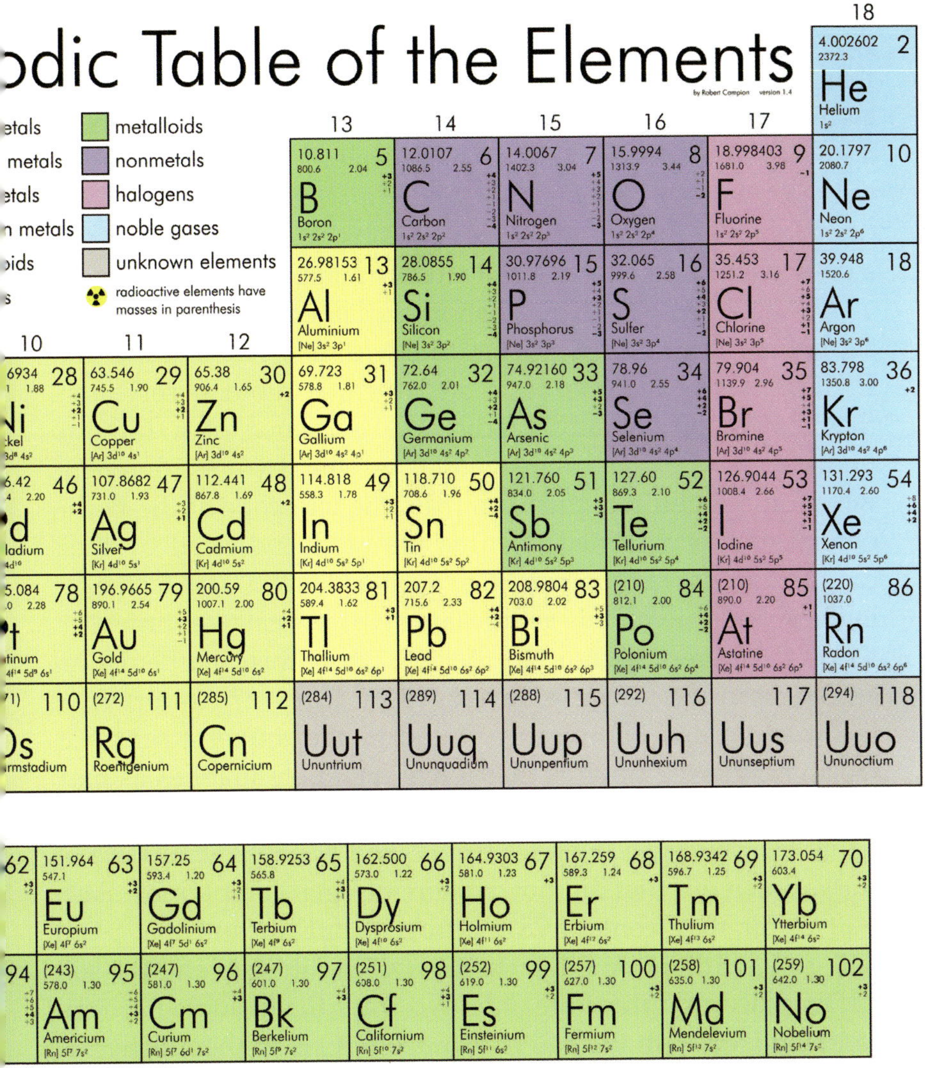
odic Table of the Elements
by Robert Campion version 1.4
etals
metals
etals
n metals
oids
metalloids
nonmetals
halogens
noble gases
unknown elements
radioactive elements have masses in parenthesis
10 11 12 13 14 15 16 17 18
4.002602 2 He Helium
10.811 5 B Boron
12.0107 6 C Carbon
14.0067 7 N Nitrogen
15.9994 8 O Oxygen
18.998403 9 F Fluorine
20.1797 10 Ne Neon
26.98153 13 Al Aluminium
28.0855 14 Si Silicon
30.97696 15 P Phosphorus
32.065 16 S Sulfer
35.453 17 Cl Chlorine
39.948 18 Ar Argon
28 Ni
63.546 29 Cu Copper
65.38 30 Zn Zinc
69.723 31 Ga Gallium
72.64 32 Ge Germanium
74.92160 33 As Arsenic
78.96 34 Se Selenium
79.904 35 Br Bromine
83.798 36 Kr Krypton
46
107.8682 47 Ag Silver
112.441 48 Cd Cadmium
114.818 49 In Indium
118.710 50 Sn Tin
121.760 51 Sb Antimony
127.60 52 Te Tellurium
126.9044 53 I Iodine
131.293 54 Xe Xenon
78
196.9665 79 Au Gold
200.59 80 Hg Mercury
204.3833 81 Tl Thallium
207.2 82 Pb Lead
208.9804 83 Bi Bismuth
(210) 84 Po Polonium
(210) 85 At Astatine
(220) 86 Rn Radon
110
(272) 111 Rg Roentgenium
(285) 112 Cn Copernicium
(284) 113 Uut Ununtrium
(289) 114 Uuq Ununquadium
(288) 115 Uup Ununpentium
(292) 116 Uuh Ununhexium
117 Uus Ununseptium
(294) 118 Uuo Ununoctium
62
151.964 63 Eu Europium
157.25 64 Gd Gadolinium
158.9253 65 Tb Terbium
162.500 66 Dy Dysprosium
164.9303 67 Ho Holmium
167.259 68 Er Erbium
168.9342 69 Tm Thulium
173.054 70 Yb Ytterbium
94
(243) 95 Am Americium
(247) 96 Cm Curium
(247) 97 Bk Berkelium
(251) 98 Cf Californium
(252) 99 Es Einsteinium
(257) 100 Fm Fermium
(258) 101 Md Mendelevium
(259) 102 No Nobelium

it for granted that the innumerable stars we see in the sky, like pinpoints of lights, are part of a vast unchanging pattern. But these "pinpoints" of light are actually colossal balls suspended in the vastness of space and, since time immemorial, have been moving in the same fixed orbits with such perfect precision that their paths (and, more recently, that of artificial satellites) can be accurately predicted at any given moment. Right from a tiny drop of water to the greatest imaginable star, the whole range of natural phenomena evinces a wonderful system and organization. The behaviour of such objects is uniform to such a degree that we have been able to formulate laws on this basis.

Newton's theory of gravitation explained the revolution of astronomical spheres. In accordance with this, A.C. Adams and U. Leverrier found the basis on which, without observation, they could successfully predict the existence of a hitherto undiscovered planet. As foretold by the two astronomers, when on a night in September 1846, the telescope at the Berlin observatory was turned towards the point indicated by their calculations, it was observed that such a planet did, in fact, exist in the solar system. This is the planet we now call Neptune.

Isn't it preposterous to believe that this mathematical exactness in the universe developed on its own? An aspect of the wisdom and significance found in the universe which is worth pondering upon is that it has such potentialities as may be exploited by man whenever the need arises. For instance, let us take nitrogen. Human beings and animals would die of starvation if our diet did not contain nitrogen compounds. Each puff of air may contain 78% nitrogen, but no nutritive plant will grow without an interaction between nitrogen and the soil taking place, and there are only two ways that soluble nitrogen can be mixed with the soil to fertilize it. One of them is by the typical bacterial process. Certain bacteria, which live in the roots of leguminous plants such as peas, beans, alfalfa and peanuts, assimilate atmospheric nitrogen. When the plant dries up, some part of this compound remains stored in the soil. Another form of fixed nitrogen, nitric acid, occurs naturally in the atmosphere when lightning discharges. The action of electrical energy on the atmosphere, which dissociates nitrogen and oxygen molecules, allows the free atoms to form nitric oxide and nitrogen dioxide, and this nitrogen compound is brought down by rainfall to our fields. The amount of nitrate obtained from nitrogen by this means, according to one estimate, is five pounds per acre of soil, in each year. This quantity is equal to 30 pounds of sodium nitrate.[13]

Both these sources have proved inadequate in meeting the nitrogen requirements of man, for fields which are repeatedly cultivated over long periods eventually run short of nitrogen. Hence the practice of crop rotation by farmers. Owing to an increase in population and intensive cultivation at the beginning of the present century, a general deficiency of nitrogen compound began to make itself felt and man appeared to be heading for a prolonged period of famine. It is strangely significant that, at such a critical time, we discovered the method of artificially preparing this compound from the air. One of the several different essays in this field entailed the artificial causation of thunder and lightning in the atmosphere. A force of about 300,000 horsepower was applied to cause this phenomenon, and, as had been estimated, a small amount of nitrogen was thus produced. Man, with his God-given wisdom, had marched one step forward. It was ten thousand years after the dawn of human history that methods had been invented to convert nitrogen gas into fertilizers. This invention placed man in a position to produce this essential part of his nutrition himself, without which, he would surely have died of starvation. It is inspiring to think that, for the first time, throughout the entire history of the earth, man had discovered a solution to the problem of food scarcity at the exact point in time when it was about to cause ultimate disaster to the human species. Many other significant aspects of divine wisdom and purpose are immanent in the universe. All that has so far been revealed by scientific enquiry is quite imaginably nothing in comparison to the facts which still await discovery. Be that as it may, whatever little, comparatively speaking, man has discovered of nature is still too vast in scope to be covered by the present volume. In fact, any attempt on the part of man to list and describe divine blessings would be inadequate. No matter how comprehensive the description may be, the moment our tongues and pens stop moving, we begin to feel that all we have done is delimit rather than describe. Indeed, no account of divine wisdom as manifested in the universe would be complete, even if all knowable facts were to come to light and all human beings, equipped with all of the resources available in the world were to join together in describing them.

> **And if all the trees in the earth were pens, and the sea, with seven more seas to replenish it, were ink, the writings of Allah's words could never be exhausted. Mighty is God and Wise.**[14]

Anyone who has attempted to make an exhaustive study of the universe will admit that there is no element of exaggeration in these words from the divine scripture. They are just a plain, unembroidered expression of the truth. In the last few pages, we have referred to the wonderful organization, meaningfulness and extraordinary wisdom which manifest themselves in the universe. The antagonists of religion will no doubt concede that these are facts, but they will insist on a different interpretation of their significance. They do not glimpse even fleetingly, an Organizer and Sustainer in this universe. On the contrary, they hold that life on earth and the existence of the universe are simply chance occurrences. As T.H. Huxley puts it:

> Six monkeys, set to strum unintelligently on typewriters for millions of millions of years, would be bound in time to write all books in the British Museum. If we examined the last page, which a particular monkey had typed, and found that it had chanced, in its blind strumming, to type a Shakespeare Sonnet, we should rightly regard the occurrence as a remarkable accident, but if we looked through all the millions of papers the monkey had turned out in untold millions of years, we might be sure of finding a Shakespeare Sonnet somewhere amongst them, the product of the blind play of Chance. In

the same way, millions of millions of stars wandering blindly through space for millions of millions of years are bound to meet with every kind of accident; a limited number are bound to meet with that special kind of accident which calls planetary systems into being.[15]

But one of the greatest of our contemporary physicists, Sir Fred Hoyle, asks if it is at all possible that chance could operate on such a large scale, and answers emphatically in the negative. As he puts it in his book, *The Intelligent Universe*:

'The Universe, as observed by astronomers, would not be large enough to hold the monkeys needed to write even one scene from Shakespeare, or to hold their typewriters, and certainly not the wastepaper baskets needed for the rubbish they would type.'

None of our sciences up till now has unearthed any such "chance occurrence" as could have accounted for such a great, meaningful and permanent phenomenon as the universe. Of course, there are certain random happenings which do explain certain aspects of nature. For instance, a gust of wind sometimes carries away pollen grains from a red-coloured rose and, with them, pollinates the stigma of a white-coloured rose. This cross pollination produces pink-coloured roses. But such an incident is only a minor event in the entire existence of the rose. Its continued presence under specific conditions in this universe, and its wonderful adaptation to the whole physical system of the rest of the world, can never be fully understood simply by ascribing these things to a random flow of air. The term 'chance occurrence' expresses one facet of the truth, but as an explanation for the existence of the universe and its processes, it is patently absurd. According to Professor Edwin Conklin, a biologist at Princeton University, "The probability of life originating from accident is comparable to the probability of the Unabridged Dictionary resulting from an explosion in a printing shop.'[16]

It is said that an explanation for the existence and working of the universe with reference to 'chance' is not just a haphazard guess but, in the words of Sir James Jeans, is based on 'purely mathematical laws of chance' (*The Mysterious Universe*, p. 3). An author writes: 'Now chance, or probability as it is termed, is a highly developed mathematical theory which  is applied to that vast range of objects of knowledge that are beyond absolute certainty. This theory puts us in possession of the soundest principles on which to discriminate truth from error, and to calculate the likelihood of the occurrence of any particular form of an event.[17]

Even if we take it for granted that matter in a crude form spontaneously originated in the universe, and that a chain of voluntary action and reaction is responsible for creation, (although such an assumption is baseless) we have no adequate explanation for the existence of the universe. Unfortunately for the antagonists of religion, the same mathematics that provides them with the golden key of the Law of Chance, rules out the possibility of the Law of Chance having been the cause of the present universe, for, in calculating the age and dimensions of our world, Science shows that Chance falls far short of explaining the facts. In a chapter on the uniqueness of our world, from his book, *Man Does Not Stand Alone*, Cressy Morrison offers a telling illustration of this point:

> Suppose you take ten pennies and mark them from 1 to 10. Put them in your pocket and give them a good shake. Now try to draw them out in sequence from 1 to 10, putting each coin back in your pocket after each draw.
>
> Your chance of drawing No. 1 is 1 to 10. Your chance of drawing 1 and 2 in succession 1 in 100. Your chance of drawing 1, 2 and 3 in succession would be one in a thousand. Your chance of drawing 1, 2, 3 and 4 in succession would be one in 10,000 and so on, until your chance of drawing from No. 1 to No.

10 in succession would reach the unbelievable figure of one chance in 10 billion. The object in dealing with so simple a problem is to show how enormously figures multiply against chance.

Sir Fred Hoyle similarly dismisses the notion that life could have started by random processes:

> Imagine a blindfolded person trying to solve the Rubik cube. The chance against achieving perfect colour matching is about 50,000,000,000,000,000,000 to 1. These odds are roughly the same as those against just one of our body's 200,000 proteins having evolved randomly, by chance.

Now, just imagine, if life as we know it had come into existence by a stroke of chance, how much time would it have taken? To quote the biophysicist, Frank Allen:

> Proteins are the essential constituents of all living cells, and they consist of the five elements, carbon, hydrogen, nitrogen, oxygen and sulphur, with possibly 40,000 atoms in the ponderous molecule. As there are 92 chemical elements in Nature, all distributed at random, the chance that these five elements may come together to form the molecule, the quantity of matter that must be continually shaken up, and the length of time necessary to finish the task, can all be calculated. A Swiss mathematician[18], Charles Eugene Guye, has made the computation and finds that the odds against such an occurrence are $10^{160}$ to 1, or only one chance in $10^{160}$, that is 10 multiplied by itself 160 times, a number far too large to be expressed in words. The amount of matter to be shaken together to produce a single molecule of protein would be millions of times greater than that in the whole universe. For it to occur on the earth alone would require many, almost endless billions ($10^{243}$) of years.
>
> Proteins are made from long chains called amino-acids. The way those are put together matters enormously. If in the wrong way, they will not sustain life and may be poisons. Professor

J.B. Leathes (England) has calculated that the links in the chain of quite a simple protein could be put together in millions of ways ($10^{48}$). It is impossible for all these chances to have coincided to build one molecule of protein.

But proteins as chemicals are without life. It is only when the mysterious life comes into them that they live. Only an Infinite Mind, that is God, could have foreseen that such a molecule could be the abode of life, could have constructed it, and made it live.[19]

Science, in attempting to calculate the age of the whole universe, has placed the figure at 50 billion years. Even such a prolonged duration is too short for the necessary proteinous molecule to have come into existence in a random fashion. 'When one applies the laws of chance to the probability of an event occurring in Nature, such as the formation of a single protein molecule from the elements, even if we allow three billion years for the age of the earth or more, there isn't enough time for the event to occur.[20]

There are several ways in which the age of the earth may be calculated from the point in time at which it solidified. The best of all these methods is based on the physical changes in radioactive elements. Because of the steady emission or decay of their electric particles, they are gradually transformed into radio-inactive elements, the transformation of uranium into lead being of special interest to us. It has been established that this rate of transformation remains constant irrespective of extremely high temperatures or intense pressures. In this way we can calculate for how long the process of uranium disintegration has been at work beneath any given rock by examining the lead formed from it. And since uranium has existed beneath the layers of rock on the earth's surface right from the time of its solidification, we can calculate from its disintegration rate the exact point in time when the rock solidified. In his book, *Human Destiny*, Le Comte Du Nouy has made an excellent, detailed analysis of this problem:

It is impossible because of the tremendous complexity of the question to lay down the basis for a calculation which would enable one to establish the probability of the spontaneous appearance of life on earth (p. 33).

The volume of the substance necessary for such a probability to take place is beyond all imaginations. It would be that of a sphere with a radius so great that light would take 1082 years to cover this distance. The volume is incomparably greater than that of the whole universe including the farthest galaxies, whose light takes only $2 \times 10^6$ (two million) years to reach us. In brief, we would have to imagine a volume more than one sextillion, sextillion, sextillion, times greater than the Einsteinian universe (p. 34).

The probability for a single molecule of high dissymmetry to be formed by the action of chance and normal thermic agitation remains practically nil. Indeed, if we suppose 500 trillion shakings per second ($5 \times 10^{14}$), which corresponds to the order of magnitude of light frequency (wavelengths comprised between 0.4 and 0.8 microns), we find that the time needed to form, on an average, one such molecule (degree of dissymmetry 0.9) in a material volume equal to that of our terrestrial globe is about $10^{243}$ billions of years (1 followed by 243 zeros) (p. 34).

But we must not forget that the earth has only existed for two billion years and that life appeared about one billion years ago, as soon as the earth had cooled ($1 \times 10^9$ years) (p. 34).

Life itself is not even in question but merely one of the substances which constitute living beings. Now, one molecule is of no use. Hundreds of millions of identical ones are necessary. We would need much greater figures to "explain," the appearance of a series of similar molecules, the improbability increasing considerably, as we have seen for each new molecule (compound probability), and for each series of identical throws.

If the probability of appearance of a living cell could be expressed mathematically the preceding figures would seem negligible. The problem was deliberately simplified in order to increase the probabilities (p. 35).

Events which, even when we admit very numerous experiments, reactions, or shakings per second, need an infinitely longer time than the estimated duration of the earth in order to have

*Nature and Science Speak about God*

one chance, on an average, to manifest themselves can, it would seem, be considered as impossible in the human sense (p. 36).

It is totally impossible to account scientifically for all phenomena pertaining to life, its development and progressive evolution, and that, unless the foundations of modern science are overthrown, they are unexplainable.

We are faced by a hiatus in our knowledge. There is a gap between living and non-living matter which we have not been able to bridge (p. 36).

The laws of chance cannot take into account or explain the fact that the properties of a cell are born out of the coordination of complexity and not out of the chaotic complexity of a mixture of gases. This transmissible, hereditary, continuous coordination entirely escapes our laws of chance.

Rate fluctuations do not explain qualitative facts, they only enable us to conceive that they are not impossible qualitatively (p. 37).

Such calculations show that at least 1400 million years have elapsed since the process of rock-solidification took place. These estimates are based on a study of those rocks which are known to be the oldest on our planet. J.W. Sullivan puts the earth's age at two thousand million years—a moderate estimate by his own account. When a period of trillions and trillions of years would be required for a single non-living proteinous molecule to develop in a purely random way, we have to ask ourselves how more than ten hundred thousand species of animals with fully developed bodies, and more than two hundred thousand species of plants could have originated upon the surface of the earth within the relatively short period of two thousand million years.

And how was it that innumerable members of each species reproduced themselves and became widespread throughout the land and the oceans? Is it really conceivable that within such a short span of time, a superior creature like man could have evolved from inferior living organisms, and all just by the merest chance?

The theory of evolution is based upon a certain incidence of chance mutations—accidental variations—among the different species. But even supposing rare mutations conferring a 1% advantage did occassionally occur, just how rapidly could they be accumulated in a species? Patan, in his *Mathematical Analysis of the Evolution Theory*, has shown that it would take about 1,000,000 generations to effect a population breeding true for this new mutation. Certainly, even granting the immense periods of time postulated by geologists, it is difficult to see how such a relatively modern animal as the horse would have evolved from its presumed five-toed dog-like ancestor since the relatively recent Eocene times.[21]

This detailed analysis has been made here simply to expose the absurdity of the "chance occurrence" theory. Neither an atom nor a molecule, nor the mind which applies itself to how the universe originated, could have come into existence by pure "chance." No matter how long a period may be presumed for it, the theory of chance occurrence is impossible, not only from the mathematical point of view, but also from the standpoint of common sense. As a theory, it just does not carry any weight.

An American physiologist, Dr. Andrew Conway Ivy writes: "It is many times more absurd to believe that this causal chain came from nothing, and was due to chance, than it would be to believe that you could get a map of the world by spilling a glass of water on the floor."[22]

It may well be asked where the floor, the gravitational force of the earth, the water and the glass came from in order to bring about this 'chance occurrence.'

Haeckel, a noted biologist, claimed, "Give me air, water, chemical elements and time and I will make a man." This claim obviously implied that God was not necessary for such a feat. But by admitting the prior presence of the man – himself – and the material conditions essential for the success of his project, he unwittingly demonstrated the vacuity of such a notion.

Dr. Morrison has rightly said: "While asserting this, Haeckel overlooked the problem of genes and life itself. To bring a man into existence, first of all he would have to obtain the invisible atoms. Then, after putting them in a specific order, he would have to construct a gene and import life to it. Even then, the

*Nature and Science Speak about God* • 111

probability of its chance creation is one in crores. But even supposing that he succeeded, he could not call it an 'accident.' On the contrary, he would regard it as the outcome of his own intelligence.[23]

In the following statement of belief, George Earl Davis, an American physicist, makes perhaps the best summing up of the situation: 'If a universe could create itself, then it would embody in itself the powers of a Creator, a God, and we should be forced to conclude that the universe itself is a God. Thus the existence of a God would be admitted, but in the peculiar form of a God that is both supernatural and material. I choose to conceive of a God who has created a material universe not identical with Himself but dominated and permeated by Himself.[24]

## Notes
1. "Je pense, donc je suis."
2. John Stuart Mill, *Autobiography* (New York, Columbia University Press, 1960), p.30.
3. *Evidence of God*, pp. 50-51.
4. *The Mysterious Universe*, p. 133.
5. Sir Arthur Stanley Eddington (1882-1944), noted British physicist and astronomer.
6. *The Mysterious Universe*, p. 169.
7. *Encyclopaedia Britannica*, Vol. I, p. 954.
8. *The Age of Analysis*, p. 85.
9. *Please Explain*, pp. 65-65.
10. *The Age of Analysis*, p. 33.
11. *Man Does Not Stand Alone*, pp. 78-79.
12. *Evidence of God*, pp. 74-75.
13. Lyon, Buckman and Brady, *The Nature and Properties of Soils*.
14. Quran, 31:27.
15. Quoted by Sir James, *The Mysterious Universe*, pp. 3-4.
16. *The Evidence of God*, p. 174.
17. *Ibid.*, p. 23.
18. Quoted by V.H. Mottram in the organ of the British Broadcasting Corporation, April 22, 1948.
19. *Evidence of God*, pp. 23-24.
20. *The Evidence of God*, p. 160.
21. *Ibid*, p. 117.
22. *Ibid*, p. 239.
23. *Man Does Not Stand Alone*, p. 87.
24. *Ibid*, p. 71.

# Argument for the Life Hereafter

One of the most important tenets of religion is the reality of the life hereafter. After death, human beings will leave this present ephemeral world, and, on the Day of Judgement, will enter another world, which will be eternal. The present world is but a place of trial where man, throughout his entire life-span, is on probation. When the time has come for the Last Reckoning, God will destroy this world and replace it by another world created on an entirely different pattern. All human beings will then be resurrected and will be brought before the Almighty to be judged: it is then that they shall be rewarded, or punished, according to the merits and demerits of their deeds on this earth.

We shall now examine this concept from different standpoints and determine whether it is right or wrong to believe in this probability.

## Probability

The question that first arises concerns the possible advent of an after-life in the present system of the universe. Do any events or indications substantiate our view?

The first thing that this concept of the other world presupposes is that man and the universe in their present form are not eternal. From the entire array of human knowledge up to the present, this fact stands out as indisputable. We all know, beyond any shadow of a doubt, that for both man and the universe, death is an inescapable fate.

The greatest desire of those who do not believe in the other world is to convert this world into a heaven of eternal bliss. Research into the cause, or causes, of death have even been carried out so that it could be forestalled and prevented, thus rendering human beings immortal. But the failure of such research has been abysmal, and, with each unsuccessful attempt, it has been borne in more and more upon researchers just how ineluctable death is.

Why does death occur? About two hundred explanations have been put forward as to its causes. Organic decay in the body; the exhaustion of constituents; the atrophying of veins; the replacement of dynamic albumens by less dynamic ones; the wearing out of the tissues; the secretion of poison by intestinal bacteria which is spread throughout the body, and so on.

The concept of bodily decay would appear to be correct. Machines, shoes, garments and all such material things do wear out with the passage of time. There is, ostensibly, the possibility of our body wearing out too, sooner or later, just as a garment does. But science only partially supports this view of bodily decay, for the human body is very different from a garment, a machine or a piece of rock. It should be likened rather to a river which has been flowing for thousands and thousands of years and continues to flow in the same fashion even today. Can we really say that a river becomes old or stagnates? An American chemist, Dr. Carl Linus Pauling (b. 1901), recipient of two Noble Prizes, one of Chemistry in 1954 and the Nobel Peace Prize in 1962, has pointed out that, theoretically man is cast to a great extent in an eternal mould, cells in the human body being just like machines which automatically remove their own defects. In spite of this, man does grow old, and he does die.

But let us leave death for a moment and look at life. Our bodies are constantly undergoing a process of renewal. Molecules of albumen present within our cells are continually being produced, destroyed and reproduced. Cells too (except the nerve cells) are regularly destroyed and replaced by newly formed cells. It has been estimated that the blood in a human body is fully renewed within the short span of about four months. And, within a few years, all of the atoms in a human body are totally replaced. It shows that man is more like a river than a mere structure of flesh and bones. In short, the human body is constantly undergoing a process of change. This being so, all concepts of the body becoming old and worn-out are seen to have no basis in fact. Consider that in the normal course of events, the indirect causes of death, such as injury, various types of deficiencies, the clogging of arteries and the wasting away of muscle, tissue etc., are generally dealt with, bit by bit by the body's own processes, (sometimes with the help of medical treatment) but, in any case are eliminated in the course of time, without either singly or jointly having caused the onset of death. It is normally much later in life that death occurs. How then can these injuries, deficiencies, etc., be held responsible for the death of the body? This would appear to imply that the cause of death does not lie in the intestines, veins or heart, but somewhere else.

Another explanation has it that nerve cells are the cause of death because they remain unchanged throughout life and are never replaced. The number of nerve cells in a human

*Argument for the Life Hereafter* • 115

body thus decline year after year, thereby weakening the nervous system as a whole. If it is correct to say that the nervous system is the Achilles' heel of the human body, it should conversely, be correct to say that a body having no nervous system at all should be able to survive for the longest period of time.

But observation does not support this view. A tree, which is devoid of a nervous system does survive much longer than a man, and in fact, survives the longest of all forms of plant-life. But wheat, which likewise has no nervous system, survives for only one year. And the amoeba, with a minute nervous system, survives for only half an hour. These examples would appear to imply the reverse—that is, animals belonging to the higher species, with perfect nervous systems, should live longer. But that is not the case either. Creatures relatively lower down the evolutionary scale, like crocodiles, turtles and fishes, are the ones who survive the longest.

All the investigations so far carried out with the objective of showing that death need not be a certainty have met with total failure. The fact still remains that, one day, all human beings will have to die. There is no avoiding death. Dr. Alexis Carrel, a French Nobel prize-winner who has done advanced research in tissue culture, has discussed this problem at length under the heading of Inward Time.

> **Man will never tire of seeking immortality. He will not attain it, because he is bound by certain laws of his organic constitution. He may succeed in retarding, perhaps even in reversing in some measure, the inexorable advance of physiological time. Never will he vanquish death.**[1]

Anomalies in the organisation of the present setup of the universe, which periodically result in minor calamities, are indicative of what is going to happen on large scale at some time in the future.

The earthquake is the terrestrial phenomenon which most obviously forewarns us of the possible advent of Doomsday. The interior of the earth is, in fact, composed of red-hot semi-molten magma, which is ejected periodically through volcanic activity in the form of lava. Sometimes strong vibrations of the earth's crust can also be felt. These are produced by the shrinking of the globe due to the cooling process which has been going on for aeons. From time to time, the wrinkling of the earth's surface assumes gigantic proportions and the resulting earthquakes are like a unilateral attack of nature upon man in which nature definitely has the upper hand. 'When we remember that only a thin, rocky crust, comparable to the skin of an apple, separates us from the red-hot, semi-molten  interior of our planet, we do not wonder that the inhabitants of its surface are so often reminded of the "physical hell" lying below the peaceful woodlands and blue seas.'[2]

Such earthquakes occur almost every day in varying degrees of intensity, some regions being more prone to earthquakes than others. The earthquakes which struck Shensi, a district in China, is the oldest of the highly destructive earthquakes recorded in history. It occurred in 1556 A.D. and took a heavy toll of more than 800,000 lives. Similarly, on the 1st November 1755, a volcano erupted cataclysmically in Portugal, totally destroying the city of Lisbon. In the course of this earthquake, within hardly six minutes, 30,000 people were killed and all the buildings were destroyed. It has been calculated that this earthquake caused an area four times the size of Europe to tremble. Another earthquake of the same intensity rocked Assam in 1877 A.D. It is reckoned to be one of the five most violent and devastating earthquakes on record. The whole of the northern part of Assam was catastrophically shaken, the course of the river Brahmaputra was diverted and Mount Everest was raised by 100 feet.

An Earthquake is, in fact, but a small reminder of the day of resurrection. When the earth is split asunder with a terrible rumbling; when buildings come tumbling down like playing cards; when the upper layers of the earth are cracked open and the interior of the earth is spewed out, when cities bustling with life are reduced to ashes in a matter of minutes; when the earth is strewn with dead bodies, like shoals of fish washed up on the sea coast, man realises his utter helplessness in the face of nature. What is most tragic about earthquakes and volcanic eruptions is the fact that no one can predict when or where they will take place. And, when they do, everything happens in a flash, leaving little or no time for escape. The day of the resurrection will come upon us all of a sudden, just like an earthquake. Such natural catastrophes demonstrate, most awesomely, God's capacity to destroy the earth at any moment.

Even more terrifying events take place in the outer reaches of the universe. In the infinitude of its space, innumerable, enormous bonfires – the stars – are rotating wildly like so many spinning tops dancing at a furious pace through unimaginable voids. Not even the very fastest of our rockets could ever hope to catch them, so rapid is their flight. In this process, celestial bodies can be likened to crores of heavily loaded bomber aeroplanes, who after flying for aeons through space may all of a sudden collide with one another. Studies in astronomy having confirmed that this is an actual possibility, it would not be surprising if they did collide. (What is surprising is that they do not collide). Our Solar System may well be the result of a collision of this type. If we can visualise such a collision taking place on a greatly enlarged scale, the day of resurrection will no longer seem impossible, nor even such a remote possibility as we had perhaps at first imagined. Believers in the concept of the life hereafter contend that a time is bound to come when the forces of destruction which are present in the universe in embryonic form will one day assume gigantic proportions. What is latent today will certainly manifest itself tomorrow, and the coming of the day of resurrection will be a reality. Today we apprehend it as a probability; tomorrow we shall witness it as a fact.

Once *qiyamah* (the Final Day) has been accepted as a probability, the second question that must be asked is: "Is there any life after death?" The answer to this tends nowadays to be in the negative because we are so used to thinking of life in terms of all the material elements of which it is apparently composed. We think of life developing when all the aforesaid elements are arranged in a particular order, and, as a corollary to that, we think of death as shattering that order and, in consequence, obviating all possibility of life after death.

T.R. Miles regards the concept of resurrection as a symbolic truth and refuses to accept it literally:

> It seems to me that there is a good case for regarding 'People have experiences after death' as a literal, factually significant assertion capable in principle of being verified or falsified by

experience. The only difficulty, in that case, is that, until we die, there is no means of discovering the true answer. Speculation, of course, is possible. It might be argued, for instance, that according to neurology awareness of the space occupied by our bodies (and of spatial relationships in general) is possible only when the brain is functioning normally, and that after death, when the brain disintegrates, no such awareness will be possible.[3]

But there are certain other assumptions which suggest that disintegration of material particles in a body does not bring life to an end. And these assumptions carry considerable weight. We should be prepared to recognise that life has a distinct and independent identity which survives in spite of the change in material particles. It is known that the human body is composed of certain specific elements called cells. These are the fundamental units of living things, and are composed of microscopic particles with a highly complicated structure. A man is made up of some million million cells. It is as if cells were the tiny bricks[4] of the human construction. But whereas real bricks remain the same as they were at the time of building, human cells undergo a constant process of transformation. This is known as our metabolism.

When a machine is in operation, it undergoes a gradual process of deterioration; in like manner, our bodily 'machine' is in a continual state of deterioration. Its 'bricks' are constantly being eroded and destroyed in the normal course of our daily lives. But we compensate for this loss by taking in food. Once digested, this produces various forms of cells which counterbalance any physical deficiency. Our bodies are, in fact, a compound of cells that is always in the process of change. It is like a large river that is always filled with water, without the water ever remaining the same. At every moment the old water is being replaced by the new. The container remains the same, but the water flows on.

Our bodies are so constantly undergoing changes that a time comes when all of the 'bricks' in our bodies have been eroded and replaced by new ones. During childhood, this is a fairly rapid process. However, as one ages, this process slows down day by day. Over an entire lifetime, on an average, all of the body cells are renewed every ten years. This process of the death and decomposition of the body goes on continually, whereas the inner man survives in his original form. At all stages of his life, he thinks of himself as being the same 'man' that he was in the past, and this, in spite of the fact that no feature of his—eyes, ears, nose, hands, legs, hair, nails, etc.—has remained the same.

Now if, along with the death of the body, the man inhabiting it died too, he should be diminished or depleted in some way by this total replacement of his cells. But this is not so. He remains quite distinct from and independent of the body, and retains his identity notwithstanding the death and decay of the body. Man is like a river. And the human personality is like an island in it, unaffected by the ceaseless flow of the cells. That is why a scientist has regarded life, or the human personality, as an independent entity that remains constant in the face of continuous change. He asserts that 'personality is changelessness in change.' Now if death means the end of the body, we might well say that whenever there is such a total replacement of cells in the body, the man actually dies on each occasion. And that if we see him moving about alive, he has really been resurrected. That is, a fifty-year old man would have experienced death at least five times within the short span of his life. If a man does not experience bodily 'death' five times in a row at ten-year intervals, how are we justified in believing that on the ultimate occasion he will have ceased quite finally to live?

Those who find this argument unacceptable—and modern philosophy is, in the main, opposed to the concept of the soul as an independent entity—will insist that the mind, or internal entity, that is called man does not, in fact, enjoy any independent existence. Man is simply the outcome of the interaction between the body and the outer world. All feelings and thoughts in man develop in the course of a material process, just as friction between two pieces of metal causes heat. Sir James Jeans is of the view that consciousness is merely a function or a process, and contemporary philosophers maintain that consciousness is nothing more than a nervous response to external stimuli. According to this concept, once a man dies, that is, when he biologically disintegrates, there can be no question of his survival, because the nerve centres which interact with the outside world and produce a set of responses which we call 'life' no longer exist after death. The concept of life after death, viewed in this way, appears irrational and unconnected with reality.

I should like to point out at this juncture that if this is the sum total of man's existence, we should certainly be in a position to create a man,—a conscious, living being. Today we are highly knowledgeable about the elements which make up the human body. All of these are obtainable in abundance beneath the surface of the earth and in the atmosphere. We have examined in great detail the internal system of the body with a microscopic 'eye' and we are very well aware of how the skeleton, veins, fibres, etc. have been constructed. Moreover, we have the services of so many expert artists who can copy the human body to perfection. If the antagonists of the 'soul'-concept are truly convinced that their views are correct, they should prove their point by constructing 'human' bodies, placing them in sets of circumstances where they receive the correct number and type of stimuli and then demonstrating to the rest of the world how these inert bodies begin to move about and talk in response to their environment. The plain fact that no man can create another man in this artificial way, that no man can breathe the spark of life into a lifeless lump of flesh, should be enough to convince them that there is a great deal more to life than permutations and combinations of cellular forms.

Apart from concerning ourselves with the probability of survival after death, we must also look at this problem from the angle of what purpose is served by having faith in such a concept. Religion makes it plain that life is not as Nietsche maintained, just a blind and meaningless cycle of life, death, and resurrection, like an hour-glass being emptied of its sand, time and time again, for no particular reason: it is, on the contrary, a time of trial for the whole of mankind, and the afterlife is the time of reward or punishment. The purpose of belief in such religious tenets, therefore, is to strengthen the moral fibre of society by inculcating the fear of God in the individuals of which it is composed.

The advent of the life hereafter assumes a high degree of credibility when we find, astonishingly, that the daily deeds of each and every human individual are being instantaneously recorded throughout the universe at all times. The human personality manifests itself in three ways: intentions, words and actions. All three manifestations are being preserved in their entirety, all being imprinted on a cosmic screen in such a manner as to make their precise reproduction an instant possibility. No detail of one's life on earth will remain a secret. It will be possible to know who opted for the path of God and who opted to follow Satan, who drew their inspiration from the angels and who trod the ways of evil.

Since we soon forget the thoughts that pass through our minds, we imagine that they have been erased from our memories forever. However, when we dream of some long forgotten event, or when someone suffering from a mental disorder begins to reveal things that relate to a distant and not even dimly remembered past, it becomes evident that the human memory is not confined just to that part of existence which is consciously experienced. One may not be conscious of certain compartments of the human memory, but they nevertheless exit. Various experiments have proved that all our thoughts are preserved for ever in the form in which they first existed. And even if we so desired, we could not eradicate them from our memory. Such investigations have revealed that the human personality does not have its basis only in the conscious part of the brain. On the contrary, there is another major part of the human personality which exists below the level of consciousness. Freud dubbed this part the subconscious, or unconscious. The human personality is rather like an iceberg whose tip—one ninth part of its total volume—is visible above the ocean's surface, while the rest—a massive eight ninths—lies submerged, and therefore hidden from view. It is in this hidden part, the subconscious, that all of our thoughts and intentions are preserved. In his thirty-first lecture, Freud elaborates:

> The laws of logic—above all, the law of contradiction—do not hold for processes in the id. Contradictory impulses exist side by side without neutralising each other or drawing apart; at most they combine in compromise-formations under the overpowering economic pressure towards discharging their energy. There is nothing in the id which can be compared to negation, and we are astonished to find in it an exception to the philosophers' assertion that space and time are necessary forms of our mental acts. In the id there is nothing corresponding to the idea of time, no recognition of the passage of time, and (a thing which is very remarkable and awaits adequate attention in philosophic thought) no alteration of mental processes by the passage of time. Conative impulses which have never got beyond the id, and even impressions which have been pushed down into the id by repression, are virtually immortal and are preserved for whole decades as though they had only recently occurred.[5]

This theory of the subconscious has gained general acceptance in psychology, this in turn giving credence to the idea that every good or bad thought that comes to mind is indelibly engraved upon the human psyche. The passage of time or different sets of circumstances do not cause even the minutest changes to occur. This process of thought registration goes on independently, and irrespective of human likes or dislikes.

Freud, however, failed to take stock of Nature's purpose in taking such great pains to preserve a record of our intentions and their outcome within the subconscious. He thus felt the necessity of inviting philosophers to ponder the matter. But when we look at this phenomenon in relation to the concept of the life hereafter, we immediately grasp its meaningfulness. It clearly shows the advent of the life hereafter as a distinct probability— as the time when every single human being will be confronted with a complete and accurate record of his deeds on earth. His own entity will be evidence of what the thoughts and intentions were which guided him in the course of his worldly existence.

"We verily created man and We know the promptings of his soul, and are closer to him than his jugular vein."[6]

Let us now consider what happens to man's words.

"Each word he utters shall be noted down by a vigilant guardian".[7]

No matter whether his words are sweet or bitter, true or false, good or evil, each and every one of them is being cosmically recorded, and man shall be held accountable for them, for this record will be consulted on the Day of Judgement.

Whenever a man moves his tongue to utter some words, this movement produces waves in the air, just as a stone dropped

into water will produce ripples. If you enclose an electric bell inside an air-tight glass jar, pump out all the air so that the bell is in a vacuum and pass an electric current through it, it will ring, but the sound will be almost inaudible, because the sound waves from the ringing bell, cannot pass through the vacuum to our ears. The only sound which will be audible will be that which comes via the wires carrying the electric current, and it will be so extremely faint as to be almost undetectable. It is only when waves can pass freely through the air to strike the tympanum of the ear that the aural devices can pick them up and transmit them to the brain, thus making it possible for us to understand what we hear, whether it be the sound of a bell ringing, a bird chirruping or a series of spoken words.

It has been proved that sound waves once produced continue to exist for ever in the atmosphere. Although our technology is not yet so advanced as to enable us to catch and reproduce these sounds, science, is making such rapid and gigantic leaps forward that it will only be a matter of a very short time before we are actually able to do so. It has been accepted, in theory, that we shall have the physical means to listen to the sounds produced in ancient times, just as we receive the sounds relayed from broadcasting stations and have them made intelligible for us by radios. The obstacles to the actual catching of sounds from ancient times are fewer than the difficulties of separating individual sounds from the complex mixture of noises produced at any given moment. The same difficulties occur in broadcasting. There are hundreds of radio stations all over the world simultaneously relaying innumerable and vastly different kinds of programmes at the enormous speed of one hundred thousand and eighty six miles per second. One might imagine that the sounds received would be confused and incomprehensible because of their speed, huge numbers and widespread diffusion. But this is not so, because the different radio stations broadcast their respective programmes on different wavelengths, some on short waves, some on long, and we have only to adjust our radios to the appropriate meter-band and we can listen to any desired programme without the interference of other sounds.

The technique of segregating natural sounds has yet to be evolved. But the very fact that techniques already exist by which radio transmitters and receivers separate artificial sounds is a strong indication that some time in the future, we shall be in a position to hear distinctly separate, naturally produced sounds. Then we shall have a first-hand account of all periods of human history through the medium of the sounds produced at that time. Once such a possibility is accepted, it becomes quite comprehensible that, man's speech having been perfectly recorded in nature, everyone will be called to account for his deeds and misdeeds.

It came to light that when a former Prime Minister of Iran was placed under detention, a recording machine, which kept working round the clock, was secretly introduced into his room, so that every single word that he uttered, would be recorded and could be used in evidence against him when he was brought into court. In a similar fashion, God's invisible angels are constantly hovering around every single individual on the face of this earth, recording with unfailing accuracy upon a cosmic disc his every thought, word and deed.

How are our deeds actually documented? Scientific studies have shown, surprisingly, that all our actions, whether in public or in a private, in broad daylight or in pitch darkness, linger in that atmosphere in photographic form. These photographs may be resorted to at any time to lay bare the innermost secrets of an entire life.

Recent investigations have shown that all objects continuously emit heat-waves, (provided the surroundings are of a lower temperature) no matter whether it is in darkness or in light, in motion or at rest. For instance, suppose that after sitting in this room, writing this text, I get up and go out of the room. The heat waves emitted from my body while I was in the room will still be there. With the help of an evaporagraph, a contrivance now in use in Britain and the U.S.A., a complete 'photograph' of me can then be taken. Since this device functions by means of infrared rays, which can penetrate darkness, it does not matter whether the shots are taken in the light or darkness. However, the evaporagraphs in use at present are only powerful enough to register heat waves emitted up to a few hours beforehand.

A few years ago in the U.S.A., there was an interesting case of an evaporagraph solving a mystery. An unidentified aeroplane was seen flying around New York City. Then, quite suddenly, it disappeared. The suspicions of the authorities having been aroused, 'photographs' were taken of it with the help of an evaporagraph. A study of these shots revealed the design of the aeroplane.[8]

Commenting on this event, The Hindustan Times, New Delhi, remarked that, in the near future, we shall be able to watch history on the screen. And it is quite probable that such a series of strange facts will come to light as will drastically change our entire conception of the past.

The remarkable performance and results of this invention show us that all our actions can be documented on a cosmic scale, just as all the actions of actors and actresses on a film set are caught and registered on film by the fast-moving, sharply-focussed cameras of the film world. Whether you strike someone or help a poor fellow to lift up his burden; whether you crusade for a noble cause or stoop to collaborate in the evil designs of others; whether you are in the light, in motion or at rest, all of your actions are being imprinted on a cosmic screen. This is happening every second of every minute in every home. There is no way of stopping it.

Once a story is filmed, it can be repeated on the screen even at far-off places and after long intervals. It is watched by people as if they were on the spot, witnessing everything as if it was actually happening there and then. In exactly the same way, a total picture of an individual's good or bad deeds in this world can come before him on the day of Resurrection in such minute detail as will make him exclaim in bewilderment: "What can this book mean? It omits nothing small or great; all are noted down!"[9]

From the above discussion it becomes clear how a complete

account of each and every deed is being unfailingly recorded. Every thought that comes to mind and every single word that we utter are preserved for eternity. We are pursued by such 'cameras' as are unaffected by darkness or light and which go on documenting our lives without interruption.

What happens is very similar to the fate of erring drivers, who blatantly commit traffic offences, unaware that their every movement is being picked up by closed-circuit television cameras. One such offender was the driver of a three-wheeler scooter rickshaw who left his vehicle in a no-parking area in Delhi, early in 1980.

The system was new at that time, so he had no idea he was being watched. When he was admonished by a policeman, he tried to pretend that he had just allowed a passenger to alight and that he was about to move on. The policeman promptly took him to the traffic inspector in the control room, where he was shown a film of all his movements—his parking (no passenger to be seen!), his strolling around, chatting to friends and finally his conversation with the policeman to whom he had put on such an air of outraged innocence! Naturally, when he saw the film, he had no defence left.

Cosmic recording is similar in effect, but it is no sporadic affair. It is a round-the-clock process. And it is as if not only our external personalities, but reflections of our inner selves were being regularly pictorialised. This astonishing phenomenon is explainable only as a means of providing evidence for or against individuals, to be used in the divine court on the Day of Judgement. Now if even such a stark reality fails to convince a man of his ineluctably being called to account on that fateful day, it is impossible to imagine what would, in the last analysis, cause the scales to fall from his eyes.

## The Concept of the Afterlife as an Imperative

In the preceding pages the concept of the life hereafter was discussed in order to ascertain whether the advent of the life hereafter, as asserted by religion was or was not a distinct probability in the context of the present setup of the universe: it was satisfactorily established that it was bound to occur. Now let us see whether or not this concept is a necessity in our present world.

First of all, let us deal with the psychological aspect. Keningham, in his book entitled, *Plato's Apology*, has described the dogma of life after death as "cheerful agnosticism."

All materialistic thinkers of the present age subscribe to the same view, in that they hold that man tends to seek out a world for himself where, free from all the restrictions and hardships of the present world, he may experience the freedom and happiness of his dreams. It is this very tendency in man, they say, which has given birth to the concept of a second life. They insist that this dogma is simply the result of wishful thinking, the desire to indulge in an imaginary solace. Who would not long, they say, to be ushered into the perfect world of their dreams after death? They would have it that the reality is otherwise and that there is no such world in existence. However, we must view man's desire for paradise and his strong urge to enter it after death as pieces of psychological evidence which support the concept of the life hereafter. If the thirst for water points to the existence of water, and signifies a correlation between man and water, in exactly the same way, the desire for a better world shows that, in fact, such a world does exist and relates directly to our lives. History bears witness to the fact that this desire for a better world has been evinced by human beings on a universal scale from the time immemorial.

Now, it seems quite unthinkable that something unreal could so impress itself upon the human mind on such a large scale and in such an eternal and all-pervasive form. This fact, in itself, indicates that another, better world must exist. It would be nothing short of perverse to disregard this as a reality.

I am at a loss to understand those who overlook the existence of such a strong psychological demand. How can they simply brush aside arguments in favour of the afterlife as being invalid? If the desire for a better world is simply the outcome of certain sets of circumstances, why should it correspond so perfectly to human aspirations. Can we cite any other thing which has remained so in consonance with human feelings over a period of thousands and thousands of years together with such unbroken continuity? The idea of the life hereafter has been deeply embedded in human psychology for as long as human beings have existed. It is inconceivable that this should be a false notion fed to uncritical, unsuspecting minds by men of superior but perverted intellect.

Many of the wishes of man remain unrealised in this world. He longs for eternal life right here in this world, but everything is terminated by death. How ironic it is that it is often just when a man, thanks to his knowledge, experience and endeavours is on the threshold of success, that he is cut short in his prime and simply disappears from the scene of life. Statistics gathered on successful businessmen in London, in the 45 to 65 age group, show that it is when they are well-established in business and have a very high level of income that one fine day their hearts suddenly fail, and they pass away from this world, bequeathing to others their greatly expanded and flourishing businesses. What then? Winwood Reade comments:

> It is question for us now to consider whether we have any personal relations towards the Supreme Power; whether there exists another world in which we shall be requited according to our actions. Not only is this a grand problem of philosophy, it is of all questions the most practical for us, the one in which our interests are most vitally concerned. This life is short, and its pleasures are poor; when we have obtained what we desire, it is nearly time to die. If it can be shown that by living in a certain manner, eternal happiness may be obtained, then clearly no one except a frenzied or a mad man will refuse to live in such a manner.[10]

But the same author rejects this great call from nature on the basis of certain trifling misgivings:

> Now this appears a very reasonable theory as long as we do

not examine it closely, and as long as we do not carry out its propositions to their full extent. But when we do so we find that it conducts us to absurdity as we shall very quickly prove. The souls of idiots, not being responsible for their sins, will go to heaven, the soul of such men as Goethe and Rousseau are in danger of hell-fire. Therefore it is better to be born an idiot than to be born a Goethe or a Rousseau and that is altogether absurd.[11]

His rejection is just like Lord Kelvin's refusal to accept the results of Maxwell's research. Lord Kelvin asserted that unless he could develop a mechanical model of whatever was under scientific consideration, he could not attest to his understanding it. That is why he did not accept Maxwell's electromagnetic theory of light as it could not be fitted into his material frame. Today such a notion seems quite absurd in the world of physics. J.W.N. Sullivan writes: "After all, why should one suppose that nature must necessarily be a thing which can be moulded by an engineer of the nineteenth century in his workshop?"[12]

In response to Winwood Reade's denigration of the concept of another world, I would say: "After all, what right has a philosoher from the twentieth century to think that the external world must necessarily be in accord with his own suppositions?"

Winwood Reade failed to understand the plain fact that reality is not dependent upon what is externally mainfest. On the contrary, the external itself is dependent upon reality. Our success lies in accepting and conforming to reality, rather than ignoring, rejecting or running counter to it. When it is a reality that there is a God of this universe and that all of us must appear before Him to be judged, it becomes the bounden duty of each and every individual, whether it be a Rousseau or an ordinary layman, to be faithful to God. Winwood Reade does not suggest that Rousseau and Goethe should bow to reality: on the contrary, he expects reality to adapt itself to them. And when reality is not ready to mould itself to conform to his ideas, he rejects reality out of hand as being absurd. It is as nonsensical as regarding the law on the safeguarding of military secrets as being absurd because its application can lead to, say, the work of an ordinary soldier being highly commended, while eminent American scientists like Rosenberg and his wife are condemned to die by electrocution for passing on war secrets to the U.S.S.R (1953). Justice is a reality, and that is what the law is concerned with, no matter how harsh the results. Similarly, the divine scheme immanent in the universe is concerned with God's justice, and makes itself manifest in many ways which may seem unpalatable or incomprehensible, but this we must nevertheless apprehend and accept as being the ultimate and incontrovertible reality.

It is a little appreciated, but highly significant fact that throughout the world as we know it, man is the only being who possesses the concept of 'tomorrow.' He is unique in thinking about the future, and not only wishing to improve his future life but actually taking steps to do so. The cerebral activity involved is far more subtle and complex than the instincts which move animals, birds and insects to be provident—for example, the ant storing food for the winter and the weaver bird weaving a nest in time for the arrival of her offspring. These activities take place, not as the result of forethought, but as the result of instinctive compulsions. There is no conscious, intellectual effort on their part. To keep 'tomorrow' in mind and then think about it and plan for it requires the capacity for conceptual thought—the privilege of man alone. No other living organism is known to have been endowed with such a capacity.

Had there been no 'tomorrow' for mankind, civilisation could never have developed in the way it has, for the concept of 'tomorrow' is inextricably linked with the desire for an improved, future life. The absence of this concept would have been a contradiction in the face of nature. The desire for a better life is often equated with the desire to escape the unpleasant consequences of failure or from general conditions of adversity, and that once a society becomes stable and prosperous, this yearning simply disappears. Roman slaves, for instance, embraced Christianity on a large scale because it offered them a haven of bliss in the afterlife. Had they not been slaves, they might have remained polytheists and idolaters. It is felt then that with the progress made in science, man will certainly become happier and more prosperous and that ultimately the concept of a second, better life will die a natural death.

The history of science and technology over the last four hundred years does not, however, bear this out. Capitalism, an economic phenomenon which went hand in hand with advances in technology, caught up ordinary people in its grip, reducing artisans and craftsmen to mere machine-minders and diverted wealth away from the proletariat and into the hands of the industrial barons. Men who had once been proud of their skills became mere labourers with no further control over their own destinies and no hope of a better life in sight. "Das Kapital" (capital) by Karl Marx, presents a gruesome picture of the exploitation of the masses which took place in the eighteenth and nineteenth centuries. It took one whole century of socialist crusading before conditions took a turn for the better. Whatever changes took place were, however, purely superficial. No doubt, the worker of today earns higher wages as compared to his predecessors. But as far as the wealth of real happiness is concerned, he is immeasurably the poorer. Modern civilisation and technology may offer certain material gains to man, but it does not bring him any mental peace. How apt is Blake's description of man in modern civilisation.

> "A mark in every face I meet, marks of weakness, marks of woe."

Bertrand Russell has plainly stated that "Animals are happy so long as they have health and enough to eat. Human beings, one feels, ought to be happy, but in the modern world they are not, at least in a great majority of cases."[13]

The tourist in New York is dazzled to see 1250 foot high skyscrapers, like the Empire State Building, which is so high that the temperature of the top floors is much lower than that of the lower floors. You go all the way up and come back down again—hardly believing that you have been right up to the top, because the whole journey takes just 3 minutes in a lift. After seeing such impressive buildings and highly sophisticated shopping centres, the tourist enters a club where he finds men and women dancing together to the strains of music. "What a fortunate lot they are!" he exclaims. But no sooner are the words out of his mouth than a woman, looking decidedly depressed, emerges from the throng of dancers and sits down in a chair beside him. Out of the blue, she shoots  the question at him, "Do I strike you as being ugly?" "No I don't think so." "I don't seem to have any glamour." "You look glamorous enough to me." "Thanks. But you know, younger men have stopped cutting in or asking for a date. Life has become so dreary!"

Man in this modern age has become a mere shadow of his former self. Progress in science and technology may have enhanced our homes in many ways and provided us with all kinds of facilities such as rapid means of transport, libraries, entertainment, etc., but to tell the truth, people have been robbed of their peace of mind. Giant technological plants have been set up, but there is mass unrest among the workers. This is the tragic culmination of four hundred years of science and technology. Why should we believe then that science and technology will ever succeed in creating that new world of peace and happiness after which man is eternally questing?

Now let us consider this problem from a moral point of view. The sordid state of affairs prevailing in the present world makes it imperative that there should be a life hereafter. The whole history of man is rendered meaningless if this concept is subtracted from it.

Human nature is such that we discriminate between good and evil, between justice and injustice. No other creature save man displays this moral sense. Yet, it is in this very world of man that we find this particular instinct being suppressed. Man exploits his fellow men, robs them, tortures them, in short, oppresses them in many different ways—even murders them. Whereas even the animals do not butcher their own species. Wolf does not eat wolf, but man has become a wolf to his own species. No doubt, the history of man shows occasional sparks of truth and justice, which are highly commendable, but the major part of human history tells heart-rending tales of cruelty, injustice, exploitation, and violation of human rights. Those who delve into history are, as a rule, disappointed to see that the hard realities of life bear no relation to the high ideals enshrined in our consciences. The following observations by famous philosophers, historians and literary men are pertinent illustrations:

Voltaire: History is nothing more than a picture of crimes and misfortunes.

Herbert Spencer: History is simply useless gossip.

Napoleon: History on the whole is another name for a meaningless story.

Edward Gibbon: History, which is, indeed, little more than the register of the crimes, follies and misfortunes of mankind.

| | |
|---|---|
| Haegel: | The only thing public and government have learnt from a study of history is only that they have learnt nothing from history. |
| G.B. Shaw: | We learn from history that we learn nothing from history. |

We must ask ourselves if this grand show of humanity was staged only in order to present a series of horrors and then come to an end for ever. Our natures obviously rebel against this idea. A deeply rooted sense of justice and fair play in man demands that the fate of our world be different. There must come a time when truth and falsehood are known for what they are, when the oppressors must be called to account and the oppressed must be given due recompense for their sufferings. This desire for justice is so strongly ingrained in human nature that it is an inalienable part of the history of man. This contradiction between man's nature and the course of events shows that there is a vacuum which demands to be filled. The difference between what should happen and what actually does happen clearly indicates that there is some other stage of life which has yet to emerge. This gap cries out for the time when this world will be brought to completion. I wonder how people agreeing with Hardy's philosophy come to regard this world as a place of cruelty and oppression and yet fail to understand that something which does not exist today can exist tomorrow—that reason and logic demand it.

"If there is no Day of Judgement, who will punish these tyrants?" Often, while reading the newspaper, this question, sadly, forms in my mind. Newspapers, mirrors of day-to-day happenings in this world, report cases of kidnappings and murders, assault and battery, thefts, burglaries, charges, countercharges, and perhaps worst of all, the propaganda of vested interests. They show how rulers oppress their own subjects, and how, in the name of so-called national interest, one nation encroaches upon the territory of another. A newspaper thus depicts the dramas strategically played out by people in high places and how the common man is affected. The tally of racial genocide, communal riots, plunder and massacre of innocent people at the instance of those in power reaches unimaginable proportions. Heinous acts of violence are a commonplace. The atrocities perpetrated during the reign of a leader who is careful to project the public image of a benefactor of humanity and prophet of peace are so shameful that even animals like panthers, wolves and wild pigs seem humane by comparison. Such things happen regularly, on a large scale, and in an organised fashion over long periods. Sometimes, they happen too quite unabashedly in broad daylight for everyone to see. In spite of this, they may not even be mentioned in the world press, and false propaganda can all too easily prevent their final inclusion in the pages of history. Was this world created simply to serve as a stage for all these hideous dramas of fraud, wickedness, ferocity and robbery? For neither is the oppressor taken to task, nor are the grievances of the victims redressed. We must face the truth: such a world viewed in its entirety, reveals itself as suffering from abysmal deficiencies. Our world is incomplete, unfinished. This being so, a time will surely come when this world will be completed to absolute perfection.

Now look at the issue from another standpoint. Right from ancient times, the problem has arisen of keeping people on the path of truth and justice. If a group is vested with strong political authority, it is possible that those subject to that authority might not commit atrocities for fear of being punished. This system places no restraints, however, on those actually in authority. How then are those in power to be guided on to the path of justice? Even if laws are made and a whole army of policemen is raised, how is it possible to control people at places and on occasions which are beyond the reach of the police and the law? If a campaign appealing to the masses is launched, no matter how persuasive its propaganda may be, it is unlikely that those who have benefited materially from corrupt practices will relinquish their hold on their ill-gotten gains, or will change their ways one whit for the better. Humane appeals all too often fall on deaf ears. Even the fear of punishment in this world is unlikely to deter the criminal and the corrupt, for everyone knows fully well that falsehood, bribery, unfair influence and a host of other such underhand strategies will eventually win the day. Well-versed as they are in such tactics, the corrupt seldom feel apprehensive about prosecution and punishment.

If a man is to be successfully deterred from corrupt practices it is his own, inner motivation which will do this best. In the case of an upright, honest man, his will will be strengthened by the thought of the rewards in the after life, whereas a weak, immoral man will find himself propelled towards the straight and narrow path of virtue by his inner fear of the punishment that awaits him after death. These motivations will be far stronger and more effective than any external, artificial sanctions. This holds for everyone, whether in a superior or a subordinate position, be it in darkness or in light, in private or in public. The moment one seriously considers the fact that tomorrow, if not actually today, one will be made to stand before God Almighty on the Day of Reckoning, and that God, having kept a watch over everyone, will indeed sit in judgement on that day, one will be stiffened in one's resolve to perform only good and right actions and to eschew all that is base and evil. On this most important of religious beliefs, Mathew Hales, an eminent jurist of the late seventeenth century commented: "To say that religion is a cheat is to dissolve all those obligations whereby civil societies are preserved."[14]

How meaningful is the concept of the life hereafter when seen even from this angle. Even unbelievers who refute the notion that a day of judgement is an inevitable reality have been forced by the lessons of history to agree that if we reject the concept of the life hereafter there remains no other deterrent strong enough to control man and oblige him to observe the rules of justice and fair play. Immanuel Kant, the noted German philosopher, rejected the belief in God's existence on grounds of insufficient proof: "Since religion must be based not on the logic of theoretical reason but on the practical reason of the moral sense, it follows that any Bible or revelation must be judged by its value for morality and cannot itself be the judge of a moral code."[15]

Voltaire likewise did not believe in any metaphysical reality, but in his view also:

> "The concept of God and the life hereafter are very important in that they serve as postulates of the moral feeling. To him by means of them alone an atmosphere of good morals may be created. In the absence of such beliefs we have no incentive for good behaviour, making the maintenance of a social order well-nigh impossible."[16]

Those who adhere to the view that the life hereafter is merely a hypothesis should pause to consider why, if it is really only hypothetical, we should find this notion so indispensable. Why is it that, without such a concept, we cannot have true social order? Why is it that if this concept is eliminated from human thinking, the whole moral structure of life disintegrates? Can any mere hypothesis be so integral to life as this? Is there any other single example in this universe of a supposedly non-existent thing looming so large in human life, as a positive reality? The concept of the life hereafter being so vital to the establishment of a just and equitable order of life clearly shows that it is the greatest and most universal of all truths. It is in no way an exaggeration to say that, seen in this way, the concept of the life hereafter is quite consistent with the standards set by empiricism.

From another standpoint, the life hereafter may be viewed as the result of a 'universal demand.' In the last chapter, the existence of God in the universe was discussed and it became clear that a purely scientific and rational study demands that we believe in God as Creator and Sustainer of the universe. Now if there is such a God, his relationship with mankind ought to be in evidence. But as far as the present world is concerned, we have to concede that this relationship is not in any way apparent. Our leaders may boast of apostasy and still remain leaders while servants of the divine cause are debased and derided and their activities even declared illegal. We do not then experience any thunderbolts from heaven, or any other sign of God's displeasure.

There are people who openly ridicule religion, uttering such inanities as "We went to the moon on a rocket, but we didn't find God on the way!" No bolt of lightning strikes them down. Innumerable institutions work for the propagation of their materialistic ideologies and they are aided and eulogised by the high and the low at home and abroad, no effort begin spared to ensure the success of their mission. In stark contrast to this, those who preach the simple, noble message of God and religion have abuse heaped upon them and are dubbed reactionaries and revivalists by contemporary scholars. They are fortunate if the worst they have to suffer is social ostracism. In what way does God show His ire? Nations rise and fall; revolutions come and go like thunderstorms and natural catastrophes occur with a depressing regularity. But nowhere in this world is the relationship between God and mankind made plain. The question then arises as to whether we should believe in God or not. If we do believe in God, we must also believe in the life hereafter, for the simple reason that we can conceive of no other set of circumstances in which the relationship between God and man can be made manifest.

Darwin recognised a Creator for this world, but his interpretation of life did not prove the existence of any relationship between the Creator and His creatures. Neither did his interpretation suggest that there was any need for a life hereafter or a day of judgement upon which the relationship between the Creator and His creatures would become a reality. I fail to understand how Darwin imagined this gap in his biological interpretation could be filled. That there should be a God of this universe without his having any relationship with this world seems too extraordinary to be even conceivable. That His Lordship over mankind may never be revealed to us; that such a vast universe has been created and will ultimately come to an end without the attributes of the power behind it ever being known—all this seems quite unimaginable and certainly deficient in logic.

Our hearts cry out that truly a Day of Resurrection is bound to come—like an unborn child that is impatient to enter the world. A rational approach will likewise lead us to the view that the Day of Resurrection is imminent and may burst upon the world at any moment.

> "They ask you about the Hour (of Doom) and when it is to come. 'None Knows except my Lord. He alone will reveal it at the appointed time. A fateful hour it shall be both in the heavens and on earth. It will come without warning."[17]

## Empirical Evidence:

To conclude this discussion, we must ask ourselves what empirical evidence there is to support the concept of a life hereafter. In actual fact, the greatest proof of the life hereafter is our present life, in which we must obviously believe, even if we do not accept that there is an afterlife. But then why should we not accept it? It should be obvious that if life is possible on one occasion, it is perfectly possible for it to come into existence a second time. There would be nothing very strange about the recurrence of our present experience of life. In truth, there is nothing so irrational as admitting to a present occurrence, while rejecting the probability of its recurrence in the future.

Modern man falls unwittingly into self-contradiction. He is sure that the gods he has forged (the law of nature, chance, etc.) can cause the recurrence of certain sequences of events, but that the God of religion is not at all in a position to cause a regenesis of the present world. Explaining that the present earth and all its attributes owe their origin to an "accident," Sir James Jeans epitomises this school of thought: "There is no wonder if our earth originated out of certain accidents. If the universe survives for a long period, any thinkable accident is likely to occur."[18]

The doctrine of organic evolution asserts that all the species of animals have evolved from the same rudimentary species. According to Darwin, the present giraffe was originally like the other hoofed quadruped, but, in the course of lengthy evolution, developed a long-necked structure after a series of minor mutations. On this point Darwin observes: "It seems to me almost certain that (if the desired process goes on for a longer period) an ordinary hoofed quadruped might be converted into a giraffe."[19]

It followed, obviously, that whosoever attempted to offer an explanation for life and the universe had no choice but to accept that, given the same set of circumstances as was responsible for their origin, the same sequence of events could certainly be repeated. The truth is that, from a rational point of view, a second life is as great a possibility as our present life and this has to be admitted, no matter who is supposed to be the creator of this universe, no matter who he may be, he can cause the same sequence of events to occur all over again. If we choose to deny this, then we must need to deny the existence of our present life as well. Once we accept the first life, we have left ourselves no basis for the denial of the second life.

In the course of the above discussion, with reference to psychological research, it has been shown how all the thoughts in the human mind remain preserved indefinitely in the memory cells, the subconscious part of the brain. This clearly shows that the human mind does not form a part of the body, the particles of which undergo a complete change every few years. Just reflect upon the fact that, even after a hundred years, there occurs no faintness, no delusion, nor any error in the record maintained at the sub-conscious level. If memory is related to the body, where is it situated, what part of the body does it occupy and when the body particles gradually disappear within a few years, why does not memory also disappear? What manner of a record is it that remains intact even when the plate on which it is engraved is broken into pieces? This advanced study of psychology clearly proves that the human entity is not in fact the body, which, of necessity, deteriorates and dies. There is, on the contrary, something over and above the body which is not subject to death or decay and which has an immutable and independent existence whose continuity remains unbroken.

As far as the present life is concerned, all our conscious

functions are subject to the laws of time and space; the world hereafter – if it exists – is beyond their preview. If, according to Freud's theory, we had an intellectual life which was free from these laws, this would clearly establish the fact that this life would continue even after death and that we would survive in spite of death. Our dying is a logical outcome of the laws of time and space. Our real entity, or, in the words of Freud, our subconscious, is totally free from these laws. That is why death does not affect it. Death affects only our mortal body. The subconscious, which is the real being, survives even after the death of man. Suppose an event which took place in my life twenty five years ago, or an idea which developed in my mind equally long ago, slipped from my memory, but that one day I recollected that very event or idea, or even dreamt of it, the psychologist's explanation would be that it had all along been preserved intact in the depths of my subconscious. Here arises the question of where the memory lies. If it were engraved upon the cells as the voice is registered on gramophone records, it could not have been perpetuated, because those very cells would have disintegrated to the point of non-existence by the time of recollection. Where then was this subconscious record maintained within my body?

This is clearly evidence of an empirical nature which shows that, apart from this visible and tangible body, there is another invisible, intangible entity which does not die with the death of the body.

The results of psychical research—a branch of modern psychology which makes an empirical study of supernatural faculties in man—likewise establishes the existence of life after death at a purely observational level. What is most interesting is that such research does not merely establish survival; rather it establishes the survival of exactly the same personality—the entity that was known to us before death.

The first institution to conduct research in this field was established in England in 1882. It exists till today under the name of "Society for Psychical Research." In 1889, it began its work on a large scale by contacting 17,000 people for the purpose of making enquiries from them and obtaining their help in carrying out studies in the field. Many other countries followed suit, and by means of various experiments and demonstrations, it was shown that even after bodily death the human personality survives in some mysterious form. In his *Human Personality and its Survival of Bodily Death*, F.W.H. Myers recounts how a travelling agent was once noting down his orders, sitting in a hotel room at the Hotel St. Joseph in Missouri (U.S.A.), when he suddenly felt that someone was seated on his right. Turning quickly, he clearly saw that it was his sister, who had died nine years ago. Soon afterwards, his sister's image disappeared. He was so badly perturbed by this event that instead of continuing on his onward journey, he caught the next train back to his home town, St. Louis, where he narrated the entire episode to his relatives. When he reached the point of saying that he had seen a red-coloured scratch on the right side of his sister's face, his mother at once got to her feet, trembling. She confessed that after her daughter's death she had accidentally scratched her face, and had been so greatly pained to see this scar that she rubbed powder on it to conceal it, and had refrained from mentioning it to anyone.

There are a great number of recorded events which testify to the survival of the personality after bodily death. We cannot simply write off these events as illusory. Just ponder upon the fact that the scratch on the girl's face was known only to her mother and, presumably, to the deceased girl. There was no third person who had any inkling of it. Such events are not confined to Europe and America. But since most of the latter-day investigations have been carried out on those continents we find ourselves obliged to refer to them, for the sake of having a sufficiently large body of scientific evidence to draw on. If people in our country were adventurous enough to come forward and start such investigations right here and now, a large number of highly credible and sound pieces of evidence could be collected.

Regarding another class of events C.J. Ducasse observes:

Another class of occurrences asserted to constitute empirical evidence of survival consists of the communications given by the persons called automatists. There are men or women, whose organs of expression – their hand, holding a pencil, or their vocal organs – function at times automatically; that is, write or speak words that are not the expression of thoughts present to their consciousness at that time or of knowledge they possess, but appear to be as independent of the thoughts of, and of the stock of knowledge possessed by another person who happens to read them. The automatist is usually in a trance at such times, but there are many cases where he is not, and where, for example, he will be engaged in conversation, with someone present, and yet his hand will at the same time be writing, on some totally different subject, a lengthy communication of whose content he knows nothing until he reads it afterwards. The communications so obtained generally purport to come—either directly or through some invisible intermediary referred to as the automatist's "control"—from a person who has died and whose spirit has survived death. Such communications, in many cases have contained numerous items of evidence, of the very kinds which, for instance, would satisfy one of the identity of a person claiming to be his brother, with whom he could communicate at the time only through the intermediary of some third person or by telephone."[20]

Most contemporary scholars are hesitant about accepting the evidence furnished by psychical research. C.D. Broad writes:

"Barring the doubtful exceptions of psychical research, none of the different branches of science prove even the remotest possibility of life after death."[21]

This argument is as unsound as saying that "thinking" is a rather dubious phenomenon because, except for man, we have never been able to place anything in the universe under observation which testifies to the phenomenon of "thinking." Since the survival or extinction of life after death is a purely psychological problem, any evidence, either for or against, must be produced by psychology alone. To seek affirmation from any other discipline of science is as meaningless as turning to botany or metallography in order to understand man's inborn capacity to think. Even a study of the parts of the body cannot serve as a basis for the affirmation or denial of this concept because the doctrine of the life hereafter asserts not the survival of the present material body, but that of the spirit which albeit dwelling in the body, has its independent existence.

Many other scholars who have objectively examined the evidence furnished by psychical research have felt compelled to accept the life hereafter as a matter of fact. C.J. Ducasse, Professor of Philosophy at the Brown University, has made a philosophical and psychological scrutiny of this concept. He does not believe in it in the sense in which it is presented by religion, yet he holds that apart from the dogmas of religion, such evidence does exist as compels us to accept the survival of life after death. After making a general survey of various investigations in the field of psychical research he observes:

> Some of the keenest-minded and best informed persons, who studied the evidence over many years in a highly critical spirit, eventually came to the conclusion, that, in some cases at least, only the survival hypothesis remained plausible. Among such persons may be mentioned Alfred Russel Wallace, Sir William Crookes, F.W.H. Myers, Ceasare Lombrozo, Camille Flammarion, Sir Oliver Lodge, Dr. Richard Hodgson, Mrs. Henry Sidgwick and Professor Hyslop, to name only a few of the most eminent.
>
> This suggests that the belief in a life after death, which so many persons have found no particular difficulty in accepting as an article of religious faith, not only may be true but is perhaps capable of empirical proof; and if so, that, instead of the inventions of theologians concerning the nature of the post-mortem life, factual information regarding it may eventually be obtained.
>
> That, in such a case, the content of this information will turn

out to be useful rather than not, for the two tasks which it is the function of religion to perform, does not, of course, automatically follow.[22]

Having travelled so far along the road towards acceptance of life after death as a reality, it seems quite extraordinary to refuse to accept the religious concept of this same phenomenon. This is on a parallel with the insistence of an ignorant villager that conversation between two people living thousands of miles apart is impossible. Even when we dial the number of one of his own relatives living at a far distant place, hand him the receiver and let him have that conversation which he had found so incredible, he responds with, "Oh, that was not necessarily my relative speaking. That could have been some kind of machine." Where belief is concerned, we can lead a horse to the water, but we cannot make him drink.

## Notes

1. *Man the Unknown*, p. 173.
2. George Gamow, *Biography of the Earth*, p. 82.
3. T.R. Miles, *Religion and the Scientific Outlook*, p. 206.
4. Here a cell is described in terms of "bricks" simply to indicate its function in the body. In actuality, the cell is a highly intricate compound having a fully developed 'body' of its own. To study the cells, a new branch of science has been developed called Cytology.
5. *New Introductory Lectures on Psycho-Analysis*, (London, The Hogarth Press, Ltd., 1949), p. 239.
6. Quran, 50:16.
7. Quran, 50:18.
8. *Reader's Digest*, November, 1960.
9. Quran, 18:19.
10. Winwood Reade, *The Martyrdom of Man*, London, 1948, p. 414.
11. *Ibid*, p. 415.
12. *The Limitations of Science*, p. 9.
13. *Conquest of Happiness*, p. 93.
14. Quoted by Julian Huxley, *Religion without Revelation*, p. 115.
15. Will Durant, *The Story of Philosophy*, 1955, p. 279.
16. Windelband, *History of Philosophy*, p. 496.
17. Quran, 7:187.
18. *Modern Scientific Thought*, p. 3.

19. *Origin of Species*, p. 169.
20. C.J. Ducasse, *A Philosophical Scrutiny of Religion*, p. 407-408.
21. *Religion, Philosophy and Psychical Research*, (London, 1953), p. 235.
22. *A Philosophical Scrutiny of Religion*, p. 412.

# Affirmation of Prophethood

The Second basic tenet of religious belief is the concept of prophethood. Throughout the ages, God has conveyed His will to mankind through men of superior virtue, whom He has singled out from amongst all other human beings to be His prophets. Since there is no visible link between God and His messengers, claims of divine revelation are often doubted. Their truth becomes apparent, though, when we compare them with other events of this nature which have come to our knowledge.

Sounds are produced around us which are aurally undetectable, either because their frequency is too low or too high, or because they are too faint to impinge on our ear drums. But we know that they are a reality, because we now have such supersensitive sound-detecting devices as can record the movements of even a fly, moving miles away, as accurately as if it were buzzing around our ears. Even the collisions of cosmic rays can be recorded. Such devices are widely available today, yet such refinements of detection and registering of sound might conceivably seem impossible to one endowed only with the five senses provided him by nature, if he had somehow remained in ignorance of modern technological advances.

Such feats are not confined only to mechanical apparatus. The study of animals reveals that they have been endowed by nature with similar powers. A dog, for instance, with its highly sensitive nose, can smell an animal at a point from which it has long since departed. The special ability to track by scent is frequently used in the investigation of crime. A lock broken open by a thief is given to a dog to sniff, then the dog is unleashed. Out of a  whole crowd of people, the dog will pick up the real culprit just by using his highly developed sense of smell. Similarly, there are many animals which can detect voices at pitches above or below the normal range of human hearing.

Investigations have revealed that animals, who were formerly considered to communicate telepathically, actually emit signals which are inaudible to the human ear. A tiny creature like a female moth can emit signals which are picked up and responded to by male moths from great distances. The male cricket rubs its wings together to produce a sound which, in the silence of the night, can be heard half a mile away, vibrating 600 tons of air in the process. This is how the cricket calls its mate. The female answers in some mysterious 'soundless' way, yet the male receives this signal and sets off unerringly to join his mate. It has been discovered that the auditory ability of the common grasshopper is so refined as to be able to detect even the slightest movements of the radicals of a hydrogen atom.

There are innumerable examples of this kind which show that invisible and inaudible means of communication do exist, being perceptible only to creatures whose sensory abilities are more highly developed than man's. In view of our acceptance of such natural phenomena, there should be no great element of mystery in someone claiming that he receives messages from God which are not heard by ordinary people. When there are voices which only mechanical devices can detect and record, and messages are transmitted which are picked up only by animals with specially developed sensory perception, why should it appear strange that God communicates His message to specially endowed individuals in ways undetectable to others? The truth is that revelation, far from running counter to our observations and experiences, is a higher and more refined form of communication than our normal senses are capable of grasping.

Studies of telepathy and clairvoyance have revealed that certain human beings can communicate with others without recourse to speech, hearing, mechanical aids, etc. This potential presumably exists in all human beings, albeit in a rudimentary form. Dr. Alexis Carrel states: "The psychological frontiers of the individual in space and time are obviously suppositions."[1]

Just think that the hypnotist can cause his subject to fall into a trance without having recourse to any external medium. He can then make his subject laugh or weep, in fact, give any response he wishes, and he can also communicate certain ideas to the mind of the hypnotised person. It is an activity in which a hypnotist and subject are linked together by an invisible bond; no other person save the hypnotist and his subject can feel the effects of it. How is it then that a contact of this nature between God and man seems so unthinkable? After having admitted the existence of God and having observed or experienced telepathic communication in human life, we are left with no grounds for denying divine revelation.

A suit was filed by the Bavarian authorities in December, 1950, against a hypnotist, one Fronter Strobel, for having telepathically interrupted a radio programme, while demonstrating his art at the Rijna Hotel in Munich. What happened was that Strobel picked out a playing card, handed it to a member of the audience and asked him to note the suit of the card without disclosing this to him or to anyone else. The hypnotist then claimed that, even without knowing the number and suit of the card himself, he would transmit these details to an announcer, who was reading the news on Radio Munich at that time. Seconds later the audience were astonished to hear the announcer say in a faltering voice, "Rijna Hotel, trump card." The member of the audience who had co-operated in the experiment confirmed that this was indeed what he had mentally noted.

The horror of the announcer was evident from his voice, but he continued reading the news. Meanwhile, hundreds of listeners were telephoning the broadcasting station to find out what had gone wrong. They had obviously grasped that these words had no place in the context of the news and many of them alleged that the newsreader had been drunk. A doctor was immediately sent for and, examining the 'patient' found him in an extremely agitated state. He told the doctor that while reading the news, he had suffered from a severe headache all of a sudden, and that later he could not remember what had followed.

Now, if a mortal being can be endowed with telepathic faculties which permit him to transfer thoughts from one person to another without there being any visible link between the two and when, moreover, they are situated at prodigious distances from each other, why is it that the same kind of communication from the Lord of the Universe is considered inconceivable? Given this demonstration of a purely human capacity, we should have no difficulty in understanding how contact between man and God can be made without any visible medium, and how ideas can be transmitted from one to the other with no loss or distortion whatsoever. The perfect form of such communication is known specifically as 'revelation' in religious terminology. Revelation, in essence, is a kind of cosmic telepathy.

Evidence of its reality clearly emerges from the migratory habits of birds, who move from one part of the world to another along well-defined routes in search of more abundant food and better lives, returning with the changing seasons to their point of departure. Unlike man who needs information and guidance about routes and destinations before he sets off on a journey, the birds fly swiftly and unerringly towards their destination along 'flyways' which take them across wide stretches of water at their narrowest points thus keeping them above land for the maximum period possible. There is no evidence that for this to happen any information-gathering process or any exchange of ideas takes place. We must assume then that their guidance is from some external source, just as, according to the Quran, God made certain revelations to the bee (16:68) which led to its existence being so highly organised. Birds do not, like man, carry out research and pass on information.

If man were to be denied access to the historical information which has been accumulating over the centuries, or to the institutions which made the exchange of ideas a fruitful reality, he would be unable to accomplish anything. For instance, it is doubtful if Columbus would have sailed west in 1492 in the hope of finding India, if he had not been influenced by the ideas about the roundness of the world which were propagated by Latin translations of the works of Al-Idrisi (1100-1165), an Arab geographer and scientist who wrote one of the greatest mediaeval works on geography. The latter in his day had derived this idea from the Hindi concept of Arin. Columbus' experiences in turn increased the knowledge of his successors, and so the chain of learning was added to the science of geography till it reached its present state of progress. If a captain with confidence sails his ship from one shore to another of a vast ocean, or a pilot makes a perfect flight across several continents, it is thanks to the accretion of centuries of experience.

The birds have no such source of knowledge or means of communicating experience. They do not exchange ideas in the way that men do. No bird can collect and write down its experiences in book form for the future guidance of its successors. In spite of this, these birds manage to travel enormous distances, just like human beings, but with much greater accuracy and economy of effort. They move from one place to another with the precision of a rocket going into space by means of radio control.

The map on this page shows the intercontinental journeys of the birds from the colder Russian and European countries to the hotter regions of Africa and Asia. During this long journey they cross the Caspian, the Black sea and the Mediterranean—three seas no less. Far from flying in just any direction in an unaware,

*Affirmation of Prophethood* • 155

haphazard fashion, they unerringly follow the shortest route over the sea. In so doing, they can spend as little time as possible above water, where they cannot alight periodically for food and rest. Have a look at this map from right to left. The first flock of birds from Europe arrives at the Caspian, makes a detour around it, splitting into two groups, one of which goes via the Karakeram, the other flying by the side of Caucasus. Both arrive in Asia and land at

Principal routes taken by the European white stork (Ciconia ciconia) between nesting grounds in Europe and wintering grounds in Africa.

their desired destinations. Exactly the same course is followed when the birds arrive at the Black Sea. There they again divide themselves into two groups, one going by the west coast and the other by the east. And onwards they go until they reach the Asian regions. The third flock travels as far as Bulgaria, then diverts its course towards Turkey and follows the coast of Palestine, Lebanon and Syria in order to reach Suez, from where it enters Egypt, then travels onwards into Africa. The fourth flock wings its way to Greece with its many long promontories which help them southwards. The birds touch down in Greece and Crete while crossing the Mediterranean—at the narrowest point geographically. It is obvious that the birds take this route so as to spend the shortest possible time over the sea. The fifth flock of birds turns towards Italy, then Sicily, making a long flight southwards above the land and crossing the remaining narrow strip of sea to reach the north coast of Africa. The sixth flock flies towards France, then Spain, then crosses over the Straits of Gibraltar where the land masses of Iberian Peninsula and the coast of Africa are only ten miles away from each other. From there they reach West Africa.

There is something quite extraordinary about these flights. An ornithologist writes: "Birds have evolved a highly efficient means for travelling swiftly over long distances with great economy of energy."[2]

But their minds are quite inferior to the human mind. And they have no way of receiving help from the various fields of science. Nor is there any evidence to indicate that the birds have acquired their abilities through a process of evolution. How is this astonishing phenomenon to be explained? A thorough examination of the subject produces only two possible suppositions: firstly, that these birds have a complete knowledge of the geography of Europe, Asia and Africa, and of their lands and seas, a notion which is purely conjectural, this never having been borne out by research; secondly, that they are being given constant geographic guidance by some invisible remote control arrangement such as is given to unmanned rockets by radio control.

This second supposition is closer to the facts and makes the concept of revelation fully understandable in terms of religion. It means, quite simply, that God sends His guidance to man by just such invisible means, to show him what he must do and what he must not do. There being no visible contact between God and man at the time of revelation, many people refuse to accept that any such thing takes place. But if we consider the lives of other creatures, in particular, those of migratory birds, it becomes clear that guidance which is in the nature of revelation does take place. The flight of these birds can have no other true explanation than that they do receive some kind of external guidance. When there exist no known causes within the birds, we have to attribute their uncanny sense of timing and direction to external causes. The claim of the prophet that he received unseen guidance from God was certainly quite extraordinary. But such unseen guidance should not seem strange in the present universe, where there are so many such examples, one very obvious example being that given to fish such as salmon and eel to enable them to return across half the world to their breeding places in order to spawn.

Once we have admitted the possibility of divine revelation, we must establish whether there is any real need for God to address Himself to particular human beings in order to have His message conveyed to the rest of humanity. The most telling evidence to this effect is the fact that the message the prophets bring – the truth – is man's greatest need. From time immemorial man has gone in search of reality, but has found it impossible to discover unaided. He longs to understand what the universe is, how our life began, and what its end will be. He seeks to understand the true nature of good and evil, and how mankind may be controlled. He needs to know how to organise life so that all aspects of human relations are given due recognition and can have a balanced growth. So far, man's attempts to find answers to these age-old problems have met with utter failure. It has taken us only a relatively short time to acquire a vast knowledge of the material world, and branches of such learning as pertain only to the physical aspect of life continue to proliferate. But in the sphere of human sciences, the most prolonged efforts on the part of the best brains have failed to determine even the most basic factors in this field. What greater proof can there be that we need the help and guidance of God? Without this, we cannot arrive at the fundamental principles on which we should lead our lives, we cannot understand what is meant by religion, and we shall certainly never discover what is ultimately the truth.

Modern man has admitted that life is still a great, unsolved mystery. He is, nevertheless, confident that one fine day he will unveil it. But the brains which are bent to the human sciences have yet to discover the reality; they are wandering adrift, in a world of their own fantasies. This is because the present environment developed by science and technology does not suit man as a living creature, and is, therefore, hardly conducive to the reception of divine inspiration. The sciences concerned with inert matter have made immense progress, but those concerned with living beings are still in a rudimentary state. The French Nobel Laureate Dr. Alexis Carrel states:

> **The principles of the French Revolution, the visions of Marx and Lenin, apply only to abstract men. It must be clearly realised that the laws of human relations are still unknown. Sociology and economics are conjectural sciences – that is pseudo-sciences.**[3]

No doubt science has developed immensely in modern times, but human confusion has not been helped by this. In *Limitations of Science*, J.W.N. Sullivan points out that the universe that is in the process of discovery by science nowadays is the most mysterious issue in the entire history of intellectual thinking, and that although our present knowledge of nature is much richer than in any previous epoch, even this is insufficient because, no matter where we turn, we are faced with ambiguities and contradictions.

Attempts by material science to discover the secret of life have been such pathetic failures that they leave us with the uncomfortable thought, finally, that it is undiscoverable by man. If the reality of life is to remain unknown, how are we ever to function satisfactorily as individuals and as communities? Our finest feelings demand to know it. The intellect – the most superior part of our being has an eternal craving for this knowledge. The whole system of life is fast deteriorating and without it, there can be no improvement. Yet there appears to be no solving of this great mystery. It is the most urgent need of the hour, but it is something which we cannot achieve on our own. Is this state of affairs not proof enough that man is badly in need of revelation?

The indispensability of the knowledge of the reality of life, and this knowledge remaining undiscoverable, are clear indications that it must be provided from an external source, just as heat and light in the form of the sun's rays are provided by nature. Once we accept both the possibility and the necessity of divine revelation, we have to ascertain whether or not the person who claims prophethood is a true recipient of God's word. We do believe that innumerable prophets have been raised up by God. In the present chapter, however, we shall deal only with the claim of Muhammad, upon whom be peace, to definitive prophethood. An affirmation of his prophethood implies an affirmation of all the prophets who came before him, because the Prophet Muhammad, instead of denying the claims of his predecessors, testifies to the bonafides of all true prophets, being the last in the long series of prophets. He continues to remain a prophet for the present as well as for future generations. From a practical point of view, the salvation or damnation of mankind thus depends solely upon the affirmation or denial of his prophethood.

Muhammad was born in the early hours of the 29th of August, 570 A.D., in Makkah. But it was not until he had attained the mature age of 40 that he announced that God had chosen him as His last prophet, that He had revealed His message to him and had entrusted him with the duty of conveying it to all of mankind. Whoever obeyed Him would be amply rewarded and whoever disobeyed would be destroyed.

This call, in all its intensity, is as relevant to us now as it was in the Prophet's day. This is not a voice to be listened to with scant attention, for it makes a great demand and calls for deep thought. If, upon reflection, we find it false, we are at liberty to reject it, but if we find it true, we must accept it wholeheartedly.

According to modern thinking, it takes three stages for any idea to be accepted as a scientific fact; hypothesis, observation, verification. First of all, an idea, or hypothesis, takes shape in the mind, then it is subjected to observation and when observation testifies to it, the hypothesis comes to be recognised as an established fact.

According to this system, the claim of prophethood by

Muhammad is now before us as a 'hypothesis,' and we have to see whether observation confirms it or not. If observation speaks in its favour, this hypothesis will acquire the status of a verified fact and we shall have, perforce, to accept it.

Let us see what observations are required in order to testify to the 'hypothetical' claims of the Prophet. In other words, what are the external manifestations in the light of which it may be determined that he really was a messenger of God? What are those qualities which come together in the personality of such a messenger, the presence of which cannot be explained except in terms of his being a prophet of God? One who claims to be such must of necessity be in possession of two special qualities.

Firstly, he must be an absolutely ideal man. One who is selected from all mankind to have a special relationship with God for the purpose of revealing the divine way of life, so that the lives of all mankind may be reformed, must surely be the most superior individual of the entire human race. He must personify to perfection every high ideal. And if his life is, indeed, adorned with such ideals this is ample evidence of the truth of his claim. If his assertion were unfounded, the ideals he preached would not be enshrined in his person to such perfection, and he would not morally stand out from the whole human race.

Secondly, his message should be replete with such truths as are beyond the reach of common men—as might be expected only from one whose source of information is the Lord of the Universe. These are the criteria by which we have to judge the claim of prophethood.

So far as the first criterion is concerned, history bears witness to the fact that Muhammad, upon whom be peace, was of an extraordinary character. There are those who, out of sheer obstinacy, will doggedly assert the reverse, but anyone who studies the facts objectively and in an unprejudiced way will surely grant that the Prophet's life was quite exemplary from the moral point of view. Prophethood was conferred upon Muhammad upon whom be peace, in his fortieth year. The whole period of his life prior to this was so markedly of a high moral character that he had earned himself the title of "As-Sadiq al-Amin," or "the truthful, the trustworthy." Throughout the entire region where he lived, he was highly thought of by everyone, being considered the most honest possible person and incapable of telling a lie. Five years before the commencement of his prophethood, the Quraysh in Makkah, decided to reconstruct the Kabah after a sudden flood had shaken its foundation and cracked its walls. The work began, and new walls were built. As the walls rose from the ground and the time came to place the sacred black stone in its place in the east wall, they differed as to who should have the honour of laying it in place. Competition was so keen that it almost led to a new civil war. Four or five days passed in this state. Then Abu Umayyah, son of Mughirah al Makhzum, suggested to the Makkans, "Let the first one to pass through the gate of the Kabah next morning be our arbitrator in this dispute." And the first one to pass through the gate was Muhammad. When people beheld him they called out, "There goes al-Amin (the trustworthy)! We shall agree with his verdict."

We know of no one in history whose life (before it became the object of controversy in the wake of prophethood) remained an open book before his fellow men for all of forty years without his extraordinary reputation for high moral values and sterling character ever once being assailed.

His first experience of divine revelation took place in the Cave of Hira. It was an astounding incident such as he had never before experienced. Trembling with fear and stricken with awe, he left for home. Shivering and shaking, he told his wife, Khadija, what has happened. She implored him not to feel afraid and reassured him by saying, "By God, He (God) will not let you down; you speak the truth, you help the needy, rescue the weary; you are kind to your kin; you are honest and trustworthy. You return good for evil and you always give people their due."

When Muhammad, upon whom be peace, conveyed the message of Islam to his paternal uncle, Abu Talib, the latter did not accept it, saying, "I cannot abjure the religion of my father." But it is interesting to note his reaction to his own son, Ali, coming under the prophet's influence. In his book, The Ideal Prophet, Khwaja Kamaluddin records him as saying, "Well, my son, he (Muhammad) will not call thee to anything save that which is good; therefore thou art free to cleave unto him" (p. 211).

After being entrusted with the divine mission, the Prophet called his people together for the first time near Mount Safa. Before conveying his message to the people assembled there, he first asked them, "What is your opinion of me?" They all replied in unison, "We have never seen anything but truth in you." This distinguished historical record of the Prophet's life prior to his prophethood is unparalleled in history, and is such as no poet, philosopher, thinker or writer can lay claim to.

When Muhammad, upon whom be peace, proclaimed his prophethood, the Makkans, who were thoroughly acquainted with his virtues, could hardly repudiate him as a liar or a fraud, because this would have been totally at variance with the life he had led uptill then. His message was regarded rather as a form of poetic exaggeration, the result of mental disorder, or witchcraft, while some held that an evil spirit possessed him. His opponents gave voice to all these misgivings, but they did not dare cast aspersions on his personal honesty, truthfulness and integrity. How remarkable it is that a people, provoked to the extreme at his call, turned into his direct enemies, expelled him from his home town, yet continued to refer to him as being 'honest and trustworthy.' In Ibn Hisham's *The Life of Muhammad*,[4] this is testified too: "It happened that whenever in Makkah anyone had to keep anything safely, he would entrust it to the Prophet, as everyone was sure of his truthfulness and honesty" (Vol.II. p. 298).

In the thirteenth year of his prophethood, at the very moment when his opponents had blockaded his house in order to assassinate him as he came out, the Prophet was instructing Ali, his cousin, to tarry in Makkah until he had returned all the things given to him for safekeeping to their rightful owners.

Nadhr ibn Harith, one of the Prophet's opponents and the most seasoned of all the Qurayshites, one day addressed his people thus: "O, Quraysh, the message of Muhammad has put you in such an awkward (difficult) position that you are left with no solution. He grew up to a mature age before your very eyes. You know very well that he was the most sincere; most honest; most trustworthy and most dear to you all. Now when his hair turned grey and he presented before you something which you have received, it was you that said, 'this fellow is a magician, a poet, an insane person.' By God, I have heard him, Muhammad is neither a magician, nor a poet, nor insane, I am sure some calamity is going to befall you."[5]

Even Abu Jahal, the Prophet's worst opponent and deadliest enemy, said, "Muhammad, I do not say that you are a liar, but I hold that the message you are propagating is not true."

Muhammad was a prophet sent not only to the Arabs but to all mankind. As such, he took it upon himself to send letters to the neighbouring kings, calling them to Islam. Dihyah ibn Khalifah al Kalbi was chosen as the Prophet's emissary to Heraclius and met him at the time of his victorious return from the war with Persia during which he had recovered the cross which had been taken away by the Persians when they occupied Jerusalem. The vow which Heraclius had made, namely, to make a pilgrimage on foot to Jerusalem and return the cross to its original place could now be fulfilled. It was on this very pilgrimage to the city of Homs that Muhammad's message was received. Heraclius was in no way upset by it and sent for some Arabs belonging to Muhammad's tribe, who had come to Syria in a caravan of Quaraish[6] traders, they duly arrived at his court and Heraclius first inquired of them as to who was the closest relative of the person who had claimed prophethood in their city. Abu Sufyan replied that he belonged to the Prophet's family. Here is a part of the ensuing dialogue.

Heraclius: Have you ever heard him telling a lie before he made this claim?

Abu Sufyan: Never.

Heraclius: Has he ever failed to keep his word?

Abu Sufyan: No, he had never broken any promise, any

agreement.

Heraclius: When it has been experienced that he never tells a lie when the matter is between men, then how can it be said that he can concoct such a great lie in the matter of God?

This dialogue took place when Abu Sufyan himself had not yet accepted Islam and had actually been leading military campaigns against the Prophet. Abu Sufyan admitted that he had not felt inclined to tell the emperor the truth, but, because of his fellow Arabs being present, he felt obliged to do so for fear of being dubbed a liar.

In the entire history of mankind we find no comparable paradox: a leader of men held in the highest of esteem by enemies so diametrically opposed to him that they were ready to assassinate him. The fact that even his deadliest antagonists could recognize his virtues is in itself ample evidence of being a Prophet of God.

M. Abul Fazal, in his *Life of Mohammad*, quotes Dt. Leitner as saying: "If there be such a process as inspiration from the source of all goodness, indeed, I venture to state in all humility, that if self-sacrifice, honesty of purpose, unwavering belief in one's mission, a marvellous insight into existing wrong or error, and the perception and use of the best means for their removal, are among the outward and visible signs of inspiration, the mission of Muhammad was 'inspired.'"

When the Prophet began to propagate his message, his own people began to persecute him in a variety of ways. On one occasion his path was strewn with thorns. On another he was pelted with filth when saying his prayers. Once, when he was in prayer at the Kabah, Uqbah ibn Abi Muayt, a dire opponent of the Prophet, twined a sheet so tightly round his neck that he fell down in a swoon. When torment upon torment failed to deter him from his resolve, the Makkans imposed a social boycott upon him and all the members of his family, who were then forced to seek refuge in one of the hilly areas on the outskirts of Makkah. In their isolation, they suffered all kinds of privations often going without food and water. During this period, no one was allowed to buy from or sell to Muhammad or his family, not even eatables. The leaves of wild bushes had to serve as their food. One day one of them came upon a piece of dried leather. He picked it up, washed it, baked it on a fire and then ate it with water. This boycott went on for three long years.

In the face of such hardness on heart of the part of the Makkans, the Prophet (when the boycott was finally revoked) chose to turn his attention to Taif, a city located three miles away from Makkah, where he hoped to call the tribe of Thaqif to Islam, and to solicit their support.

The people of Taif not only refused to hear him, but repudiated him and his teaching outright. They made such insulting remarks as, "Couldn't God find anyone but you for prophethood?" And that was not all. They incited the street urchins to jeer at him in the public thoroughfares. They pelted him with so many stones that his shoes were overflowing with blood. Whenever he sat down hoping to have some relief, the townspeople forced him to keep walking so that they could stone him on the move. They kept this up for three long miles until he was enveloped by the darkness of night. Bleeding and exhausted, he walked on until he came to the vineyard of 'Utba ibn Rabia, a nobleman of Makkah, where he finally took shelter.

Once he said to his wife, Aisha, "I have suffered what I have suffered from your people, but the hardest of these days was the day of Taif." The Prophet continued to preach the word of God even in the face of such terrible persecution. Finally, the chiefs of all the tribes unanimously agreed that assassination was the only way to bring his missionary activities to an end. The house of the Prophet was then laid siege to by young men selected by the Quraysh from different tribes to waylay him and murder him. But, by the grace of God, the Prophet was able to slip away from his house and reach Madinah in safety.

The Quraysh then resolved to wage war on him, and thus kept the Prophet and his companions embroiled in wars for ten long years. In these battles, the Prophet was badly wounded, even losing some of his teeth, and witnessed the martyrdom of many of his best companions, not to speak of all the suffering, misery and hardship which are inflicted on people in war-time conditions.

Makkah was finally conquered towards the end of the Prophet's life, but only after twenty-three years of trials and tribulations. His enemies, who had shown themselves obdurate and unrelenting then stood before him in a state of utter helplessness. That was the moment to crush them completely. But this was not the way of the Prophet Muhammad. What other, lesser men would do in such a situation is common knowledge, but the Prophet did not avenge himself upon them for their past offences. He quite simply asked them, "O people of the Quraysh, how do you think I shall deal with you?" They replied, "You are our noble brother and son of our noble brother." The Prophet then said, "Go, you are all free." Stanley Lane-Poole, in his introduction to E.W.Lane's *Selection from the Quran* elaborates upon the Prophet's remarkable self-discipline:

> Now was the time for the Prophet to show his blood-thirsty nature. His old persecutors are at his feet. Will he not trample on them, torture them, revenge himself after his own cruel manner? Now the man will come forward in his true colours: We may prepare our horror, and cry shame beforehand. "But what is this? Is there no blood in the streets? Where are the bodies of the thousands that have been butchered? Facts are hard things, and it is a fact that the day of Muhammad's greatest triumph over his enemies was also the day of his grandest victory over himself. He freely forgave the Quraysh all the years of sorrow and cruel scorn they had infected on him: he gave an amnesty to the whole population of Makkah. Four criminals, whom justice condemned, made up Muhammad's proscription list when he entered as a conqueror the city of his bitterest enemies. The army followed the example, and entered quietly and peaceably and no house was robbed, no woman insulted.

Had such an example of superior conduct survived from pre-historic times, perhaps in the form of a myth, it would have been regarded as fiction, being too astonishing to be a fact. History, indeed, has no match for the magnanimity of the Prophet. Sir William Muir, speaking of the treatment meted out to the prisoners of Badr by the Muslims, gives another such shining example:

> In pursuance of Muhammad's commands, the citizens of Madinah and such of the refugees as possessed houses, received the prisoners and treated them with much consideration. 'Blessings be on the men of Madinah!' said these prisoners in later days. 'They made us ride, while they themselves walked; they gave us wheat and bread to eat, when there was little of it, contending themselves with dates!'

The sincerity of purpose and selflessness that he displayed throughout his life have, indeed, no parallels in history.

Prior to his prophethood, he had been a successful merchant and had entered into marriage with a wealthy widow, Khadija. But when he was entrusted with the divine mission, he gave up trading and even used up Khadija's wealth in the propagation of the faith, entering upon a period of untold suffering and persecution. The very necessities of life like food and water became scarce and it was no uncommon thing for his followers to go without them altogether.

Although the prospects of a far more comfortable life were always there before him, the Prophet continued to suffer all kinds of privations for the sake of his divine mission. During his stay in Makkah, Uqba was once sent to the Prophet on behalf of the Quraysh. He said, "Son of my friend, be it thy aim to acquire wealth by this affair, we will assess ourselves to make thee our lord, and will do nothing without thee. If it be the Jinn that has taken possession of thee, we will bring thee the most able physicians, and we will pour out our gold until they cure thee." "Is that all?" asked the Prophet. "Yes." "Well, now listen to me." Then the Prophet, in answer, simply recited some verses from the Quran.[7]

In Madinah, the Prophet was the ruler of a state and had such a faithful band of followers as would be hard to find again in the whole history of mankind. But events show that right to the very last moments of his life, his daily existence was humble in the extreme.

Umar, one of his close companions, narrates how one day he went to see the Prophet at his home. "When I entered his room, I saw that he was resting on a mat of date palms and had no shirt on. The marks of the mat were visible on his back. Besides the mat, his only possessions were three skins, some bark placed in a corner and small quantity of barley. On seeing this, I could not help but weep. 'What makes you weep? the Prophet asked. "The Roman and Persian emperors enjoy all worldly comforts, yet you—the messenger of God—are suffering so much,' I replied. On hearing these words, the Prophet sat up and said, 'Umar, what on earth do you mean? Don't you want those people to have the world and we to have the Hereafter?"

Often, month after month would pass without a fire being lit in the Prophet's kitchen. When Urwah, one of his companions, asked the Prophet's wives how they survived with food in such short supply, they answered that their diet consisted of dates and water. At times the Ansars (Madinan neo-converts) would send them some milk. It seldom happened that the Prophet's family had enough wheat in store to last out three days in succession. When the Prophet finally left this world, the material conditions of his life were in no way better.

In spite of having access to all power, he passed his life in this state and left nothing behind him for his family. Neither did he leave a will. All he left behind him was the simple dictum: "We prophets have no heirs, whatever we leave behind is to be given in alms", These were the words of the founder of the world's greatest empire, knowing fully well that it was soon to annex Asia and Africa and cross the borders of Europe.

These glimpses of his words and character, of his sincerity and self-sacrifice are not trifling exceptions. His whole life was lived out in this way. It will hardly be surprising then if we accept such an extraordinary man to have been a messenger of God. What would be surprising, on the contrary, would be to refuse to accept him as such. In our acceptance of him as a prophet, we find an explanation for his miraculous personality. Conversely, if we do not accept his prophethood, we are left with no answer as to the source of his astonishing qualities, particularly when we know that in the whole of recorded history, he is absolutely unique. Bosworth Smith's words are at one and the same time a recognition of the reality and a call to mankind to believe in his prophethood. "What more crowning proof of his sincerity is needed? Muhammad to the end of his life claimed for himself that title only with which he had begun, and which the highest philosophy and the truest Christianity will one day, I venture to believe, agree in yielding to him, that of a Prophet, a very Prophet of God."[8]

## Notes

1. *Man the Unknown*, p. 242.
2. *Encyclopaedia Britannica*, Vol. 12, p. 179.
3. *Man the Unknown*, p. 37.
4. The oldest known biography of the Prophet Muhammad.
5. *Seerat Ibn Hisham*.
6. The Arabian tribe from which the Prophet Muhammad, upon whom be peace, had descended, and of which his grandfather was chief. This tribe occupied a very prominent place on account of its strength and importance amongst the tribes of Arabia.
7. *Seerat ibn Hisham*, vol. 1. p.314.
8. Bosworth Smith, *Mohammad and Mohammadanism*, p.340.

# The Challenge of the Quran

'All of the prophets were given such miracles as inspired people to believe. And the miracle that I have been given is the Quran.'

These words of the Prophet recorded by Bukhari in the first century of Islam, give proper direction to our quest. They make it clear that the Quran, which he presented to the people as having been revealed to him, word by word, by God is itself a compelling proof of his being a true prophet.

What are those features of the Quran which prove it to be the word of God? There are many, but I shall refer briefly to only a few.

The one which is bound to make the immediate impact upon a student of the Quran is the challenge it made fourteen hundred years ago to produce a book, or even a chapter, which is its equal.

**And if you are in doubt of what We have revealed to Our servant, produce one chapter comparable to it. Call upon your helpers besides God to assist you, if what you say be true.**[1]

Needless to say, this challenge has not to this day been met. Those who feel that the authorship of the Quran was human and not divine should consider also that no ordinary mortal would deliver himself of such a challenge for fear of being instantly proved a posturer and a braggart. Neither the Quran, nor the challenge it flings down to humanity, can be of human origin, for no human work is ever complete; it can always be added to, improved upon and emulated. Purely human standards are always re-attainable. This, however, has proved the Quran to be quite unique in that it is both definitive and inimitable.

Attempts were, of course, made to meet this challenge. The first was that of Labid Ibn Rabiyah, a contemporary of the Prophet and the last of a series of seven renowned poets of the time. He was so eloquent that once, when he recited a poem at the famous annual fair of Ukaz, the other poets present fell in prostration before him—they were so enchanted by his verses. In pre-Islamic days, outstanding poets used to be honoured after annual gatherings by having their works hung on the wall of the entrance to the Kabah, so that the public could read them, the whole year round.

Before his acceptance of Islam, Labid once composed a poem in reply to the Quran which was thus displayed. Shortly after this, a Muslim brought some verses from the Quran and hung them alongside Labid's poem. The following day, when Labid read them, he was so moved that he declared that they must be the work of some superhuman mind, and, without further ado, he embraced Islam. But this was not the end of the matter. Famous as he was as an Arabian poet, he was so greatly impressed by the literary excellence of the Quran that he decided to give up writing poetry altogether. When asked why he did not continue to write poetry, he replied, 'What? After the Quran?' Once, when asked by Umer, the Second Caliph, to recite a poem, he said, 'When God has given me such compositions as are enshrined in the Quran, it does not behove me to recite poems.'

Stranger still is the case of Ibn-al Muqaffa (died 727 A.D.), a great scholar and celebrated writer of Persian origin, who was called upon by the unbelievers to counteract the widespread influence the Quran was having on great throngs of people. A man of extraordinary genius, he felt quite confident that he could produce such a work in one year's time, provided that all his practical requirements were taken care of, so that he could give his undivided attention to the composition. Six months passed and, naturally, certain people were eager to know how much work had been accomplished. When they went to see him, they found him sitting, pen in hand, staring at a blank sheet of paper. Around him were scattered innumerable pieces of paper. This great, learned and eloquent writer had done his best to write a book comparable to the Quran, but had failed pathetically. Highly embarrassed, he admitted that even after working for all these six months, he had not been able to produce even a single sentence which could match up to the excellence of the Quran. Ashamed and hopeless, he gave up the task he had been entrusted with. This incident was recounted by the orientalist Wollaston, in his book, *Muhammad, His Life and Doctrines*, (p.143) to show that 'Muhammad's boast as to the literary excellence of the Quran was not unfounded.'

The challenge of the Quran has yet to be answered. Centuries have rolled by without anyone ever having been able to match it. This uniqueness of the Quran undoubtedly proves that it is of divine origin. If man has the ability to think objectively, this should be enough to convince him of the truth. Such was the miraculous nature of the Quran that the Arabs, who had no peers in eloquence and fluency, were so proud of their rhetoric that they called all non-Arabs dumb—*ajamis* were compelled to bow before the superior qualities of the Quran.

## Predictions

Another factor which testifies to the divinity of the Quran is its predictions which, astonishingly enough, came true in the course of time. We come across many intelligent and ambitious people in the pages of history who have dared to predict their own or other's futures. But seldom has time confirmed their predictions. Favourable circumstances, extraordinary capabilities, a host of friends and supporters and initial successes have often singly, or together, deluded people into thinking that nothing could stop them from attaining certain cherished goals, and so they have ventured to prophesy that they were destined to scale great pinnacles of success. But history has almost refused to fulfill their predictions. On the other hand, in spite of totally unfavourable and quite unthinkable circumstances, the words of the Quran have come true, time and time again, and in such a manner that no human science is able to offer an explanation for it. These events can never be understood in the light of human experience. The only way to rationalize them is to attribute them to a super human being.

Napolean Bonaparte was one of the greatest generals of his time. His initial successes showed signs of his surpassing even such renowned conquerors as Caesar and Alexander. It was not unnatural that his phenomenal success should foster the idea that he was the master of his own destiny. He then became so over-confidant that he stopped consulting even his closest advisers. He believed that nothing short of total victory was to be his lot in life: but how did his career end? On June 12, 1815, Napoleon set off from Paris with a huge army, which was intended to annihilate the enemy. Just six days later, Napoleon and his army were given a thorough trouncing at the Battle of Waterloo by the Duke of Wellington who was leading the forces of Britain, Holland and Germany. His hopes and aspirations shattered, he abandoned his throne and attempted to flee to America to seek asylum. But no sooner had he reached the harbour than he was arrested by enemy guards and forced to board a British ship. He was subsequently taken to the Island of St. Helena in the Southern Atlantic, where he was compelled to live in isolation, bitter and frustrated, till he breathed his last on 5th of May 1821.

Another example of the hazards of human prophecy is the Communist Manifesto of 1848 in which it was presaged that Germany would be the first country to witness a communist revolution. But even after one hundred and thirty eight years, this prophecy has still to be fulfilled. Karl Marx wrote, in May 1849, that in Paris, red democracy was just around the corner. More than a century has passed, but the dawn of red democracy has yet to rise over that city.

Another important, but ill-fated prophecy was made in 1798 by the British economist, Robert Malthus (1766-1834), more than a thousand years after the Quran was revealed. In his book, *An Essay on the Principle of Population as it Affects the Future Improvement of Society*, he set forth his famous theory on the growth of population. 'Population, when unchecked, increases in a geometrical ratio. Subsistence only increases in an arithmetical ratio.'

Simply stated, growth in population and growth in sustenance are not naturally equal. Human population grows geometrically, that is at a ratio of 1-2-4-8-16-32, while the growth of food supplies maintains an arithmetical ratio: 1-2-3-4-5-6-7-8. Sustenance, therefore, cannot keep up with the astronomical growth in human population. The only solution to this problem, according to Malthus, was for mankind to control its birth rate. The population should not be allowed to exceed a certain limit. If it did, the number of people on earth would become greater than the amount of sustenance available, ushering in an age of famine in which countless people would starve to death.

Malthus' book made a powerful impression on human thought, winning substantial support among writers and thinkers, and leading to the launching of birth-control and family-planning schemes. Recently, however, researchers have come to the conclusion that Malthus was quite wrong in his calculations. Gwynne Dyer has summarised this research in an article which appeared in *The Hindustan Times* (New Delhi) on

December 28, 1984. The provocative headline read: 'Malthus: The False Prophet.' In it he wrote:

> It is the 150th anniversary of Malthus' death, and his grim predictions have not yet come true. The world's population has doubled and redoubled in a geometrical progression as he foresaw, only slightly checked by wars and other catastrophes, and now stands at about eight times the total when he wrote. But food production has more than kept pace, and the present generation of humanity, is on average the best fed in history .

Malthus was born in an age of 'traditional agriculture.' He was unable to envisage the approach of an age of 'scientific agriculture', in which amazing advances in production would become possible. Over the 150 years since Malthus's death, methods of cultivation have been radically altered. Crops under cultivation are chosen for their particularly high yield. Cattle are able to produce a far higher amount of dairy food than before. New methods have been discovered to increase the fertility of land. Modern machinery has brought vast new areas under cultivation. In technologically-advanced countries of the world there has been a 90% fall in the number of farmers: yet at the same time a tenfold increase in agricultural produce has taken place.

As far as the third world is concerned, 3 billion people inhabit these under-developed countries, but the third world also possesses the potential to produce food for 33 billion—ten times the present population. According to F.A.O. estimates, if the increase in the population of the third world continues unabated, reaching over the 4 billion mark by the year 2000 A.D., there will still be no cause for alarm. The increase in population will be accompanied by an increase in production: the means will be available to provide food for 1½ times more than the number of people who have to be fed. And this increase in food production will be possible without deforestation. So there is no real danger of a food crisis, either on a regional or on a universal scale. Gwynne Dwyer concludes his report with the following words:

'Malthus was wrong. We are not doomed to breed ourselves into famine.' Fourteen hundred years before this, the Quran had said: 'And fearing hunger, do not slay your own offspring. We provide for them and for you. Surely, it is a great error to slay them.'²

Where Malthus' book on population and sustenance—the work of a human mind working within the confines of time and place—was very far out in its predictions for the human race, (and this was proved to the world just 150 years after the author's death), the Quran, on the other hand—the work of a superhuman mind—still bears out external realities to this very day.

Nearer to our times, one of the most famous unfulfilled prophecies was that which the German dictator, Adolf Hitler made about himself.

In a famous speech delivered in Munich on the 14th of March, 1936, he declared that he was marching ahead with full confidence that victory would come his way. The world knows, however, that after several brilliant victories, the destiny that awaited him was a final crushing defeat, and an ignominious death by suicide.

If we look at the historic prophecies which have been made in this world, those made in the Quran stand out from all the rest in that they all came quite literally true. This fact is ample proof that their origin was a superhuman mind which, with its eternal knowledge, controls the course of cosmic events—in short, they were the words of God.

Of particular interest are the predictions concerning the victories respectively of the Prophet of Islam over his antagonists and of the Romans over the Persians.

When the Prophet Muhammad began propagating the message of Islam, almost the whole of Arabia turned against him. On the one hand were the idolatrous tribes, who were thirsty for his blood and, on the other, were the rich and powerful Jews who were determined to foil every attempt on his part to propagate his message. A third group consisted of Muslims who made a public show of having embraced the faith, while concealing their intention to infiltrate the ranks of the genuinely faithful in order, without arousing any suspicion, to bring about the downfall of the Islamic cause.

Thus the Prophet was carrying on his mission in the face of three inimical groups, two of which openly displayed their power and resources, while the third, the conspirators, donned the mask of hypocrisy. Leaving aside a small band of slaves and few people from the lowest rungs of society, no one was willing to rally to his cause. Out of all the highly placed people of Makkah, those who answered his call were almost negligible in number, and when they converted, they too incurred the wrath of their people, so that, in spite of having come from the nobility, they were destined to become just as helpless as the Prophet was.

The Islamic mission went on, however, irrespective of the obstacles placed in its path. But a time came when circumstances became so critical that the Prophet and his companions were forced to leave their home town, Makkah. These neo-converts were already defenceless and almost without resources, but their situation became even worse when they emigrated to Madinah, for whatever their meagre possessions, they had all to be left behind in Makkah. The helpless state in which they reached Madinah can be imagined form the fact that some of the emigrants did not even have so much as a roof over their heads. They had to live out in the open with only a curtain stretched above their heads to make a kind of shed. Because of this they were known as 'the companions of the shed.' The number of those who lived in this shed from time to time has been placed at four hundred. Abu Huraira, one of their members said he had seen seventy of them together. All they owned was one piece of coarse cloth, which they wore from neck to knee. He himself was reduced to a pitiable state during those days. He would often lie so still in the Prophet's mosque that people thought he was unconscious. But the truth was that continuous starvation had weakened him so much that he was hardly fit to do anything else but just lie motionless.

When this forlorn little caravan was camping of Madinah, there was the danger that at any moment their enemies, who were all around them, would suddenly swoop down on them and there would be a massacre. But God repeatedly gave them the good tidings that they were His representatives and that, therefore, no one could overcome them.

> **They seek to extinguish the light of God with their mouths; but God will perfect His light, much as the unbelievers may dislike it. It is He who has sent His apostle with guidance and the Faith of Truth, so that He may exalt it above all religions, much as the Pagans, may dislike it.**[3]

Shortly after this prediction, the whole of Arabia surrendered before him. The believers, who were far fewer in number and completely lacking in resources, overpowered the unbelievers, who greatly exceeded them in numbers and in material resources.

In material terms, no explanation can be offered as to how, exactly according to the prediction, the Prophet came completely to dominate Arabia and the neighbouring countries. The only explanation possible is that he was God's emissary, and that purely on the strength of God's assistance, he was able to gain a victory over his enemies. And such was the victory granted by God to his mission that all his enemies came over to his side and became his helpers. The fact that, in face of extraordinary opposition and enmity, this unlettered prophet's mission bore fruit, is sound evidence that he was a representative of the Lord of the Universe. Had he been an ordinary man, it would have been impossible for his words to have made the impact that they did, and they would certainly never have made history—and history which, till today, has no parallel. J.W.H. Stobart, in his book, *Islam and its Founder*, underlines the fact that, when seen in terms of the scarcity of resources at his disposal, his far-reaching and permanent achievements make his name stand out as the most radiant and prominent in the whole of human history (p.228). There is such compelling evidence of his being a messenger of God that even Sir William Muir, the distinguished orientalist, has accepted him as such, albeit indirectly. In his book, *The Life of Mahomet* he speaks of how 'Muhammad, thus holding his people at bay, waiting, in the still expectation of victory, to outward appearance defenceless, and with his little band, as it were, in the lion's mouth, yet trusting in His Almighty power whose messenger he believed himself to be, resolute and unmoved—presents a spectacle of sublimity paralleled only in the sacred records by such scenes as that of the Prophet of Israel, when he complained to his Master, "I, even I only, am left."'[4]

Another prediction of the Quran worth mentioning here is the overpowering of the Iranians by the Greeks (who at that point formed part of the eastern Roman Empire). This is recorded in the thirtieth chapter of the Quran. "The Greeks have been defeated in a neighbouring land. But after the defeat, they shall themselves gain victory within a few years." The Persian empire, known as the Sassanid empire, lay to the east of Arabian peninsula on the other coast of the Persian Gulf, while the Roman empire, known as the Byzantine empire, was situated on the western side, stretching from the shores of the Red Sea to the Black Sea. The frontiers of both the empires met on the banks of the Tigris and the Euphrates in the north of Arabia. These empires were the super powers of their times and Edward Gibbon, the noted historian, holds that the Roman empire, whose history dates back to the early part of the second century B.C., was the most civilized empire of its time.

More than any other civilzation, the Roman empire has attracted the attention of historians, one of the most famous historical works being Edward Gibbon's *Decline and Fall of the Roman Empire*. The second chapter of the fifth volume is of particular concern to us. Constantine, a former Roman emperor, having embraced Christianity in the year 325 A.D. made this new faith the state religion. Thus the majority of the Romans became Christians, following in the footsteps of their king. The Persians, on the contrary, were worshippers of a sun-god. Eight years before Muhammad, upon whom be peace, attained prophethood, Maurice, who was the head of this Roman empire, thanks to his lack of administrative ability, suffered an insurrection of his army, lead by Captain Phocas, in the year 602 A.D. This coup being successful, he was usurped by Phocas, who then acceded to the throne of Rome. Once in power, Phocas, brutally assassinated the Roman emperor and other members of his family. After consolidating his hold, he deputed one of his envoys to proclaim his recent coronation in the neighbouring state of Persia. At that time, Nao Sherwan Adil's son, Chosroes II, was the emperor of Persia. Once in 590-91 A.D., Chosroes had had to flee from Persia because of an uprising of his own people. During this period, the Roman emperor, who had been so brutally murdered, had given him asylum, helped him to regain his throne, and given his daughter to him in marriage. Maurice, therefore, was like a father to him, and he was greatly enraged when he learnt of the overthrow and assassination of his father-in-law. He therefore imprisoned the Roman envoys, refused to recognize the new government and promptly declared war against the Roman empire.

In the year 603, his troops crossed the Euphrates and entered Syrian cities. Phocas failed to arrest this unexpected advance and the Persian troops continued their march until they had finally captured the city of Antioch and seized the sacred city of Jerusalem. Within no time, the boundaries of the Persian empire were extended up to the Nile Valley. Because of the policy of inquisition pursued by the erstwhile Roman State, the anti-Church sects like the Nestorians, the Jacobites and the Jews were already simmering with discontent, so they supported the Persian conquerors in over-throwing the Christian regime—a factor which was of considerable help in the Persian conquest. On seeing the failure of Phocas to combat the Persians, some nobles of the Roman Court sent a secret message to the Roman governor of the empire's African colony, begging him to save the empire. The governor, therefore, appointed his son, Heraclius, to lead the military campaign. He marched with his troops from Africa in such secrecy that no hint of their approach was received until, from his castle, Phocas, himself could see their ships approaching the coast. Heraclius captured the capital, Constantinople, after a minor battle and Phocas was killed.

Although Heraclius succeeded in eliminating Phocas, he failed to counteract the Persian menace, which eventually proved insuperable. By 616, the Romans had lost the entire territory in the east and west, save the capital, to the Persian emperor. In Iraq, Syria Palestine, Egypt and Asia Minor, the Zoroastrian flag replaced the Christian flag. Heraclius was besieged on both sides by these implacable enemies and the Roman empire was eventually reduced to what lay within the walls of Constantinople. After the loss of Egypt, the capital was afflicted by famine and pestilence. Thus the situation was worsening day by day. Only the trunk of the Roman empire's huge tree had survived, and even that had begun to wither away. The public lived in fear and horror of the Persians who might lay siege to Constantinople at any moment. Normal transactions came to a standstill and public places, which at one time had been bustling with activity, now wore a deserted look.

After capturing the Roman territories, the fire-worshippers' regime took a series of oppressive measures to eradicate Christianity. The offerings of the devout over a period of three hundred years were rifled in one sacrilegious day, the patriarch Zachariah and the true cross were transported into Persia and ninety thousand Christians were massacred. The Christians of the East were scandalized by the worship of fire and the impious doctrines of the conquerors. Gibbon comments: 'If the motives of Chosroes had been pure and

honourable he must have ended the quarrel with the death of Phocas, and he would have embraced as his best ally the fortunate African who had so generously avenged the injuries of his benefactor Maurice. The prosecution of the war revealed the true character of the barbarian; and the suppliant embassies of Heraclius, to beseech his clemency, that he would spare the innocent, accept a tribute, and give peace to the world, were rejected with contemptuous silence or insolent menace.'[5]

What a marked difference there now was in the balance of strength between the Roman and Persian empire, and how far superior the Persian conqueror supposed himself to be to his Roman counterpart we may judge from the tone in which Chosroes II addressed a letter to Heraclius from Jerusalem: 'From Chosroes, the supreme god of all gods, the lord of the earth, to his mean and block-headed slave, Heraclius. Thou sayest that thou hast confidence in God. Why did not thy God save Jerusalem from my hands.[6]

Heraclius, incapable of resistance and hopeless of relief, had resolved to transfer his person and government to the more secure residence of Carthage. His ships were already laden with the treasures of the palace, but the flight was arrested by the Patriarch, who armed with the powers of religion in the defence of his country, led Heraclius to the altar of St. Sophia, and extorted a solemn oath that he would live and die with the people whom God had entrusted to his care.[7]

'During this time, the friendly offer of Sain, the Persian general, to conduct an embassy to the presence of the Great King, was accepted with the warmest gratitude...... but the lieutenant of Chosroes had fatally mistaken the intentions of his master. When Chosroes learnt about this peace mission, he said: 'It was not an embassy,' said the tyrant of Asia; 'It was the person of Heraclius bound in chains, that he would have brought to the foot of my throne. I will never give peace to the emperor of Rome till he has abjured his crucified God and embraced the worship of the sun.[8]

'However, a six-year long battle finally inclined the Persian monarch to make peace on certain conditions: 'A thousand talents of gold, a thousand silk robes, a thousand horses and a thousand virgins.'[9]

Gibbon rightly describes these terms as ignominious. Heraclius would definitely have accepted these terms, but, in view of how circumscribed and depleted the territory was and considering in how short a time he was expected to meet these terms, it was preferable for him to employ those very resources in preparation for a final decisive battle with the enemy.

These events that were taking place in Rome and Persia, the greatest empires of the time, had their repercussions in Makkah, which occupied a central place in Arabia. The Iranians worshipped a sun god and fire, whereas the Romans believed in revelation and prophethood. It made sense psychologically for the Muslims to side with the Christian Romans, whereas the Makkan idolaters sided with the Zoroastrians, they too being nature worshippers. The conflict between the Romans and Persians, therefore, took on a symbolic value for the believers and unbelievers of Makkah, in the sense that both looked to the outcome of this transfrontier war as a precursor to their own future.

In 616 A.D., the Iranians emerged victorious and all the territories of the Roman Empire were annexed to Persian territory. When this news reached Madinah, the opponents of Islam made capital out of it and began to demoralize the Muslims. They taunted the Muslims with the fact that their Persian brothers had prevailed over the Romans who were adherents of a religion which was similar to Islam. They claimed that in the same way they would uproot the Muslims and their religion. In the weak and helpless state the Muslims were in, these sardonic words from the non-believers were like salt to their wounds. It was at this time that the Prophet had a highly significant revelation made to him:

> The Greeks have been defeated in the neighbouring land. But after their defeat they shall themselves gain victory within a few years. God is in command before and after. On that day the believers will rejoice in God's help. He gives victory

to whom He will. He is the Mighty one, the Merciful. That is God's promise. He will never be untrue. Yet most men do not know it.[10]

At the time this prediction was made, no series of events could have been more inconceivable for, according to Gibbon, 'the first twelve years of Heraclius were proclaiming the dissolution of the empire.

Clearly, this prediction had come from a Being both omniscient and omnipotent. No sooner had the Prophet received God's message, than pronounced changes in Heraclius began to become evident. Writes Gibbon, 'Of the characters conspicuous in history, that of Heraclius is one of the most extraordinary and inconsistent. In the first and last years of a long regime, the emperor appears to be the slave of sloth, of pleasure, of superstition, the careless and impotent spectator of public calamities. But the languid mists of the morning and evening are separated by the brightness of the meridian sun: the Arcadius of the palace arose the Caesar of the camp; and the honour of Rome and Heraclius was gloriously retrieved by the exploited trophies of six adventurous campaigns. It was the duty of the Byzantine historians to have revealed the causes of his slumber and vigilance. At this distance we can only conjecture that he was endowed with more personal courage than political resolution; that he was detained by the charms, and perhaps the arts, of his niece Martina, with whom, after the death of Eudocia, he contracted an incestuous marriage' (p.82).

The same Heraclius who had abandoned all hope and courage, and whose mind had become so confused, then planned a military expedition which was entirely successful. Since the days of Scipio and Hannibal, no bolder enterprise has been attempted than that which Heraclius achieved for the deliverance of the empire. In Constantinople, all the might and power which he could muster went into preparations for war. In the year 622, however, when Heraclius set sail with a select band of five thousand soldiers from Constantinople to Trebizond, people felt they were witnessing the final acts of the grand drama of the Roman empire.

Heraclius, knowing that the Persian navy was weak, first deployed his own fleet to take the enemy from the rear. Charting a perilous course through the Black Sea and braving the hazards of the mountains of Armenia, he penetrated into the very heart of Persia, to the very point where Alexander the Great had defeated the Persians in the course of his famous march from Syria to Egypt. This surprise attack played havoc with the Persian army, and before they could counter-attack with a strong reserve force of theirs positioned in Asia Minor, Heraclius launched another unexpected offensive from the northern coast. Subsequently to this attack, Heraclius returned by a sea route to Constantinople. On the way, he entered into a pact with the Avars, who then helped in arresting the advance of the Persian troops beyond their own capital. These two Roman attacks were followed by three more expeditions between 623 and 625 A.D. Invading from the southern coast of the Black Sea, the Romans penetrated into the heart of the Persian empire and went as far as Mesopotamia. The Persian aggression had by now received a deathblow, and all the occupied territories were vacated. The conclusive battle, however, was fought at Nineveh, on the banks of the River Tigris, in December 627.

By this time, Chosroes II had no fight left in him. He planned to flee from Dastgard, his favourite palace, but his flight was rudely arrested by rebellion against him from within his own palace. Eighteen sons were massacred before his very eyes, and he was thrown into a dungeon by his own son, Siroes, where he expired on the fifth day. The glory of the house of Sassan ended with the death of Chosroes; his unnatural son enjoyed the fruits of his crimes for only eight months, and in the space of four years, the regal title was assumed by other pretenders to the throne, who disputed with the sword or the dagger the last remnants of an exhausted monarchy. In such a state of anarchy, the Persians were clearly in no position to launch another expedition against the Romans. Cabades II, the son of Chosroes II, entered into a peace treaty with the Romans and handed over all Roman territories. The wood of the Holy Cross was restored at the urgent entreaties of Constantine's successor. Chosroes' son abandoned the conquests of his father with no apparent regret.

'The return of Heraclius from Tauris to Constantinople was a perpetual triumph. After a long impatience, the senate, the clergy, and the people went forth to meet their hero, with tears and acclamations, with olive branches and innumerable lamps; he entered the capital in a chariot drawn by four elephants'.[11]

Thus the Quranic prediction about the Romans regaining their lost territories came true, to the letter, within the specified period of ten years. Gibbon expressed astonishment at this prediction but at the same time, in order to lessen its importance, he has quite wrongly related it to the epistle sent by the Prophet Muhammad to Chosroes II. Gibbon observes: 'While the Persian monarch contemplated the wonders of his art and power, he received an epistle from an obscure citizen of Makkah inviting him to acknowledge Mahomet as the apostle of God. He rejected the invitation, and tore up the epistle. It is thus, exclaimed the Arabian Prophet, that God will tear the kingdom, and reject the supplications of Chosroes. Placed on the verge of the two great empires of the East, Mahomet observed with secret joy the progress of their mutual destruction; and, in the midst of the Persian triumphs, he ventured to foretell that, before many years should elapse, victory would again return to the banners of the Romans. At the time when this prediction is said to have been delivered, no prophecy could be more distant from its accomplishment, since the first twelve years of Heraclius announced the approaching dissolution of the empire'.[12]

But other historians are in agreement that his prediction does not relate to the epistle addressed to Chosroes II, because this having been sent to the emperor of Persia in the seventh year of Hijrah, in 628 A.D., whereas the prediction of the Roman victory had been made in 616 A.D. in Makkah, before the emigration.

# The Mummy of Merneptah

One of the most intriguing predictions made by the Quran concerns a Pharaoh of Egypt, called Merneptah, who was the son of Rameses II. According to historical records, this king was drowned in pursuit of Moses in the Red Sea. When the Quran was revealed, the only other mention of Pharaoh was in the Bible, the sole reference to his having drowned being in the Book of Exodus; 'And the waters returned, and covered the Chariots, and the horsemen, and all the host of Pharoah that came into the sea after them; there remained not so much as one of them'.[13]

Amazingly, when this was all the world knew about the drowning of Pharaoh, the Quran produced this astounding revelation: 'We shall save you in your body this day, so that you may become a sign to all posterity.[14]

How extraordinary this verse must have appeared when it was revealed. At that time no one knew that the Pharaoh's body was really intact, and it was nearly 1400 hundred years before this fact came to light. It was Professor Loret who, in 1898, was the first person to find the mummified remains of the Pharaoh who lived in Moses' day. For 3000 years the corpse had remained wrapped in a sheet in the Tomb of the Necropolis at Thebes where Loret had found it, until July 8, 1907, when Elliot Smith uncovered it and subjected it to proper scientific examination. In 1912, he published a book, entitled *The Royal Mummies*. His research had proved that the mummy discovered by Loret was indeed that of the Pharaoh who knew Moses, resisted his pleas, pursued him as he took flight, lost his life in the process. His earthly remains were saved by the will of God from destruction to become a sign to man, as is written in the Quran.[15]

In 1975, Dr. Bucaille, made a detailed examination of the Pharaoh's mummy which by then had been taken to Cairo. His findings led him to write in astonishment and acclaim:

> Those who seek among modern data for proof of the Holy Scriptures will find a magnificent illustration of the verses of the Quran dealing with the Pharaoh's body by visiting the

Royal Mummies Room of the Egyptian Museum, Cairo![16]

As early as the seventh century A.D., the Quran had asserted that the Pharaoh's body was preserved as a sign for man, but it was only in the 19th century that the body's discovery gave concrete proof of this prediction. What further proof is needed that the Quran is the Book of God? Certainly, there is no book like it, among the works of men.

## Survival of Arabic Language

The very language Arabic in which it is written is a kind of miracle, being an astonishing exception to the historical rule that a language cannot survive in the same form for more than 500 years. In the course of five centuries, a language changes so radically that the coming generations find it increasingly difficult to understand the works of their distant predecessors. For instance, the works of Geoffrey Chaucer (1342-1400), the father of English poetry, and the plays and poetry of William Shakespeare (1564-1616), one of the greatest writers of the English language, have become almost unintelligible to twentieth century readers, and are now read almost exclusively as part of college curricula with the help of glossaries, dictionaries and 'translations.'

But the history of the Arabic language is strikingly different, having withstood the test of time for no less than 1500 years. Wording and style have, of course, undergone some development, but not to such an extent that words should lose their original meaning. Supposing someone belonging to the Quranic times of ancient Arabia could be reborn today, the form of language in which he would express himself would be as understandable to modern Arabs as it was to his own contemporaries.

It is as if the Quran had placed a divine imprint upon Arabic, arresting it in its course so that it should remain understandable right up to the last day. This being so, the Quran is never just going to collect dust on some obscure 'Classical Literature' shelf, but will be read by, and give inspiration to people for all time to come.

In the field of science, despite the great and rapid advances in knowledge in recent years, we come back to what was asserted in the Quran, so many centuries ago, as having arrived at the quintessence of the matter. Just as the Arabic language seems to have been crystallised at a particular point in time—in fact, at the moment of divine revelation, so also does sciences seem to have been arrested in its course, the Quran having the final say on matters which for centuries lay beyond man's knowledge and which still, in many important cases, elude man's intellectual grasp. The most significant of these is the origin of the universe.

It is interesting to note how this theory of the origin of the universe affected a group of Chinese graduate students who were pursuing their studies at the University of California under government sponsorship. Some twelve members of this group went to the pastor of the First Presbyterian Church of Berkeley and asked to have a Sunday School Class arranged for them—not that they wished to become Christians, as they explained quite frankly, but because they wanted to learn to what degree Christianity had influenced American culture. This being a rather special type of class, the pastor arranged for the mathematician and astronomer, Peter W. Stoner, to organize and instruct it. Just four months later, all of those young students accepted Christianity! What could have been the reason for his extraordinary response? Peter W. Stoner explains it is this way: "I was immediately faced with the problem as to what should be presented to a group of this type. Since these young men had no faith in the Bible, ordinary Bible teaching seemed useless. Then I hit upon an idea. I had noticed in my undergraduate work a very close relation between the first chapter of Genesis and the sciences, and decided to present this picture to the group.

'The students and I naturally were aware of the fact that this Genesis material had been written thousands of years before science had any of its present-day knowledge and concepts regarding the universe, and the earth, and the life upon it. We realized that many of the teachings of people back in the days of Moses and for thousand of years thereafter were very absurd when looked at in the light of modern knowledge available also to this group of students. Nevertheless, we "tackled" the subject with a will.

We spent the whole winter in Genesis I. The students took assignments to the university library, and then brought back papers marked by thoroughness such as a teacher usually only dreams of. At the end of that winter the pastor invited me to his office and told me that the entire group had come to him saying that they wished to become Christians. It has been proved to them, they had said, that the Bible was the inspired Word of God."[17]

One sentence of the Book of Genesis regarding the beginning of the world reads: ...and darkness was upon the face of the deep.'

According to recent discoveries, this gives the best description of the time when the earth was still hot and all water had evaporated. All throughout that time all our seas were suspended in the atmosphere in the form of dense clouds, as a result of which light was not able to penetrate to the surface of the earth. As A. Cressy Morrison says in his book, *Man Does Not Stand Alone*:

> Can science pick a flaw in this briefest story ever told? We must accord our homage to the writer, unknown and unheralded, in complete humility bow to his wisdom and admit his inspiration. In the face of the simple truth here told, let us not quarrel over details due to translation and human interpolation or over the question of how God did His work or the time it took. Who knows? The facts as told have come down through the ages and are facts.

It is our belief that the Old and New Testaments were originally divine, as the Quran still is today and that they still contain sparks of divine knowledge, but the scriptures have lost their pristine qualities in the process of translation and interpolation.

As Dr. Maurice Bucaille writes in his book *The Bible, the Quran and Science*, 'A revelation is mingled in all these writings, but all we possess today is what men have seen fit to leave us. These men manipulated the texts to please themselves, according to the circumstances they were in and the necessities they had to meet.

'When these objective data are compared with those found in various prefaces to Bibles destined today for mass publication, one realizes that facts are presented in them in quite a different way. Fundamental facts concerning the writing of the books are passed over in silence, ambiguities which may mislead the reader are maintained, facts are minimalised to such an extent that a false idea of reality is conveyed. A large number of prefaces or introductions to the Bible misrepresent reality in this way. In the case of books that were adapted several times (like the Pentateuch), it is said that certain details may have been added later on. A discussion of an unimportant passage of a book is introduced, but crucial facts warranting lengthy expositions are passed over in silence. It is distressing to see such inaccurate information on the Bible maintained for mass publication (pp. 9, 10).

Later, on p. 42, he says, 'At a time when it was not yet possible to ask scientific questions, and one could only decide on improbabilities or contradictions, a man of good sense, such as Saint Augustine, considered that God could not teach man things that did not correspond to reality. He therefore put forward the principle that it was not possible for an affirmation contrary to the truth to be of divine origin, and was prepared to exclude from all the sacred texts anything that appeared to him to merit exclusion on these grounds.

'Later, at a time when the incompatibility of certain passages of the Bible with modern knowledge has been realized, the same attitude has not been followed. This refusal has been so insistent that a whole literature has sprung up, aimed at justifying the fact that, in the face of all opposition, texts have been retained in the Bible that have no reason to be there.'

This certainly can never be said of the Quran. In the more ancient scriptures we find only glimpses of the truth, whereas in the Quran the truth is enshrined in all its original glory. Had the Quran been the work of man, and not of God, its assertions would certainly have been proved wrong, or irrelevant, in the light of modern scientific discoveries.

Professor Arberry has translated the Arabic word 'ikhtilaf' as 'inconsistency.' Other renderings of the word include contradiction, disparity and difference.

Total consistency is an extremely rare quality, one that can only be found in God. It is beyond any human being to compose a work of absolute consistency. For a work to be free of inconsistency, the composer has to command knowledge which encompasses the past and the future, and extends also to all objects of creation. There must be no shadow of doubt in his perception of the essential nature of things. Furthermore, his knowledge must be based on direct acquaintance, not on information indirectly received from others. And there is another unique quality he must possess: he must be able to see things, not in a prejudiced light, but as they actually are.

Only God can possess all these extraordinary qualities. For this reason, only His Word will remain perennially free of all inconsistency and contradiction. The work of man, on the other hand, is always marred by imperfection, for man himself is imperfect; it is beyond him to compose a work free of contradiction.

## Contradictions in Human Reasoning

It is not by chance that the work of man is fraught with contradictions. It is inevitable, given the inherent limitations of human thought. Such is the nature of creation that it accepts only the Thought of its Creator. Any theory that is not in consonance with His thought cannot find its place in the universe. It will contradict itself, for it stands in contradiction to the universe at large; it will be inconsistent, for it is not in accord with the pattern of nature.

For this reason, intellectual inconsistency is bound to afflict any theory conceived by man. We shall illustrate this point by several examples.

## Darwinism

Charles Darwin (1809-1882), and other scientists after him, developed the Theory of Evolution from their observations of living creatures. They saw that the various forms of life found on earth outwardly appeared different from one another. Yet, biologically, they bore a considerable resemblance to each other. The structure of a horse, for instance, when stood up on its two hind feet, was not unlike the human frame.

From these observations they came to the conclusion that man was not a separate species, and that along with other animals, he had originated from a common gene. All creatures were involved in a great evolutionary journey through successive stages of biological development. While reptiles, quadrupeds and monkeys were in an early stage of evolution, man was in an advanced stage.

For a hundred years this theory held sway over human thought. But then further investigations revealed that it has loopholes. It did not fully fit in with the framework of creation. In certain fundamental ways, it clashed with the order of the universe as a whole.

For instance, there is the question of the age of the earth. By scientific calculation, it has been put at around two thousand million years old. Now this period is far too short to have accommodated the process of evolution envisaged by Darwin. It has been shown scientifically that for just one compound of protein molecule to have evolved it would have taken more than just millions and millions of years.

There are over a million different forms of animal life on earth and at least two hundred thousand fully developed vegetables species. How could they all have evolved in just two thousand million years? Not even an animal low down in the evolutionary scale could have developed in that time, let alone man, an advanced life form which could have developed only after passing through countless evolutionary stages.

A mathematician, by the name of Professor Patau, has made certain calculations concerning the biological changes postulated by the theory of evolution. According to him, even a minor change in any species would take one million generations to be completed. From this, one can gain an idea how long a period would elapse before a dog, for example, turned into a horse. The multiple changes involved in such a complicated evolutionary process would have taken much too long for them to have happened during the human lifespan of the world.

As Fred Hoyle puts it, in *The Intelligent Universe*: Just how excruciatingly slowly genetic information accumulates by trial and error can be seen from a simple example. Let us suppose very conservatively, that a particular protein is coded by a tiny segment in the DNA blueprint, just ten of the chemical links in its double helix. Without all ten links being in the correct sequence, the protein from the DNA doesn't work. Starting with all the ten wrong, how many generations of copying must elapse before all the links—and hence the protein—come right through random errors? The answer is easily calculated from the rate at which the DNA links are miscopied, a figure which has been established by experiment.

"To obtain the correct sequence of ten links by miscopying, the DNA would have to reproduce itself on an average, about a hundred thousand billion times! Even if there were a hundred million members of the species all producing offspring, it would still take million generations before even a single member came up with the required rearrangement. And if that sounds almost within the bounds of possibility, consider what happens if a protein is more complicated and the number of DNA links needed to code for it jumps from ten to twenty. A thousand billion generations would then be needed, and if one hundred links are required (as is often the case), the number of generations would be impossibly high because no organism reproduces fast enough to achieve this. The situation for the neo-Darwinian theory is evidently hopeless. It might be possible for genes to be modified slightly during the course of evolution, but the evolution of specific sequences of DNA links of any appreciable length is clearly not possible' (p.110).

And in any case, as Hoyle had earlier stated, 'Shufflings of the DNA code are disadvantageous because they tend to destroy cosmic genetic information rather than to improve it.'

To solve this problem, another theory, called the Panspermia Theory, was formed. It held that life originated in outer space. From there it came to earth. But as it turned out, this theory created new problems of its own. Where in the vastness of space was there a planet or a star with the conditions needed for life to develop? For example, there is nothing more essential to life than water. Nothing can come into existence or continue to survive without it. Yet no one knows of anywhere in the entire universe, except the earth, where it exists. We then had a certain body of intellectuals who favored a theory of Emergent Evolution, according to which life—or its various forms—came into being all of a sudden. But this theory is empty of meaning. How can there be sudden appearance of life without the intervention of an outside force—or Creator—to discount which all these theories were originally invented.

The fact of the matter is, without taking a Creator into account, one cannot give a valid explanation of life. There is simply no other theory which fits in with the pattern of the universe. Being inconsistent with the nature of life, other theories fail to take a firm root. It is indeed significant that eminent scholars from various fields have thought it fit to contribute to an Encyclopaedia of Ignorance, which has been published in London. The book has the following introduction.

'In the *Encyclopaedia of Ignorance* some 60 well-known scientists survey different fields of research, trying to point out significant gaps in our knowledge of the world.'

What this work really amounts to is an academic acknowledgement of the fact that the Maker of the world has fashioned it in such a way that it just cannot be explained by any mechanical interpretation. For instance, as John Maynard Smith has written, the theory of evolution is beset with certain 'built-in' problems. There appears to be no solution to these problems, for all we have to go by are theories. And without concrete evidence, there is no way we can back up our theories.

According to the Quran, man and all other forms of life have been created by God. The theory of evolution, on the other hand, holds that they are all the result of a blind mechanical process. The Quranic interpretation explains itself, for God can do as He wills. He can create what He wishes without material resources. Such is not the case with the theory of evolution, which demands that there should be a cause for everything that happens. Such causes cannot be found, with the result that the theory of evolution is left without an explanation,—in an intellectual vacuum, one might say, while the same cannot be said of the explanation of life offered by the Quran.

## Political Philosophy

The same has been the case with political philosophy. According to the 1984 edition of *Encyclopaedia Britannica*: 'Political philosophy and political conflict have evolved basically around who should have power over whom' (14/697).

For five thousand years, eminent human brains have addressed their efforts towards finding an answer to this question. Yet they still have not been able to produce what Spinoza termed a 'scientific base' on which to form a coherent political philosophy.

Altogether, there are more than twelve schools of political thought, which fall into two broad categories: despotism and democracy. The first is strongly objected to on the grounds that no good reason can be found for one single individual to tyrannise the entire population of a country or countries. Although democracy had wide popular support, it has also been subjected to sharp criticism on a theoretical plane. The entire basis of democracy is the belief that people are born equal, with equal rights and that they are free. But the problems afflicting democracy are alluded to in the very first lines of Rousseau's *Social Contract*: 'Man was born free and everywhere he is in the chains.'

The literal meaning of democracy—a word of Greek origin—is rule by the people. But in practice it is impossible to establish rule by all the people. How can all the people govern and be governed at the same time? Furthermore, man is said to be a social animal. Far from being alone in this world with the liberty to live as he pleases, he is part of the body of society. One philosopher puts it like this: 'Man is not born free. Man is born into society, which imposes restraints of him.'

How, then, can a popular government be formed, when all the people cannot have power at the same time? Various theories have been propounded, the most popular of which is Rousseau's i.e. that it should be left to the General Will, which can be determined by plebiscite. So, in effect, government by the people becomes government by a few elected individuals. People may be free to vote as they please, but after they have voted, they are once again subjected to the rule of a select group. Rousseau explained this by saying: 'To follow one's impulse is slavery, but to obey the self-prescribed law is liberty.'[18]

Clearly, this leaves much unanswered. Seeing how easily democratic systems deteriorated into elective monarchies, people were not satisfied with Rousseau's explanation. Once they had secured people's votes, democratically elected rulers began to assume the same role as monarchs had before them.

All political philosophers have been caught up in contradictions of this nature. And there appears no way out of the impasse. In theory, all of them cherish the ideal of human equality. Yet human equality, in the true sense, is forthcoming neither in monarchies nor in democracies. If the one is a dynastic monarchy, the other is an elective oligarchy. In the 18th and 19th centuries, people rose in great rebellion against monarchic government. But free of the yoke of kingly rule, they found that they were not much better off in that they had to resign themselves to rule by a select group of 'representatives of the people,' while the old monarchs had laid claim to being 'representatives of God on earth.' This was the only difference between the two.

Even the so-called 'representation' of the people is open to question. Take the example of the British conservatives who, in one year, won a decisive victory, winning an overall majority of 144 seats. In terms of votes, however, the conservative share of the vote (43%) has fallen since 1979, i.e. as far as seats were concerned the conservatives had won a massive overall majority. But, as far as votes were concerned, they could muster only 43%. Could this be said to be truly representative of the people? Man's failure in this field has been summed up in these words: "The history of political philosophy from Plato until the present day makes plain that modern political philosophy is still faced with the basic problems."[19]

In both democratic and despotic systems of government, power is handed over to a single or a few select individuals. In neither system, then, can men be said to be equal, not even under democracy, which has failed to produce equality although formulated in its name. Due to inherent contradictions, this system had likewise produced the opposite of what was intended.

In fact, there is only one political philosophy that does not contradict itself and that is the philosophy put forward by the Quran. The Quran says that only God has the right to rule over man: 'Have we any say in the matter?' they ask. Say to them: "All is in the hands of God" (3:154).

The idea of God as Sovereign makes for a coherent system of thought, free from all forms of contradiction. But when man is considered sovereign, there are bound to be contradictions and inconsistencies in the political theories that evolve. The aim of all political theories has been to eradicate the division between ruler and subjects. Yet no human system, whatever its nature, has been able to do this. In both the democratic and despotic systems, human equality has remained an unattainable ideal, for power has always had to be put in the hands of a few individuals, with others becoming their subjects. This disparity can only disappear when God is considered Sovereign. Then the

*The Challenge of the Quran* • 199

only difference that remains is between God and man. He is the Ruler, all are His subjects. All men are equal before Him. There is no division and no distinction, between man and man.

## The Quran

If the different parts of a book contradict each other, the book is inconsistent within itself. If the contents of a book, as a whole, or in part contradict outward realities, the book is externally inconsistent. The Quran claims—with justice—to be free of either type of inconsistency, whereas no work of human origin can be free of either. It follows, therefore, that the Quran must be superhuman in origin. Had it been written by a human being, it would have been beset by human failings and there would have been inconsistencies in it of the type so frequently found in the works of man.

Contradictions within a work arise basically from the deficiencies of its author. If inconsistencies are to be avoided, two things are essential: absolute knowledge and total objectivity. There is no human being who is not sadly deficient in both of these areas. It is only God who is omniscient, and flawless as a Being, and while works wrought by the human hand are invariably marred by inconsistencies, His book, and His book alone never contradicts itself.

Because of man's inherent limitations, there are many things which, intellectually, he cannot grasp. He is forced, therefore, to speculate, and this frequently leads him into making erratic judgements and unfounded contentions.

Every human being graduates from youth to old age, and when a man grows old, he often contradicts things he asserted as facts when he was young and immature. With age, his knowledge and experience increase, hence his final verdict being at variance with his initial judgements. But even when death finally comes to take him away, he still has much to learn, and often the assertions of his maturer age are proved wrong after his death. Truth is not arrived at purely through experience and reasoning.

Human beings, in addition to making inadvertent and unwitting errors (for the simple reason that they are humans, and not God!) are all too prone to make deliberate misrepresentations of facts when they are motivated by the base emotions of greed, envy, jealousy, revenge and fear. One such notorious instance in which the entire western scientific establishment were made dupes of for about half a century was that of the "discovery" of the Piltdown Man, a supposedly "missing link" (according to the evolutionists) between man and his ancestor, the ape. In 1912, the English newspapers trumpeted the news that a fragment of an ancient skull, half ape and half man dating back to some nebulous pre-historic period, had been found at Piltdown, thus providing material evidence which confirmed Darwin's theory of evolution.

This Piltdown man achieved instant popularity. The name appeared in standard textbooks such as R.S. Lull's *Organic Evolution*. Leading intellectuals counted the discovery among the great triumphs of modern man. In authoritative works such as H.G. Well's *Outline of History* and Bertrand Russell's *History of Western Philosophy*, it was mentioned as though there was no doubt about the Piltdown Man's existence.

For nearly half a century scholars remained enthralled with this "great discovery." It was only in 1953 that some scientists became doubtful. They extracted the Piltdown man from its iron fire-proof box in the British Museum and subjected it to detailed modern scientific analysis, studying it from every relevant angle. Their final conclusion was that the Piltdown Man was a forgery. The great acclaim it has received was totally unfounded. What had actually happened was that someone, who wished to discredit a rival by playing a trick on him, and taken the jaw of a chimpanzee and dyed it to make it look ancient and had then filed its teeth to make them look human. He then submitted his "find" to the British Museum, saying that he had come across it in Piltdown, England. He intended at a later stage to reveal the whole affair as a hoax, in order to make his rival look foolish, but when he saw the seriousness with which his trick has been taken by the entire body of western scientists, he was afraid to own up, and his silence then perverted positive thinking on evolution for several decades.

Human moods and passions are often to blame for people turning a blind eye to the truth and falling a prey to faulty reasoning. Love and hate, friendship and hostility all have their influence on human thinking. A man's inability to be dispassionate, his elation or depression, his triumph or despair, his successes and frustrations all colour the quality of his thought. Such fluctuations of mood, caprice and wilfulness, can deflect the very best minds from the truth.

The only one who is free of all such caprice and all such limitations is the Almighty. That is why His word is of an impeccable consistency.

## Biblical Inconsistency

It is unfortunate that the same cannot be said for the Bible, which, as a book of revelation was the forerunner of the Quran. Initially the Bible was the word of God, but in later years it suffered from human interpolations, with the result that many internal contradictions began to sully its pages. A case in point is the genealogy of the Messiah, which has been given in several places in that part of the Bible known as the *Injil*, or New Testament. The Gospel according to Matthew begins with this abridged genealogy: "The book of the generation of Jesus Christ, the son of David, the son of Abraham" (Matt.1:1). The genealogy of Christ is then given in detail, beginning with Joseph who, according to the New Testament was "the husband of Mary, of whom was born Jesus." (Matt.1:16) When the reader turns to the Gospel according to Mark, he finds these words: 'The beginning of the gospel of Jesus Christ, the Son of God' (Mark.1:1).

According to one chapter of the New Testament, Jesus was the son of a person named Joseph, while another chapter of this very New Testament says he was the Son of God.

Undoubtedly, in its original form, the *Injil* was the Word of God and free of all contradictions. It was only in later years, that human beings made additions of their own, introducing contradictions into a formerly consistent text. The Christian Church has evolved another extraordinary contradiction in order to explain away this contradiction in its sacred book. The description given of Joseph in the *Encyclopaedia Britannica* (1984 edition) is as follows: 'Christ's earthly father, the Virgin Mary's husband.'

## Secular Contradictions

For an instance of serious internal contradiction in secular writings, I turn to the works of Karl Marx, who commands an immense following in the modern world. The famous American economist, John Galbraith, has written of him:

> 'If we agree that the Bible is a work of collective authorship, only Mohammad rivals Marx in the number of professed and devoted followers recruited by a single author. And the competition is not really very close. The followers of Marx now far out number the sons of the Prophet.'[20]

But Marx's enormous popularity does not change the fact that his work is little better than a collection of glaring contradictions. For example, Marx considers the existence of class as the root of all evil in the world. According to his philosophy, class distinction is derived from the system of private ownership, and the control exercised by the bourgeoisie over the means of production which enables them to plunder the lower labouring class.

The solution prescribed by Marx consisted of confiscating the properties of the capitalist class and putting them under the administration of the laboring class. Thus, he claimed, a classless society would come into being. But herein lies the basic contradiction of Marx's philosophy. For what comes into existence as a result of this transfer is not a classless society, but a society in which one class takes over where the other leaves off. Where one class previously controlled the economy by virtue of ownership, another class now controls it by virtue of administration. Marx's so-called classless society was in fact one in which capitalist ownership was replaced by communist ownership.

What Marx had condemned in one place, he condoned in another. But due to his great antipathy for and antagonism towards the capitalist class, he was unable to see his own contradiction in thought. He was in favour of taking the control of economic resources away from capitalists and entrusting it to officials. But, blinded by prejudice, he did not see what he was doing. He gave separate names to two different forms of the very same phenomenon: in the one case, he called it plunder of the many by the few, in the other, he termed it 'social order.'

The Quran, on the other hand, is completely free of self-contradiction of this nature, and there is absolute harmony in its discourses. Yet, even so, opponents of the Quran have tried to prove that there are contradictions in it. All the examples they cite in this regard, however, have absolutely no connection with the case they are trying to prove. They say, for instance, that in the sermon of his Farewell Pilgrimage, the Prophet stated that all men were from Adam, and Adam was from the earth. According to this principle women should enjoy the same status as men. In practice, however, this is not the case, say opponents of the Quran. On the one hand, Islam says that men and women are equal, yet at the same time women are allotted an inferior position in Islamic society. They then cite the fact that the testimony of two women is considered equal to that of one man. This is a total misunderstanding. It is true that in Islam the testimony of two women is, under normal circumstances, considered equal to that of one man. But the basis of this rule is not discrimination between the sexes. It is something quite different, as is made clear in the verse of the Quran where it has been laid down. The verse deals with the written recording of debts:

> 'And take two male witnesses. If there are not two men, then one man and two women—you may select the witnesses of your choice. If one woman forgets, the other will be able to remind her.'[21]

The wording of the verse shows quite clearly that the basis of this rule is—not discrimination between the sexes—but rather the memorizing ability of women. The verse alludes to a biological fact—that women are not as good at remembering things as men. This is why, if one is going to accept women's testimony in loan cases, there should be two of them: so that if at any time in the future, they are required to give evidence, one of them should be able to compensate for the other's poor memory.

It is good to remember here that modern research has confirmed what the Quran said—that women's memory is weaker than that of men. Russian scientists have gone into this matter in great detail, and their conclusions have been published in book form. A summary appeared in the New Delhi edition of the Times of India on January 18, 1985, under the caption, 'Memorizing Ability':

> 'Men have a greater ability to memorize and process mathematical information than women, but females are better with words, a Soviet scientist says, reports UPI. 'Men dominate mathematical subjects due to the peculiarities of their memory,' Dr. Vladimir Knovalov told the Tass news agency.

The Quranic rule, far from evincing any contradiction, proves in fact that the Quran has come from One who has absolute knowledge of the facts of nature. He sees things from every angle, and so is in a position to issue commandments that are in total harmony with nature.

Now we turn to external inconsistency. External inconsistency in a literary work occurs when what it asserts is contradicted by some reality in the outside world. It is illuminating in this connection to make comparisons of the differing accounts of historical facts given by the Quran and the Bible.

## Historical Inaccuracy

In the 20th century B.C., during the time of the Prophet Joseph, the Children of Israel entered Egypt. Seven centuries later they left Egypt along with Moses, crossing over into the Sinai Peninsula.

These events are mentioned in both the Bible, and the Quran. But, while the account in the Quran is entirely consistent with external history, the Bible relates several incidents, which do not correspond to historical records. This has created problems for believers in the Bible. Should they accept what is written in the Bible, or should they go by history? Since the two contradict one another, they cannot accept both at the same time.

On January 12, 1985, a gathering was held in the Indian Institute of Islamic Studies at Tughlaqabad in New Delhi, which was addressed by Ezra Kolet, president of the Council of Indian Jewry. His topic was: 'What is Judaism?' Naturally, he dealt with Jewish history in his talk, mentioning among other things, the Jews' entrance into Egypt and their exodus from that country. The names of both Joseph and Moses figured in his talk as well as the kings who were ruling in Egypt in their respective times. For both kings, the contemporaries of Joseph and Moses, used the term 'Pharaoh.'

As everyone acquainted with the period knows, this nomenclature is historically incorrect. The reign of the kings known as Pharaohs only began in Moses' time; in Joseph's day, a different line of monarchs ruled in Egypt.

When Joseph entered Egypt, the kings of a dynasty known as the Hyksos ruled there. They were ethnically Arabs, and had usurped the Egyptian throne, ruling in that country from 2000 BC until the end of the 15th century BC. The indigenous population then rebelled against foreign rule and the Hyksos dynasty came to an end.

Home rule was then established in Egypt. The clan that took over sovereignty chose for itself the name of Pharaoh, which literally means son of the sun-god, for in those days Egyptians worshipped the sun, and in order to vindicate their right to rule over the Egyptians, they made themselves out to be incarnations of the sun-god.

In effect, Mr. Kolet was calling the Hyksos Kings, Pharaohs. He had no choice but to do so, for that is what they are called in the Bible, with reference to both Joseph's and Moses' respective periods. The Jewish speaker could either accept the Bible or history, but not both simultaneously. Since he was speaking in his capacity as president of the Jewish Council, he put history aside and based his talk on biblical accounts.

But in the Quran we do not find accounts which clash with history in this way, and those who follow the Quran are not compelled to forsake history in order to uphold their Holy Book. When the Quran was revealed, people had no knowledge of ancient Egyptian history. Only in later years did archeological excavations make it possible for Egyptologists to compile a record of the history of that country's ancient kings.

Yet despite this, we hear mention in the Quran of the Egyptian monarch who was a contemporary of Joseph. For him, the Quran uses the title 'King of Egypt.' As for the king who ruled in Moses' day, the Quran repeatedly calls him Pharaoh. We thus have a Quranic account that corresponds exactly with historical facts, unlike the biblical account, which is historically inaccurate. This shows that the Quran is written by One who had direct recourse to true facts, without dependence on human sources of knowledge.

## Natural Phenomena

The Quran was revealed at a time when little was known about nature. Rainfall, for example, was believed to come from a river in heaven, which gushed down on to the earth. The earth was thought to be flat and the heavens a kind of vault resting on the hilltops which provided a roof over the earth. Stars were considered to be shining silver nails set in the vault of heaven, or thought of as tiny lamps which were swung to and fro at night by means of a rope. The ancient Indians held that the earth rested upon the horns of a cow and when the cow shifted the earth from one horn to the other, this caused earthquakes. Up till the time of Copernicus (1473-1543 A.D) it was generally believed that the earth was stationary and that the sun revolved around it (Two thousand years earlier, Aristarchus of Samos had anticipated this theory, but his ideas did not gain ground.)

With the advances made in the field of science and technology, the range of human observation and experiment were vastly increased, opening up great vistas of knowledge about the universe. In all spheres of existence and in all disciplines of science, previously established concepts were proved wrong by later research and were discarded. This means that no human work dating back 1500 years can boast of total accuracy, because all 'facts' must now be re-evaluated in the light of recent information. No such book has, in fact, been found to be totally free of errors, with the notable exception of the Quran, whose authenticity has withstood all challenges over the centuries. This constitutes conclusive evidence of the Quran having had its source in an Omnipresent and Eternal Mind—one who knows all facts in their true forms and whose knowledge has not been conditioned by time and circumstances. Had it been a human fabrication it could not have withstood the test of time, human vision being, by contrast, narrow and limited.

The basic theme of the Quran is salvation in the life hereafter. That is why it does not fall into the category of any of known arts and sciences of the world. But since it addresses itself to man, it touches on almost all the disciplines which concern him. In spite of the breadth of its scope, none of its statements has ever been shown to have been made on the basis of inadequate knowledge. Bertrand Russell, in his *Impact of Science on Society* makes the point that, renowned philosopher as he was, Aristotle, while 'proving' the inferiority of women to men, stated that 'women have fewer teeth than men,' thus revealing his ignorance of the fact that men and women have an equal number of teeth. No such ignorance or misconception is ever evinced in the Quran. This clearly shows that the origin of this work is a superior Being whose knowledge pre-dates time itself and goes infinitely far beyond present knowledge, no matter how advanced the latter may appear to be.

At this point, I propose to give some examples from different disciplines to show how, while dealing with any given science, the Quran surprisingly encompassed truths which were to be discovered and confirmed much later. Before launching upon this discussion, it should be borne in mind that the correspondence between modern research and Quranic words is based on the presumption that modern research has, indeed, succeeded in finding out the truth of the facts in question, thus, providing us with the necessary material to make an up-to-date and correct interpretation of Quranic assertions about the material universe. Now, if further research proves our contemporary research wrong, even in part, it will amount in no way to proving the Quran at fault. It will simply mean that, that particular interpretation of the Quran in the light of scientific discoveries was wrongly angled, or inadequate. I feel certain that with the more accurate information which will be available in the future, an interpreter of the Quran will feel better equipped to explain those verses which contain scientific truths; correct information about any given fact can never be contrary to Quranic assertions, whatever they may be.

Assertions of this sort, fall into two separate categories, one relating to matters on which there existed no prior information whatsoever at the time the Quran was written, and the other to matters on which the information available was either superficial or inadequate.

Dr. Maurice Bucaille, in his *The Bible, the Quran and Science*, describes as 'bizarre' the notion that 'if surprising statements of a scientific nature exist in the Quran, they may be accounted for by the fact that Arab scientists were so far ahead of their time and Muhammad was influenced by their work. Anyone who knows anything about Islamic history is aware that the period of the Middle Ages which saw the cultural and scientific upsurge in the Arab world came after Muhammad and would not therefore indulge in such whims' (p.121).

There were many aspects of the universe about which ancient peoples had only partial knowledge, this having been demonstrated by modern scientific findings, but it should be made clear at this point that the main purpose of the Quran was not to expound scientific theories in order to explain natural phenomena, but to elucidate the divine symbolism of the workings of nature in order that people should be purified in mind and soul and become so imbued with feelings of awe and reverence of God's will, that a veritable moral revolution would ensue. The Quran was never meant to be just a book about the physical sciences. And had it disclosed totally new and unheard of scientific facts to the people, this would have sparked off unending and quite irrelevant discussions about the nature of these facts, while the real aims of the Quran would have been thrust into the background. It is little short of miraculous that, centuries before science had made such gigantic leaps forward, the Quran clarified for the common people such scientific facts as illustrated the highest moral principles without using terminology which would in any way confuse them or obscure the issue. And it is those very facts that we now find are entirely consistent with the results of modern investigations.

An interesting example of this is the Quran's description of the behavior of water so as to illustrate the particular physical law that governs it.

**He has let loose the two seas: they meet one another. Between them stands a barrier which they cannot overrun. (55:19-20)**

Two rivers meeting and flowing onwards together without their waters mingling with each other was a phenomenon which had obviously been observed and partially understood by ancient peoples. We can observe this today in the waters of the two rivers which flow together from Chatagam in Bangladesh to Arakan in Burma. All along their course the waters are quite distinct from one another, a 'stripe' being visible between them dividing salt water from fresh. This same phenomenon can also be seen at the confluence of the Ganges and the Jamuna at Allahabad. Both the rivers course onwards together, yet are distinctly separated from one another. Rivers which flow down to coastal areas and are affected by the ebb and flow of the sea, have large quantities of salt-water gush upstream at high tide but, again the waters do not mix. The salt water forms an upper layer, the fresh water remaining below it. At ebb tide, the salt water recedes, leaving the fresh water, as it was before.

Man had observed such natural phenomena from ancient times, but he did not know the laws of nature which governed them. It has recently been discovered by modern research that the way liquids flow is governed by a difference in salinity and thus density because saline water is denser than fresh water; when two water bodies converge, the more saline of the two flows beneath the less saline. Thus, a river flowing into the sea flows on the surface, sometimes for great distances; the Mississippi, for example, appears as a brown, fresh-water stream in the blue waters of the Gulf of Mexico. Salinity variations in the oceans and seas are partially responsible for large-scale seawater circulation.

A well-known example is the flow to the Mediterranean Sea, which is separated from the North Atlantic by a sill, 320 metres (1,050 feet) deep, at the Strait of Gibraltar. The Mediterranean is saltier than the North Atlantic because its evaporation exceeds its replenishment by rivers; the more saline water of the Mediterranean thus flows at depth over the sill into the North Atlantic, where it sinks to a depth of 1,000 metres; and less saline water from the North Atlantic flows near the surface. Current

### Gateway into the Sea

A satellite view of the Gibraltar Straits showing Spain to the left and Africa to the right, with the Atlantic in the foreground and the Mediterranean stretching away into the distance. The Rock of Gibraltar itself is the tip of the tiny promontory just inside the Straits. (Below) surface water from the ocean is continually flowing into the Mediterranean to compensate for evaportion, but denser saltier water is also followig out at depth.

speeds as high as two metres per second have been recorded.²²

It is as if there were a barrier between the waters of different densities, and 'barrier' is the exact expression used by the Quran.

## Examples From Astronomy

The firmament is another aspect of the universe which is described in the Quran in terms which are quite consistent with modern science: 'It was God who raised the heavens without visible pillars' (13:2).

Such was human observation in ancient times. Man could see that above his head the sun, moon and stars had no visible supports. And these words are equally meaningful for the scientific man of today, because the latest observations show that the celestial bodies exist in an infinite space with the invisible pull of gravity that hold them in position. Of the sun and other celestial bodies, the Quran says, "Each floats freely in an orbit of its own" (21:3).

Ancient man was familiar with the movement of celestial bodies, so he was not confused by this, "floating" being the most appropriate term to describe the movement of celestial bodies in a vast and subtle space. And how much more significance had been lent to this word by recent discoveries. Day and night, the results of such movement by a celestial body, are depicted thus in the Quran: 'He throws the veil of night over the day. Swiftly they follow one another' (7:54).

Dr. Maurice Bucaille, in his *The Bible, the Quran and Science*, lists a number of similar extracts from the Quran, which gave accurate descriptions of the alternation of day and night, long before modern deductions or the observations of cosmonauts bore this out. He then makes the important point that at a time when it was held that the Earth was the center of the world and that the Sun moved in relation to it, how could anyone have failed to refer to the sun's movement when talking of the sequence of night and day? This is not however referred to in the Quran (p. 163). He then discusses the special significance of the Arabic verb *kawwara*, (Quran 39:5), the original meaning of which is to coil or wind a turban round the head, when describing the change from night to day, evidently conveying the idea of the rotation of the earth (Most translators seem to have misinterpreted this). 'This purpose of perpetual coiling, including the interpretation of one sector by another is expressed in the Quran just as if the concept of the earth's roundness had already been conceived at the time—which was obviously not the case' (p.164).

There are many descriptions in the Quran of a similar nature, some of them being scientific statements about phenomena of which seventh century men had no knowledge whatsoever. I should now like to present recent examples from a variety of disciplines which bear out the truth of these Quranic assertions.

Up until barely a century ago, the concept of this material universe as having a beginning and an end was something which appeared to have its origin in religiously inspired texts, but which did not seem to have any scientific basis in fact. Of the origin of the universe, the Quran said:

> "Do not the disbelievers see that the heavens and the earth were one solid mass which was tore asunder, and that we made every living thing of water? Will they not have faith?" (12:30).

But now we find that modern studies in astronomy have confirmed the truth of this concept, various observations having led scientists to postulate that the universe was formed by an explosion from a state of high density and temperature (the "big-bang" theory) and that the cosmos evolved from the original, highly compressed, extremely hot gas, taking the form of galaxies of stars, cosmic dust, meteorites and asteroids. The present outward motion of the galaxies is a result of this explosion. According to the *Encyclopaedia Britannica* (1984), this is "the theory now favoured by most cosmologists." Once the process of expansion had set in—about six billion years ago—it had to continue, because the more the celestial bodies moved away from the center, the less attraction they exerted over one another. Estimates of the circumference of the original matter place it at

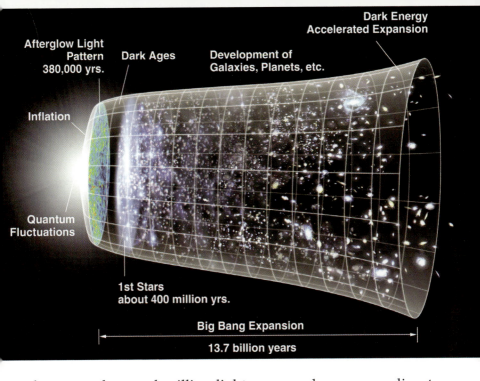

about one thousand million light years and now, according to Professor Eddington's calculations, the present circumference is ten times what it was originally. This process of expansion is still going on. Professor Eddington explains that the stars and galaxies are like marks on the surface of a balloon, which is continuously expanding, and that all the celestial spheres are getting further and further apart. Ancient man supposed quite wrongly, that the stars were as close to one another as they appeared to be. How significant that the Quran should state in Sura 51, verse 47, "The heaven, We have built it with power. Verily we are expanding it." Now science has revealed that since the universe came into existence 90 thousand million years B.C., its circumference has stretched from 6 thousand to sixty thousand million light years. This means that there are inconceivably vast distances between the celestial bodies. And it has been discovered that they revolve as part of galactic systems, just as our earth and the planets revolve around the sun.

Just as within the Solar systems, many planets and asteroids are situated at great distances from each other, yet revolve according to one system, likewise every material body is composed of innumerable 'Solar Systems' on an infinitesimally small scale. These systems are called atoms. While the vacuum of the Solar System is observable, the vacuum of the atomic system is too small to be visible. That is, all things, however solid they appear, are hollow from the inside. For instance, if all the electrons and protons present within the atoms of a six foot tall man were to be squeezed in such a manner that no space were left, his body would be reduced to such a tiny spot as would be visible only through a microscope.

The farthest galaxy that has been observed is situated several million light years away from the sun. Yet it is held that if the total quantum of cosmic matter as worked out by astrophysicists—and it is enormous—were to be compressed so as to eliminate all space, the size of the universe would be only thirty times the size of the sun. In view of how recently these calculations have been made, it is quite extraordinary that 1500 years ago the Quran asserted that not only had the universe expanded from a condensed form but that its original quantum of matter had remained constant, so that it could conceivably be re-condensed into a relatively small space. It describes the end of the universe thus: "On that day, we shall roll up the heaven like a scroll of writing" (21:104).

The moon is our nearest neighbour in space, its distance from the earth being just two hundred and forty thousand miles. Due to this proximity, its gravitational force affects the sea waves, causing an extraordinary rise in the water level twice a day. At certain points these waves rise as high as sixty feet. The land surface too is affected by this lunar pull, but only in terms of a few inches. The present distance between the earth and moon is optimal from man's point of view, there being several advantages. If this distance were reduced, for example to only fifty thousand miles, the seas would be so stormy that a major part of the earth would be submerged in them and, moreover, the continual impact of the stormy waves would cut the mountains into pieces and the earth's surface, more fully exposed to the moon's gravitation would start to crack open.

Astronomers estimate that at the time the earth came into existence, the moon was close to it and the surface of the earth had, therefore, been exposed to all kinds of upheavals. In the course of time, the earth and the moon drew apart, to their present distance from one another, according to astronomical laws. Astronomers hold that this distance will be maintained for a billion years, then the same astronomical laws will bring the moon back closer to the earth. As a result of conflicting forces of attraction, the moon will "burst when close enough and glorify our dead world with rings like those of Saturn."[23]

This concept bears out the Quran's prediction to a remarkable degree. The following lines, in addition to presenting this phenomenon as a physical fact, explain its religious significance:

> **The Hour of Doom is drawing near, and the moon is cleft in two. Yet, when they see a sign, the unbelievers turn their backs and say, 'Ingenious magic!'**[24]

## The Quran Explains Geology

Geology is another field in which the Quran is truly the forerunner of modern scientific discovery.

In several parts of the Quran, it is stated that the mountain were raised in order to keep the earth in equilibrium, "He raised the heavens without visible pillars and set immovable mountains on the earth lest it should shake with you" (31:10).

Fifteen hundred years ago, at the time these words were recorded, man had no understanding of the importance of the mountains. It is only recently that geographers have formulated the concept of isostasy, which is defined by the *Encyclopaedia Britannica* as the "theoretical balance of all large portions of the Earth's crust as though they were floating on a denser underlying layer, about 110 kilometers (70 miles) below the surface. Imaginary columns of equal cross-sectional area that rise from this layer to the surface are assumed to have equal weights everywhere on Earth, even though their constituents and elevations of their upper surfaces are significantly different. This means that an excess of mass seen as material above sea level, as in a mountain system, is due to a deficit of mass, or low-density roots, below sea level.

"In the theory of isostasy a mass above sea level is supported below sea level, and thus there is a certain depth at which the total weight per unit area is equal all around the world; this is known as the depth of compensation" (V/458).

The apparent unchangeability of the mountains—the 'immovable mountains' of the Quran—is explained by the *Encyclopaedia Britannica* (1984) in terms of this naturally occurring balance:

> "Most of the Earth's crust is approximately in hydrostatic equilibrium in this way, so that when erosion occurs and rivers transport large quantities of weathered material away from the upland areas to be deposited in the oceans, there is a tendency for the hinterland to rise isostatically, and for the adjacent ocean floor to sink" (6/44).

O.R. Von Engeln gives perhaps the most direct explanation of this phenomenon:

> "Geologists hold that the lighter matter on the surface of the earth emerged in the form of mountains, and heavier matter got depressed in the form of deep trenches which are now filled with sea water. Thus this elevation and depression together maintain the balance of the earth."[25]

Similarly it is said in the Quran that the earth had passed through a stage when God has caused the land masses to drift apart:

**And the earth he extended after that; and then drew from it water and pastures (79:3).**

These words from the Quran correspond exactly to the latest theory of drifting continents. This means that all our continents at one time were parts of one consolidated land mass, then, following an explosion, they were scattered all over the surface of the earth and a world of continents emerged from the sea and oceans.

This theory was first properly expounded in the year 1915 by a German geologist, Alfred Wegener. Together, they could be fitted into one another like a Jigsaw puzzle. For instance, the eastern coast of South America joins with the western coast of Africa, etc.

There are several other such resemblances to be found on opposite coasts of vast oceans, e.g. mountains of the same kind, rocks dating back to the same geological period, animals, fishes and plants of the same type and so on.

Professor Ronald Good, in his book entitled, *Geography of the Flowering Plants*, writes that botanists are almost unanimous in their view that the presence of certain types of plants in various regions of the earth cannot be explained unless we suppose that, at some point in the past, these tracts of land were joined together.

Some fossil magnetism having supported this theory, it

has become an established scientific doctrine. A study of the particular direction of stone particles reveals the altitude and latitudes of the rock of which they formed a part in ancient times. This study thus reveals that, in the past, certain tracts of land were not situated where they are today; on the contrary, they were situated exactly at places where the theory of drifting continents would suggest. P.M. Blacket, Professor of Physics at the Imperial College, London, writes that measurements of Indian stones definitely show that seventy million years ago, India was situated south of the equator and that examination of South African rocks reveals that the African continent split off from the land mass at the South Pole three hundred million years ago.

The word which is used in the Quranic verse to describe this phenomenon of drift and dispersal is *dahw*. It has the same connotations as the English word 'drift' in, for example, "The rain water caused the sand particles to drift away from the land. "Such a wonderful similarity between this version, from the remotest past, of major geological changes and the discoveries of the present day cannot be explained in any other way than that the Quran springs from a Being whose knowledge far surpasses the limitations of time and space.

## The Evidence of Biology

In the field of biology, Quranic descriptions of embryonic development are truly remarkable. These were headlined in the newspapers towards the end of 1984. The Canadian newspaper, *The Citizen* (22 November, 1984) published this news under the heading: Ancient Holy Book 1300 Years Ahead of its Time.

Similarly *The Times of India,* New Delhi (10 December, 1984) published this news under this headline: Koran Scores Over Modern Sciences.

Dr. Keith More, a famous embryologist and professor at Toronto University, Canada, has studied some verses from the Quran (23:14, 39:6), making a comparative study of the Quranic verses with modern research. In this connection he also visited the King Abdul Aziz University in Jeddah, Saudi Arabia, several times, along with his colleagues. He found that the statements of the Quran, astonishingly corresponded in full with modern discoveries. He was very surprised that facts contained in the Quran were brought to light by the Western World as late as 1940. In a paper written in this connection, he says: "The 1300 year old Koran contains passages so accurate about embryonic development that Muslims can reasonably believe them to be revelations from God."

Convincing supportive details can be had from the analysis Maurice Bucaille makes in his book, *The Bible, The Quran and Science* which was published in 1970. We reproduce here some excerpts from the chapter entitled 'Human Reproduction.'

## Evolution of the Embryo inside the Uterus

The Quranic description of certain stages in the development of the embryo corresponds exactly to what we today know about it, and the Quran does not contain a single statement that is open to criticism from modern science.

After 'the thing which clings' (an expression which is well founded, as we have seen) the Quran informs us that the embryo passes through the stage of 'chewed flesh', then osseous tissue appears and is clad in flesh (defined by a different word from the preceding which signifies 'intact flesh').

> **"We fashioned the thing which clings into a chewed lump of flesh and We fashioned the chewed flesh into bones and We clothed the bones with intact flesh." (23:14)**

'Chewed flesh' is the translation of the word *mudga*; 'intact flesh' is *lahm*. This distinction needs to be stressed. The embryo is initially a small mass. At a certain stage in its development, it looks to the naked eye like chewed flesh. The bone structure develops inside this mass in what is called the mesenchyma. The bones that are formed are covered in muscle; the word *lahm* applies to them.

It is known how certain parts appear to be completely out of proportion during embryonic development with what is later to become the individual, while others remain in proportion.

This is surely the meaning of the word *mukallaq* which signifies 'shaped in proportion' as used in verse 5, sura 22 to describe this phenomenon.

> "We fashioned ... into something which clings... into a lump of flesh in proportion and out of proportion."

More than a thousand years before our time, at a period when whimsical doctrines still prevailed, men had a knowledge of the Quran. The statements it contains express in simple terms truths of primordial importance which man has taken centuries to discover (pp. 205-06).

## Dietetics in the Quran

In the Quran, certain foodstuffs are declared unfit for human consumption and are, therefore, prohibited. One of these items is blood. At the time of revelation, man had no idea of the dietetic importance of this law. Much later, when laboratory research had isolated the components of blood, the wisdom of this prohibition became clear. Far from refuting the law, scientific investigation illustrated its benefits.

The analysis showed that blood contains an abundance of uric acid, a pernicious substance the intake of which is injurious to human health. This is the reason for the special method of slaughter prescribed in Islam. The wielder of the knife, having taken the name of God, makes an incision in the jugular vein; leaving the other veins of the neck intact. This causes death by a total loss of blood from the body, rather than by injury to any vital organ. Were the animal's brain, heart, liver or any other vital organ to be crippled, the animal would die immediately, and its blood would congeal in its veins and eventually permeate the flesh. The animal's flesh would thus be contaminated with uric acid and would become poisonous.

Pork has also been prohibited in the Quran. At that time the reasons for this prohibition were not fully understood. Nowadays, people are much more well informed about its harmful effects. Uric acid, as we have seen, is present in all animals. The human body too has its share, which is extracted by the kidneys and excreted by means of urination. Ninety per cent of the uric acid collected in the human body is extracted in this way. But the pig's biochemistry is such that it excretes only two percent of its uric acid. The rest remains an integral part of the body. It is this factor which causes the high rate of rheumatism found in pigs, and those who eat pork are also especially prone to this disease.

Another matter of considerable medical importance touched on by the Quran is the utility of honey.

We are told that in honey 'there is a healing for men' (16:69). In the light of this verse the Muslims made much use of honey while preparing medicine. But to the western world its medical importance was unknown.

Up till the 19th century in Europe, honey was considered only a liquid food. It was as late as the 20th century that European scholars discovered that honey contained antiseptic properties. We shall quote here in brief what an American magazine has to say about modern research on honey:

"Honey is a powerful destroyer of germs which produce human diseases. It was not until the twentieth century, however, that this was demonstrated scientifically. Dr. W.G. Sackett, formerly with Colorado Agricultural College at Fort Collins, attempted to prove that honey was a carrier of disease much like milk. To his surprise, all the disease germs he introduced into pure honey were quickly destroyed. The germ that causes typhoid fever died in pure honey after 48 hours exposure. Enteritidis, causing intestinal inflammation, lived 48 hours. A hardy germ which causes broncho-pneumonia and septicemia held out for four days. Bacillus coil Communis which under certain conditions causes peritonitis, was dead on the fifth day of experiment. According to Dr. Bodog Beck, there are many other germs equally destructible in honey. The reason for this bactericidal quality in honey, he said, is in its hygroscopic ability. It literally draws every particle of moisture out of germs. Germs,

like any other living organism, perish without water. This power to absorb moisture is almost unlimited. Honey will draw moisture from metal, glass and even stone rocks."[26]

The account which modern physiology gives of how milk is produced has led to a reinterpretation of a Quranic verse on this subject which early translators had found difficult to render for the lack of scientific knowledge. Modern translation, backed up by science, now gives us this interpretation: 'Verily, in cattle there is a lesson for you. We give you to drink of what is inside their bodies, coming from a conjunction between the contents of the intestine and the blood, a milk, pure and pleasant for those who drink it."[27]

In *The Bible, the Quran and Science*, (p. 196,197) Dr. Maurice Bucaille explains that "the constituents of milk are secreted by the mammary glands. These are nourished as it were by the product of food digestion brought to them via the bloodstream.

Blood therefore plays the role of collector and conductor of what has been extracted from food and it brings nutrition of the mammary glands, the producers of milk, as it does to any other organ. He writes:

"Here the initial process which sets everything in motion is the bringing together of the contents of the intestine and blood at the level of the intestinal wall itself. This very precise concept is the result of discoveries made in the chemistry and physiology of the digestive system. It was totally unknown at the time of the Prophet Muhammad and has been understood only in recent times. Harvey made the discovery of the circulation of the blood roughly ten centuries after the Quranic revelation.

"I consider that the existence in the Quran of the verse referring to these concepts can have no human explanation on account of the period in which they were formulated."

## Modern Physics and the Quran

Another point on which human intelligence appeared to have arrived at a major scientific truth was that of the true nature of light. It was Sir Issac Newton (1642-1727) who put forward the theory that light consisted of minute corpuscles in rapid motion which emanated from their source and were scattered in the atmosphere. Owing to the extraordinary influence of Newton, this corpuscular theory held sway over the scientific world for a very long time, only to be abandoned in the middle of the nineteenth century in favour of the wave theory of light. It was the discovery of the action of photon, which delivered the final blow to Newton's theory. "Young's work convinced scientists that light has essential wave characteristics in apparent contradiction to Newton's corpuscular theory."[28]

It had taken only 200 years to prove Newton wrong. The Quran, on the contrary, gave its message to the world in the 7th century, and even after a lapse of 1400 years its truth emerges unscathed. The reason for this is that it is of divine, not human origin: the absolute truth of its statements can be proved at all times—an extraordinary attribute that no other work can claim.

Einstein's theory of relativity declares that gravity controls the behavior of planets, stars, galaxies and the universe itself, and does so in a predictable manner.

This scientific discovery had already been developed into a philosophy by Hume (1711-1776) and other thinkers, who declared that the whole system of the universe was governed by the principle of causation, and that it had only been when man had not been aware of this, that God had been supposed to control the universe. The principle of cause and effect was then thought logically to dispense with the idea of God.

But later research ran counter to this purely material supposition. When Paul Dirac, Heisenberg and other eminent scientists bent their minds to analysing the structure of the atom, they discovered that its system contradicted the principle of causation which had been adopted on the basis of studies made of the solar system. This theory, called the quantum mechanics theory, maintains that at the sub-atomic level, matter behaves randomly.

The word 'principle' in science means something which applies in equal measure throughout the entire universe. If there is even one single instance of a principle failing to apply to something, its academic bonafides have to be called in question. It followed then that if matter did not function according to this principle of causation in an exactly similar manner at the subatomic level as it did in the solar system, it should have to be rejected.

Einstein found this idea unthinkable and spent the last 30 years of his life trying to reconcile these seeming contradictions of nature. He rejected the randomness of quantum mechanics, saying, "I cannot believe God plays dice with the universe." Despite his best efforts, he was never able to resolve this problem and it seems that the Quran has the final word on the reality of the universe. The fact that the universe cannot be explained in terms of human knowledge is aptly illustrated by Ian Roxburgh when he writes:

The laws of physics discovered on earth contain arbitrary

numbers, like the ratio of the mass of an electron to the mass of a proton, which is roughly 1840 to one. Why? Did a creator arbitrarily choose these numbers?[29]

When the Quran specifically states that God is the absolute Sovereign Lord of this universe, that He "accomplishes what He pleases" (14:27) and that He is the Executor of His own will (85:16), we need not even ask ourselves the kind of question Ian Roxburgh put. For thousands of years, this concept of God was an established one, quite beyond dispute. Now, from the point of extreme materialism the pendulum of belief has swung back to the immutable and unassailable laws of the Quran.

There are innumerable examples in the Quran and in the Traditions of the Prophet, which are extremely strong indications that the Quran's inspiration is superhuman. To sum up, here is an incident which occurred in England, as related by Inayatullah Mashriqi. "It was Sunday," he writes, "the year 1909. It was raining hard. I had gone out on some errand when I saw the famous Cambridge University astronomer, Sir James Jeans, with a Bible clutched under his arm, on his way to Church. Coming closer I greeted him, but he did not reply. When I greeted him again, he looked at me and asked, 'What do you want? 'Two things, I replied. 'Firstly, the rain is pouring down, but you have not opened your umbrella. 'Sir James smiled at his own absent-mindedness and opened his umbrella. 'Secondly', I continued, 'I would like to know that a man of universal fame such as yourself is doing—going to pray in Church?' Sir James paused for a while, then, looking at me, he said, 'Come and have tea with me this evening.' So I went along to his house that afternoon. At exactly 4 o'clock, Lady James appeared. 'Sir James is waiting for you', she said. I went inside, where tea was ready on the table. Sir James was lost in thought. 'What was your question again?' he asked, and without waiting for an answer, he went off into an inspiring description of the creation of the celestial bodies and the astonishing order to which they adhere, the incredible distances over which they travel and the unfailing regularity which they maintain, their intricate journeys through space in their orbits, their mutual attraction and their never wavering from the path chosen for them, no matter how complicated it might be. His vivid account of the Power and Majesty of God made my heart begin to tremble. As for him, the hair on his head was standing up straight. He eyes were shining with awe and wonder. Trepidation at the thought of God's all-knowing and all-powerful nature made his hands tremble and his voice falter. 'You know, Inayat-ullah Khan', he said, 'when I behold God's marvellous feats of creation, my whole being trembles in awe at His majesty. When I go to Church I bow my head and say, "Lord, how great you are," and not only my lips, but every particle of my body joins in uttering these words. I obtain incredible peace and joy from my prayer. Compared to others, I receive a thousand times more fulfillment from my prayer. So tell me, Inayat-ullah Khan, now do you understand why I go to Church?"

Sir James Jeans's words left Inayat-ullah Mashriqi's mind spinning. "Sir," he said, "your inspiring words have made a deep impression on me. I am reminded of a verse of the Quran which, if I may be allowed, I should like to quote." "Of course." Sir James replied. Inayat-ullah Khan then recited this verse:

> "In the mountains there are streaks of various shades of red and white, and jet-black rocks. Men, beasts and cattle have their different colours, too. From among His servants, it is the learned who fear God" (35:27-28).

"What was that?" exclaimed Sir James. "It is those alone who have knowledge who fear God. Wonderful! How extraordinary! It has taken me fifty years of continual study and observation to realize this fact. Who taught it to Muhammad? Is this really in the Quran? If so, you can record my testimony that the Quran is an inspired Book. Muhammad was illiterate. He could not have learnt this immensely important fact on his own. God must have taught it to him. Incredible! How extraordinary!"[30]

And how significant that Sir James Jeans should have concluded his book, *The Mysterious Universe* with these words:

"We cannot claim to have discerned more than a very faint glimmer of light at the best; perhaps it was wholly illusory, for certainly we had to strain our eyes very hard to see anything at all. So that our main contention can hardly be that the science of today has a pronouncement to make, perhaps it ought rather to be that science should leave off making pronouncements: the river of knowledge has too often turned back on itself" (p.138).

## Notes

1. Quran, 2:23.
2. Quran, 17:31.
3. Quran, 61:8-9.
4. *Life of Mahomet*, Vol.II. p. 228.
5. *The Decline and Fall of the Roman Empire*, p. 80.
6. *Ibid*, p. 76.
7. *The Decline and Fall of the Roman Empire*, pp. 80-81.
8. *Ibid*, p. 76.
9. *Ibid*, p. 82.
10. Quran, 30: 1-6.
11. *The Decline and Fall of the Roman Empire*, p. 94.
12. *Ibid*, pp. 79-80.
13. *Exodus*, 14:28.
14. Quran, 10:92.
15. Maurice Bucaille, *The Bible, The Quran and Science*, p.241.
16. *Ibid*, p. 241.
17. *The Evidence of God*, pp. 137-38.
18. *Encyclopaedia Britannica*, Vol.15, p. 1172.
19. *Encyclopaedia Britannica*, Vol.14, p. 695.
20. John Kenneth Galbraith, *The Age of Uncertainty*, p. 77.
21. Quran, 2:282.
22. See *Encyclopaedia Britannica*, Vol. VIII, p. 811.
23. A.C. Morrison, *Man Does Not Stand Alone*, p. 19.
24. Quran, 54:1,2.
25. O.R. Von Engeln, *Geomorphology*, (New York, 1948), p. 262.
26. *Rosicrucian Digest*, September, 1975, p. 11.
27. Quran, 16:66.
28. *Encyclopaedia Britannica* 1984, Vol. 19, p. 665.
29. *Sunday Times*, London, 4 December, 1977.
30. *Nuqoosh Shakhsiyat*, (Impressions of Personalities), pp. 1208-209.

# Religion and Society

Society is based on a delicate network of human relationships which, under the slightest of provocations, may become tangled, broken or distorted. Injustice of a greater or lesser gravity is the usual result of such aberrations. What then does it take to keep the balance of justice? Clearly, laws must be framed which correspond to moral imperatives, which are enforceable and which maintain a proper equilibrium between the permanent and the peripheral. Despite the urgent need for such laws, society has failed—even after the experiences of two thousand five hundred years—to evolve a universally acceptable principle on which a viable set of laws might be based.

As L.L. Fuller put it, the law has yet to discover itself. In his aptly entitled book, *The Law in Quest of Itself*, he points out that, in modern times, great minds have addressed their considerable talents to this subject, and innumerable weighty volumes have been written as a result. "Through being fashioned into a formidable science," says the *Chambers Encyclopaedia*, "law has made great advances." Yet all these efforts have failed to produce a unanimous concept of law. One legal expert puts it this way: "If ten constitutionalists were asked to define what they meant by law, it would be no exaggeration to say that we would have to be prepared for eleven different answers." Leaving aside technicalities, these schools of thought can be broadly divided into two categories of jurisprudence: the ideological, whose quest is 'Law as it ought to be,' and the analytical, which interprets 'Law as it is.' The history of the principles of law shows that neither has arrived at any acceptable conclusion. When jurists attempt to interpret the law in terms of the second category, objections are raised that logical justification has escaped their attention, and when they attempt to understand it within the framework of the first category, they are forced to the conclusion that it is something which is impossible to discover.

One school of thought views the law simply as an external structure of human society which can be built according to known rules and regulations exactly like a cage that is built to confine animals in the zoo. This theory was supported by John Austin (1790-1859) who said: "Law is what is imposed by a superior on an inferior, be that superior the king or the legislature."

While this appears to be a practicable theory, it is actually bereft of any valid logic, in that it accords the jurist a superior position without any necessary insistence on the criteria of justice being adhered to. But the human intellect could never concede that justice as a concept might be separated from the law. When the law imposes a judgement on someone, it is considered valid only when it is based on justice. As G.W. Paton observes, Austin's definition of the law reduces it to the "command of a sovereign."[1]

Although in practice, all over the world, laws are made and brought into force through political power, a number of eminent jurists have felt it necessary to carry out academic research on the principles of law. Their quest, however, has led them no further than the conclusion that, in this matter, arriving at an agreed upon criterion is a sheer impossibility. The reason is that the aim of the quest calls for the determination of legal norms on the basis of human values. Scholars are agreed that this discovery of values is not possible by purely rational methods, and constitutionalists have not even found the correct structure within which to frame the laws they propose. They may be agreed that there are certain fundamental values which they feel it would be desirable to incorporate in the law, yet, try as they may to do so, they find that while some values may be maintained, there are always others which elude them. It is rather like a man trying to weigh five frogs up with five others. He gathers five frogs on one end of the scale. Then he turns his attention to the other five. In the meantime the first five jump off. And so it has happened with all our efforts to frame a perfect set of laws. The establishment of one set of laws has led to the forfeit of others. There is no end in sight to our predicament. The only 'solution' that western civilization has found, says, W. Friedmann, is to "keep wavering from one extreme to the other."[2]

One latter-day extreme which we have reached is the sanctioning or repeal of laws according to whether they find favour with the public or not. Some laws, in spite of being ethically and academically sound, have been abandoned simply because people did not want them. Alcohol, for instance, was prohibited for some time in the U.S.A, but this law was eventually repealed because of public pressure. The death sentence in Britain was commuted for similar reasons, and homosexuality has had to be legalized despite opposition from judges and other responsible members of society, who recognized it for the evil it was.

Gustav Radburch (1878-1949) observes that the desired law can only be adopted by concession, and not for the reason that it is 'scientifically known.' Radburch's views are not an exception, and on this basis a permanent school of thought had come into existence known as the Relative School of Thought, according to which, "absolute judgements about law are not discoverable." What the law seeks relates directly to human values, and that is precisely where the human intellect has failed to find a universal solution. Yet man's instincts about right and wrong are so strong that neither the mechanical philosophy of the eighteenth century nor the utilitarian Russian system could destroy them. They are so deeply rooted in human nature, that even the Russians, who have had such a prolonged opportunity—extending over half a century—to mould human beings to their concepts in their theoretical workshop, have not been able to extirpate them, and western countries are still faced with the dilemma that even after an interminable struggle on the part of their best brains, they have wholly failed in their quest after an agreed criterion. The progress of science is making it more and more evident that we live in a world where values have no objective status.

The task of inquiry into the principles of law began, according to historical records, with Greek philosophers, one of whom was Solon (c. 638-558.), a renowned Athenian legislator. The most famous ancient book in law is by Plato (427-347 B.C.) and the legal profession had its beginnings in Rome around 500 B.C. Up till the 15th century, however, law was considered a part of theology. It was in the sixteenth century that the new trend developed which finally separated law from religion. It still, however, remained a part of politics. It was only in the 19th century that legal philosophy was separated from political philosophy, and jurisprudence was developed into an independent branch of knowledge, thus becoming a subject for specialization.

The ancient philosophers derived their legal principles from certain axioms, which they called natural rights. After the 16th century, the intellectual revolution of Europe demonstrated that these 'axioms' were actually only suppositions for which there existed no rational basis. Individual freedom subsequently came to be established as the greatest good, which could provide the basis for forming laws. But the consequences of the industrial revolution showed that, given individual freedom as the summum bonum, it leads us only to the exploitation of humanity, and to anarchy. Then the social good came to be considered the highest good which could provide guiding principles for legislation. But when this concept was first carried into effect it led to the most horrific political repression, in the name of public ownership. High hopes had indeed been held out that this new social order would guarantee greater justice for individuals, but a long experiment revealed that not only did the system of public ownership—being an unnatural system— produce violence, but it was also an inhibiting factor in human endeavor. The country where the effects of this policy could be seen on the largest scale was the U.S.S.R., where one of the first departments to come under the influence of this "ideal" was that of agriculture. Ever since the Bolshevik revolution of 1917 there had been continual attempts in Russia and in other communist countries to collectivize agriculture, and bring farming entirely under the control of the state.

The greatest thrust towards collectivization was initiated in the 1930's by Joseph Stalin (1879-1953). It soon became clear, however, that the transition from private to public ownership would not be smooth. In order to ward off the threat of starvation, the state awarded plots averaging 0.3 hectares each, to collective farmers. These plots were to be farmed privately, in order to augment the farmers' income and ensure that they were not swamped by the wave of sudden transition from individual to collective farming. This was considered as a "temporary evil," a concession to necessity, which would be disbanded once the legacy of the previous economic system disappeared.

Far from being a temporary evil, however, such measures proved to be a permanent part of the economic situation. It is always painful for man to be torn away from his natural environment, and this was no exception. An estimated 5.5 million people died of hunger and related diseases when they were forced into state and collective farms on Stalin's orders.

But an even more conclusive indictment of the state-owned system of agriculture is the fact that despite massive investments in the public sector, the private sector continues to flourish in the Soviet Union. Thousands of private farmers own small plots of land in Georgia and central Asia. According to a November 1984 article in *Questions of Economy*, a monthly journal published by the Academy of Sciences, Moscow, plots and small holding account for 25% of total agricultural production in the Soviet Union. More than half the nation's potatoes, and roughly a third of its meat, eggs and other vegetables are produced privately. These figures are even more astounding when one compares them to the proportion—just 2.8%—that private plots constitute of all the farm land in the country.

The prices that privately-grown vegetables fetch in Moscow central market make a mockery of the communist ideal of free food for all. According to a Reuter report from Moscow, dated December 28, 1984, tomatoes from Georgia were fetching 15 roubles a kilo on the Moscow market. Cauliflowers from central Asia were going for 12 roubles a piece. Muscovites complain about the high prices but it is a question of paying them or going without vegetables:

> **While Muscovites complain at the swarthy 'millionaries' from the South whose big houses and flashy cars are legend, without them fruit and vegetables would be hard to find at all.**[3]

All this goes to show that the communist state has failed to provide people with their basic needs of life, let alone provide them free of cost. People have to fall back on the private sector for elementary provision. The private sector continues to outstrip the public sector, despite the advantages, which the latter enjoys under the patronage of the communist state. Even Russian leaders, faced with the reality that the state alone simply cannot meet the nation's needs, have admitted the importance of the private sector. State planning chief Nikoli Baibakov told the latest session of Soviet parliament: "Economic leaders should devote more attention to giving help to collective farm workers in managing their private plots."

Thus communism had done a complete U-turn since the days of Stalin when complete collectivization was considered the ideal. Now there is a grudging acceptance of the inevitability of private enterprise, and the need to assist it. It is not very difficult to see why the system of private enterprise should be so resilient in face of encroachment by the state. It is because private enterprise is not a man-made system; it is an integral part of human nature, and efforts to change human nature are doomed to failure.

It had thus emerged that while excessive individual liberty could be detrimental to society, totalitarianism left the individual helpless and suppressed with his material needs uncatered for.

The new man-made laws had certainly not produced justice for all, and while the latter half of the twentieth century has seen attempts to reconcile the demands of the individual and society, this experiment likewise seems to be leading nowhere. Indeed, what man so urgently requires is not one experiment after another, but an eternal law, applicable to all peoples, all situation and valid for all times. But human reasoning, when not underpinned by religion, leads us in exactly the opposite direction. As Kohler states quite unequivocally in, *The Philosophy of Law*, "Here there is no eternal law. Inevitably, the very law that is suitable for our age cannot be suitable for another. All we can do is make an effort to provide every culture with a suitable legal system. Something which is beneficial for one culture might be harmful for another."

This concept takes away all stability from the philosophy of law. The idea that people must have a law which suits their own particular culture is one that leads human thought to blind relativism. Bereft of any foundation, it is a concept, which may controvert all basic human values.

The result of all this is that we are back where John Austin left us, with no clear idea of what justice is, or how it can be defined. Centuries of investigation and research have failed to provide mankind with a set of clear principles on which to base his laws. As G.W. Paton says: "What are the interests that a perfect legal system has to protect? This is a question that has to do with values and comes within the scope of legal philosophy, but we require more help from legal philosophy in this matter than philosophy seems prepared to give us. Consequently we have been unable to come up with an acceptable scale of values. In fact, only in religion we find such values, but religious dogmas are accepted on faith or intuition, not on the basis of rational argument."[4]

In the same work he later remarks (p. 109), "The Orthodox Natural Law Theory based its absolutes on the revealed truths of religion. If we attempt to secularize jurisprudence, where can we find an agreed basis of values?"

In ancient times, religion had a major role to play in the

framing and enactment of laws. On this, the legal historian, Sir Henry Maine, has this to say. "From China to Peru, we can find no written constitutional system of government that was not, from its very inception, tied up with religious rituals and devotion."[5]

In the face of the vacillations of philosophers, legal experts and psychologists, modern jurists having stated quite finally that "a purely logical interpretation of legal rules is impossible," we must necessarily turn to the precision, stability and universality of revealed law. This had been perfectly preserved in its original authentic form in the Quran, the holy book of Islam, which asserts that revelation from God is the only true source of law. It clearly states that there is a God of this universe, who has revealed His law to His messenger. This law is the most correct set of laws for man, on the basis of which further laws can be formed by *Qiyas*, i.e. the analogical reasoning of the learned based on the teachings of the Quran, *Hadith* and *Ijma* (the unanimous consent of a council of divines) and by *Ijtihad*, i.e. by logical deduction on a legal or theological question by a religious scholar. This does not involve digression from the basic principles and, as a method of attaining to a certain degree of authority for the purpose of inquiring into the principles of jurisprudence, it has been sanctioned by the Traditions. The word *Ijtihad* literally means 'extortion' and it is interesting to see how it applied to an actual situation in the time of the Prophet. When Muaz bin Jabal was on the point of leaving for Yemen to take over as a governor of that province, the Prophet asked him how he would judge matters. "With the help of the Quran" was his reply. The Prophet then asked him what he would do if guidelines were not to be found in the Quran. Muaz replied that he would consult the Sunnah, or sayings and deeds of the Prophet. "And what," the Prophet asked," if you do not find the necessary guidelines in the Sunnah?" "Then," said Muaz, "I will exercise my own judgement to the best of my ability."

I am prepared to admit that making claims about the effectiveness of *Qiyas* and *Ijtihad* is, from the academic point of view, a matter of great complexity. But I must stress that the reason for this complexity is not inherent in the law itself, but in the limitations of the human intellect. Fortunately I am supported in this by modern science, which makes it clear that there is a great deal more to the universe than can come under our direct observation, and that what is not knowable is much greater and more significant than that which is actually known. American Professor Fred Berthold very simply, but very profoundly sums up the philosophy of logical positivism: "The important is unknowable, and the knowable is unimportant."

In the nineteenth century, it was supposed that man was heading towards absolute reality, although at that time it was actually even farther from his grasp than it is today. But, at least it was felt that man was sure to discover it one fine day. Now the scientists of the twentieth century tell us, under the banner of positivism or operationalism, that such a supposition was entirely wrong, as science cannot tell us about ultimate reality or ultimate good. Sir James Jeans in his book, *The Mysterious Universe*, makes the point that "our earth is so infinitesimal in comparison with the whole universe, we, the only thinking beings so far as we know, in the whole of space, are to all appearance so accidental, so far removed from the whole scheme of the universe, that it is a *priori* all too probable that any meaning that the universe as a whole may have, would entirely transcend our terrestrial experience, and so be totally unintelligible to us" (p.112). Existentialism too convinces us that man, with his limitations, does not know how to discover a norm, which is beyond him.

"Man is an ethical animal in a universe which contains no ethical element." This is an often-quoted statement of Joseph Wood Krutch (1893-1970) who writes in his best-seller, *The Modern Temper*, that no matter how great an effort a man makes, the two halves of his soul can hardly come together. And he does not know how to think as his intellect tells, or how to feel as his emotions tell him. And thus in his ruined and divided soul, he has become a laughing stock."

In this, Krutch is in error. And this is because he has stepped out of his domain. The basic point that I feel needs stressing here is that what has been proved is not that values do not exist, but that man is not capable of discovering them. In the book, *Man the Unknown*, Dr. Alexis Carrel has shown that the question of values requires complete acquaintance with the different branches of knowledge, but that owing to man's limitations, this is an impossibility. He has even rejected the idea of a committee of experts reaching any sound conclusions because while "a superior art comes into being by one mind, it has never been produced by an academy."

The fact that only partial knowledge has been granted to man is a reality which must be accepted. It is a fact supported by modern science, particularly since the time of the first world war, that man is subject to certain biological and psychological limitations and cannot, therefore, apprehend all facts through his senses. To borrow Locke's phrase, "the real essence of substances" is forever unknowable. Even Einstein advocated scientific contemplation, and not just observation, if the more profound aspects of the universe were to be understood. Einstein's view is thus summed up by a colleague:

**"In dealing with the eternal varieties, the area of experiment is reduced and that of contemplation enhanced."**

Agreement has now been reached that absolute reasoning can apply only to fields of research which, according to Bertrand Russell (1872-1970), concern 'Knowledge of things.' 'Knowledge of truths' is a separate field of study and, in this, direct argument is impossible: certainties cannot be arrived at. We can only attempt to arrive at probable judgements. This is not limited only to non-material facts, but to many things which fall into the category of the material, like light, or the interpretation of gravity.

I venture to assert at this point that the basis of judgement provided by modern knowledge is indubitably in favour of revealed law.

The notion of revealed law presupposes that there is a God

of this universe, and this is obviously not unintelligible to man, for most of the great scientists have believed in God in one form or the other. Newton (1642-1727) saw a 'divine hand' in things which caused the movement of the Solar System. Darwin (1809-1882) considered a 'creator' necessary for the origin of life. There was a 'superior mind,' observed Einstein (1879-1954) which manifested itself in the universe. Sir James Jeans (1877-1946) was led by his studies to the conclusion that the universe was a 'great thought' rather than a 'great machine.' According to Sir Arthur Eddington (1882-1944), modern science was leading us to the reality that 'the stuff of the world is mind-stuff.' To Alfred North Whitehead (1861-1947) the body of information obtained through modern research proves that 'nature is alive.' So far as revelation is concerned, however, I admit that from the purely academic point of view, this is a very complex belief, not being one which is verifiable. But we do have, within the totality of our experience, a body of facts from which it can be inferred that revelation is reality. Modern methodology supports the idea that inferred facts can be as certain as observed facts. The importance of our argument is not, therefore, diminished, by stating that it is the result, not of observation, but of inference.

In the nineteenth century, the principle of causation was considered to be the alternative for the Creator. But in the present century many events have come to the notice of science, which are not explainable in terms of the common principle of material causes. For instance, all efforts have failed to explain the disintegration of the radium electron according to known laws. It has even been said by scientists that no one can be absolutely certain which piece of radium will disintegrate at which point of time. As one scientist put it, "It may rest on the knees of whatever gods there be."

Animal life too has its inexplicable aspects. It has been proved that animal instincts are innate and not an acquisition. Our proofs do not, however, tell us why this should be so. The bee makes each section of its honeycomb octagonal. It was not taught in a training center about which particular geometrical figure would be the most appropriate for its purpose. It is not, so far as we know, even conscious of the significance of this shape. Yet it constructs mathematically, as if it had been commanded to do so. Says the Quran:

> "And thy Lord inspired the bees, saying: Choose thou habitations in the hills and in the trees and in that which they thatch" (16:68).

There are innumerable such instances which show the probability of there being some consciousness outside things which instructs them as to their mode of living.

Sir Arthur Eddington has asserted that the modern quantum theory is a scientific affirmation of revelation. This statement of the Quran—"And He inspired in each heaven its mandate" (41:12)—is perhaps far more understandable to the 20th century man than it could have been to the 7th century man at the time when Quran was revealed.

If we admit that the source of the laws of nature that govern everything from the stars and planets to the biological aspects of human life, is the revelation which is received by everything from the universal consciousness, we have less difficulty in accepting the parallel belief that, for the psychological part of man too, laws must stem from that same external consciousness.

From the purely rational point of view, it can quite rightly be said that the basis of this argument is inference. In fact it has been proved that man's mental make-up is such that he cannot escape inferential argument. His only alternative is scepticism, which takes him nowhere.

The time has come to accept the fact that we are just not able to formulate laws on our own. There is no point in continuing in this endeavour, for our efforts will achieve nothing unless we have recourse to divine guidance. As W. Friedmann puts it, religion provides us with a uniquely true and simple framework within which we can formulate a perfect concept of justice.[6]

The Quran stresses the reason for man's incapacity to frame laws:

"They are asking thee concerning the Spirit. Say: The Spirit is by command of my Lord, and of knowledge ye have been vouchsafed but little" (17:85).

It then claims that, for man's guidance, God has made a revelation of His laws, and to support this claim, it challenges anyone who wills to produce a book of similar quality.

"And if ye are in doubt concerning that which We reveal unto Our slave (Muhammad), then produce a chapter of the like thereof, and call your witnesses beside God if ye are truthful" (2:23).

"Say: Verily, though mankind and the Jinn (a race of spirits) should assemble to produce the like of this Quran, they could not produce the like thereof though they were helpers one of another" (17:88).

Over the last 1300 years there have appeared on the scene immumerable enemies of the Quran and Islam who could easily have prepared a book like the Quran in Arabic in answer to this challenge, and indeed, some of them did attempt to do so. But history shows that from the time of Musailima (d.633) and Ibn Muqaffa (724-761) to the Crusades (1095-1271) no one, including Christian orientalists has succeeded in such an attempt. More astonishing is the fact that the legal principles laid down by the Quran so many centuries ago have retained their veracity till today. It has of course happened that revealed laws have been rejected in favour of man-made laws, but in the course of an experiment which lasted over 200 years, the man-made laws have proved a failure, and enlightened opinion is again veering back towards revealed law as being eternal in character. This particular quality can only be grasped when we believe that its source lies in an Eternal Mind rather than than in a human mind.

If we have not known where to allocate the power to make laws, it is because, as true religion tells us, it is God's prerogative and His alone to do so. He is the true Sovereign. No man has the right to rule over others and order their lives. Only God—man's Creator and natural Lord—has that power.

According to revealed law, freedom of the individual is subject to divine command.

**They ask: Have we any part in the cause? Say: The cause belongeth wholly to God (3:154).**

The Renaissance—the great intellectual revolution which took place in Europe in the fifteenth and sixteenth centuries—regarded this concept of freedom as little better than slavery. It proclaimed that freedom was the greatest of human values. Since the time of the French revolution till today, this new concept of freedom has held sway. But the undeniably negative end-results have now brought scholars to the point of declaring this concept meaningless. Professor B.F. Skinner, the well-known American psychologist, who developed the theory of programmed and social learning based on conditioning, is now of the view that "we can't afford freedom." Contrary to the opinion of 18th and 19th century thinkers, Skinner says that freedom is not the summum bonum. What man needs is not unlimited freedom, but "a disciplined culture." This reversal in human thought is an indirect admission of the eternal character of revealed laws.

Much heated controversy centres nowadays on the status of women vis-a-vis men. The emergence of women from their homes in order to seek equality has led to severe clashes in many fields and very often to their own degradation. A great deal of stress and strain could be avoided by simply bowing to revealed law, which assigns men and women different and separate spheres in practical everyday matters, and places men in a position of dominance. 'Men have authority over women....'[7]

This principle was latterly rejected by man-made law as totally wrong and unjust. But the experience of one hundred years has shown that, in this matter, revealed law is closer to reality. In spite of all the so-called successes of the women's lib movement, man, even today still enjoys the position of the dominant sex in the civilized world. The champions of women's emancipation have all along asserted that the difference between men and women was a factor produced and perpetuated by social environment alone. But in modern times, this issue has become the object of in-depth studies in various interrelated fields, and it has been demonstrated that the difference in the sexes is explained by biological factors. Harvard University's Professor of Psychology, Jerome Kagan, concludes that, "Some of the psychological differences between men and women may not be the product of experience alone, but of subtle biological differences."

An American surgeon, Edgar Berman, says: "Because of their hormonal chemistry women might be too emotional for positions of power."[8]

Dr. Alexis Carrel goes even deeper into the matter:

**The differences existing between man and woman do not come from the particular form of the sexual organs, the presence of the uterus, from gestation, or from the mode of education. They are of more fundamental nature. They are caused by the very structure of the tissues and by the impregnation of the entire organism with specific chemical substances secreted by the ovary. Ignorance of these fundamental facts has led promoters of feminism to believe that both sexes should have the same education, the same powers and the same responsibilities. In reality woman differs profoundly from man. Every one of the cells of her body bears the mark of her sex. The same is true of her organs and, above all, of her nervous system. Physiological laws are as inexorable as those of the sidereal world. They cannot be replaced by human wishes. We are obliged to accept them just as they are. Women should develop their aptitudes in accordance with their own nature, without trying to imitate the males.**

In the U.S.A., the women's 'lib' movement may be very powerful, but its supporters have now begun to feel that the real obstacle in their way is neither society, nor law, but nature itself, for the difference in male and female hormones has existed from the very first day they opened their eyes on this world. It is natural that women should be subject to the limitations of biology, but now enthusiastic supporters of women's 'lib' hold nature 'guilty' and say that nature is 'cruel.' They have even asked for the genetic code itself to be changed with the help of the science of eugenics in order to produce a new species of men and women! The American women's slogan, "Make policy, not Coffee!" tells us a great deal about their worldly aspirations, but, pushed to their logical extreme, these aspirations have culminated in a distortion of the very nature they hold culpable. This shows, quite clearly, that revealed law is more in consonance with nature than man-made law.

This social system which has ignored the distinctly separate roles of men and women, has been beset by great evils, not the least of which is the disappearance of the notion of chastity which has gone hand in hand with the rise in promiscuity. The whole of the younger generation likewise seems affected by various moral and psychological ailments. Today it is common for an unmarried girl complaining only of headache or insomnia to be told by her physician that she is pregnant. The free mixing of men and women has rendered the concept of purity meaningless. As a western doctor so pertinently says, "There can come a moment between a man and a woman when control and judgement are impossible." Marion Hilliard, an eminent doctor, severely criticizes free intercourse. She writes: "As a doctor, I don't believe there is such a thing as a platonic relationship between a man and a woman who are alone together a good deal." She goes on to say. "I cannot be so unrealistic as to advise young boys and girls to stop kissing. However, most of the mothers do not tell their daughters that a kiss simply stimulates the desire rather than satisfies it."[9]

By subscribing to this view, she indirectly admits the truth of religious law, yet finds it difficult to regard the initial manifestations of free intercourse as illegal.

Despite so may arguments in favour of revealed law, there are still a number of very vexed questions which arise in connection with it, and in fact with any established system of law. One of the most important of these is whether law is relative in its entirety, or whether there is some part of it which is constant in nature. Or, more simply, can a law which applies today be altered in the future? And are there any parts of the law that are not subject to change? There has been much intellectual foraging into this question, but no one had arrived at any concrete conclusions. In principle, jurists are at one on the need in legal systems for a workable alliance of constancy and flexibility, permanence and change. Certain basics must remain the same, while there inevitably be certain peripheral elements that can be altered to suit changing conditions. But how is a balance to be maintained between the two? Justice Cordoza of U.S. maintains that a philosophy reconciling the conflicting demands of permanence and change is one of the most urgent needs of law today, (The Growth of Law). As Roscoe Pound puts it in his *Interpretation of Legal History* (p. 1), the law should be stable, but not rigid, and there has to be a balance between the two forces. Philosophers may have made mammoth efforts to achieve this balance, by reconciling the dual necessities of stability and flexibility, but recent history has shown what lopsidedness can be the result. The long established idea that punishment should be inflicted, not only to deter the offender from committing further criminal acts, but to discourage others with similar propensities, was one of the most time-honoured and hallowed traditions, and its being tampered with has yielded highly dubious results.

The first notable person who advocated mitigation of the punishment of criminals was Cesare Beccaria (1738-1794), an Italian expert in criminology. A great deal of research has subsequently been carried out in this field, the upshot being that many experts have come round to the view that the committing of a crime is not an "intentional event," and that the underlying causes must be looked for biological structuring, mental disease, economic pressures, adverse social conditions, etc. Therefore, instead of the criminal being punished, he should be 'treated.' These ideas proved so influential that more than three dozen countries abolished the death sentence in the case of moral crimes. (It was still, however, considered necessary in the case of political and military crimes to retain the death penalty as a deterrent.) This approach to crime may have seemed more human, but it did not have the desired effect.

Since the Second World War, crime has actually been on the increase, all the 'treatment' schemes having failed to restrain people from evil. The death sentence has even had to be reintroduced in places like Delaware and Sri Lanka where it had supposedly been abolished for good. It was only when on 26th September 1959, Sri Lanka's Prime Minister, Mr. Bandara Naike himself was brutally murdered, that the law-makers came to their senses. Immediately after the funeral rites, an emergency session of the Sri Lankan Assembly was called and, after a 4 hour discussion, the decision was taken to reintroduce the death sentence.

Legal experts everywhere are now coming back to the view that punishment, to be effective, must be severe. A man who knows that he risks a death sentence if he kills someone, is less likely to perpetrate this hideous crime than one who feels that he is only going to be subjected to psychiatric treatment. This was something which was understood and accepted many centuries ago when Islam prescribed the death sentence for wilful murder. Even greater was its realism in making it permissible for the heirs, or next of kin of the deceased person to forgive the murderer on the acceptance of blood-money. Although the death penalty was meant to extirpate evil from the very roots, it was recognized that measures had also to be taken to prevent the destitution of the surviving members of the deceased's family. In special cases the state has the right to raise a sufficient amount of money as compensation.

Human perceptions had obviously been at fault in determining which laws should remain inviolable. To establish the inviolability of a law, there must be proof of its permanent effectiveness and relevance. No such proof can be offered by purely human jurisprudence. A law that people of one age considered immutable might well be called in question by people of a later age.

Divine law is the only answer to this problem, for we can derive from it all those basic principles upon which our legal systems are permanently to rest. Divine law addressed itself specifically to basic issues, remaining silent on secondary matters. In this way, it defines what part of the law is inviolable, and what part may be subjected to changes. What makes this definition take pride of place over the others is the fact that it comes directly from God. It is for this reason that we can have full confidence in its validity. In providing a solution to this problem, divine law has conferred the most immense of benefits upon humanity. No equivalent alternative could ever be fabricated by man himself.

If we consider some of the alternatives to divine law which have emerged over a period of centuries, we see that, if they have certain strength, they also have inherent weaknesses. In every constitution, there are some deeds that are classified as "crimes." As there has to be some sound cause for criminalizing an action, human law has defined such actions as anything which disturbs the peace, or interferes with administration of the realm. Any action, therefore, which does not fall into this category cannot be made illegal by society. In what light then are we to consider adultery? It cannot be defined as illegal in terms of conventional law. Yet adultery causes massive corruption in society. Other major problems are the ensuing illegitimacy of the children of such unions, and the weakening of the bonds of marriage. Unchecked, it fosters a frivolous, sensual attitude to life, which inclines people to go to any lengths to achieve what they desire. The permissiveness of society opens up all kinds of avenues to such evils as theft, deceit, kidnapping—even murder. Yet even the degeneration of public standards which results from open fornication cannot lead to its being illegalized. For as long as force is not used, and these acts take place between consenting adults, society has no grounds on which to frame laws prohibiting them. It is not, in fact, adultery, which is frowned upon, but the use of force, or other compulsions. It is felt that, just as it is a crime to take someone's property by force, so it is a crime to wrest someone's honour from him by force. Conversely, just as one person's property can be legally transferred to another provided both parties agree to the transaction, so when both parties agree to commit adultery, society sees nothing wrong in this. In fact, in cases of mutual consent, the law actually takes the side of the adulteress, and if a third party attempts to intervene, it is he who is regarded as the criminal.

Islam has solved this problem by sanctioning polygamy, a practice which has been severely criticized by modern civilization as uncivilized. But experience has shown that this Islamic principle is in conformity with human nature. After all, if the doors of legalized polygamy were closed, it would merely open the floodgates of illegal prostitution.

The U.N.O. Demographic Report of 1959, shows that the modern world is producing more children out of wedlock than ever before, the illegitimacy rate in Western countries being as high as 60%. In Panama, for example, three children out of four are born without the parents having had either a civil or a religious ceremony. Latin America, with an illegitimacy rate of 75%, tops the list. This same report shows that Muslim countries have almost no illegitimate children. In Egypt, which has been most exposed to western influence, there are less than one percent. How is it that Muslim countries have not succumbed to this modern 'epidemic'?

The editors of the report say: "Since polygamy is in practice in Muslim countries, the business of illegitimate relations is not flourishing. The principle of polygamy has saved the Muslim countries from the storm of the time." (From an article, 'More Out than In')[10]

Human law-makers have likewise had difficulty in finding grounds for the prohibition of alcohol. Eating and drinking are looked upon as fundamental rights, not to be tampered with by law. Society does not see anything wrong with drinking liquor nor, indeed, with becoming intoxicated. Only when one disturbs the peace under the influence of drink, say, by fighting with and abusing others does the law step in. Similarly, those who drive in a drunken condition are punishable by law because they are liable to harm others. It is not then the practice of drinking which be punished, but the harm which is done, or could be done to other people. Yet, not only alcohol harmful to the health, but it is also a great drain on one's financial resources. Whole families can be reduced to destitution by one man's alcoholism. By paralyzing the finer instincts alcohol makes it easier for a person to commit crimes such as murder, theft, rape and robbery. In fact, it so reduces one's sense of propriety that one becomes little better than an animal. Society is fully aware that such things are happening, but is not able to prohibit alcohol by law. Why is this so? Because it cannot find a solid justification for clamping restrictions upon what people eat and drink.

Divine law, being an expression of the will of God Almighty, provides a solution to this problem. The very fact that its origin is God is sufficient reason for its application in the world of man. It does not require any further justification. God is All-knowing and All-seeing. When He prohibits something, it is because, quite simply, it is bad for man, and whatever is bad for man should be considered as a crime and at all times eschewed.

A certain deed may be decreed an offence and, therefore, punishable by law, but it is not enough for the words of prohibition to be inscribed in the statute book. For something to be considered an offence, and a punishment attached to it, it has to be viewed with general abhorrence by society at large. Anyone committing an offence can then be made to feel that he is doing something wrong, for his action will be condemned by the whole of society, and law-enforcement authorities will then be able to apprehend him with full confidence; judge and jury will be in a position to deliver their verdicts, confident that they are punishing one who is deserving of punishment.

What is an offence in the eyes of the law must be a sin in the eyes of men. As the historical school of legal thought maintains, law-making can only succeed when it complies with the inner convictions of the generation by whom and for whom the law is made. A system of law, which does not do so is bound to fail.[11]

This statement may not constitute a valid argument in support of that particular school of legal thought, but it does contain an element of external truth.

Moreover, for the law to be effective, there also have to be forces at work in society, which discourage crime. Apart from punishment, there has to be prevention, for the activities of law enforcement bodies in themselves do not necessarily inspire sufficient fear to act as deterrents. This is largely because, all to often, punishment can be eluded by resorting to bribery and corruption. Anyone who is confident of being able to escape in this way will pay no heed to the law or its enforcement.

In divine law lies the answer to all the shortcomings of man-made law. We have seen how an atmosphere in which people are encouraged to uphold the truth has to be engendered in society as a whole, for the penal code cannot, merely by its existence, induce correct attitudes. This has to originate elsewhere—from a source effective enough to ensure that, in the last analysis, anyone who perjures himself will not escape self-recrimination. In a Western Circuit Court in England, there is a stone which commemorates a unique event which took place there many years before. A certain witness took the oath in the normal way, then added: "May God take my soul here and now if what I say be false." And he fell down dead on that very spot.[12]

Other events of this nature have also occurred, providing poignant reminders of the much direr punishment that awaits people in the next world. If people in their hearts dread such retribution, they will take very good care to do nothing which will bring it down upon their own heads. A common consciousness of what is wrong must emerge in society, something which does not and cannot stem from legislation alone. This can only come from religion, which gives us not only a law, but a faith to go with it. Through this faith, we become aware that it is One who is omniscient who has made the Law. Knowing everything that we do, He has a record of all our thoughts, words and deeds. After death we shall be brought before Him, at which time all will be laid bare. We may use worldly resources to escape worldly punishment but there will be no such escape route when we stand before God. There will be no escaping the infinitely greater punishment that awaits us in the next world.

An incident, which occurred during the reign of King James I of England, is a good illustration of how indispensable religious faith is to justice. King James had proclaimed himself an absolute monarch, which meant that he could decide cases himself, without having recourse to courts of law. The Lord Chancellor, Lord Coke—a religious man, famed for the long hours he spent in worship—cautioned the King that he had no right to take final decision, and that all cases should be decided in courts of law. "It is my opinion," the monarch countered, "and I have heard as much from others, that your laws are based on common sense. Tell me, do I have less of that than judges?" "There is no doubt of your masterly intellect and statesmanship," said the Lord Chancellor; "but one has to have much practical experience and specialist knowledge in order to dispense justice.

Only then can one wield the golden scales of justice, by which the rights of the people are weighed, and by which even the sovereign's rights are safeguarded." "What, am I too subject to the law?" demanded an extremely incensed King James. "To say so is treason." Quoting Bracton, Lord Coke replied: "The monarch is subject to no man; but he is subject to God and the Law."[13]

The fact is, when we subtract the divine element from justice, we are left with no logical grounds for saying that the monarch (or anyone else for that matter) is subject to the law. The same goes for groups of individuals. When the law has been devised by a number of human minds; when it is by their sanction that laws are exacted; when they, as legislators, can annul the law or maintain it at will: can there be any basis on which they themselves may be subject to that law?

When man himself is the law-maker, he is entitled to assume the powers of lord and sovereign. He himself is God. He himself is the law. How is it possible then that he be made subject to the law?

The principle of all men being equal is accepted in modern

democratic countries, but in practice, all are not equal in terms of their own legal systems. In India, for instance, it is not as easy to initiate legal proceedings against the president, a provincial governor, a minister or a senior officer, as it is against an ordinary citizen. Clause 361 of the Indian Constitution protects the president and provincial governors from prosecution without the permission of parliament, and the government has to give its clearance if cases are to be brought against ministers. Furthermore, Clause 197 of the Indian Ordinances decrees that no judge, magistrate or civil servant may be dismissed from his post without the prior permission of the central or provincial governments. In case of corruption, there can be no hearings in court until the central or provincial government—whichever the employer—grants permission. In other words, if you want to take a prominent politician or administrator to court, you have to have his permission first.

This is not so much a fault of Indian law as a fault of human law, and it is to be found wherever human beings make their own laws. Only when divine law is followed it is possible for each and every individual to be equal in the eyes of the law. There is no difference then even between the ruler and his subjects. Both can be prosecuted with equal ease, for neither is the law-maker. The law-maker is God and all human beings are equal before God's law.

For centuries, jurists have been searching for just, equitable principles on which to base human laws. When one considers how successful man has been in discovering physical laws and how dismally he had failed in finding social laws, it becomes evident that something is very far wrong. The world's first photograph was taken by a French scientist in 1826. It took him eight hours, and all he was attempting to photograph was the verandah outside his room. Nowadays photography has made such great advances that an automatic camera can take more than two thousand photographs in a second. In the length of time it took to take the first photograph, sixty million photographs can now be taken. At the beginning of the century, there were just four motor cars in the U.S.A. Now, over 100 million motor cars ply the thoroughfares of that country. Our technology is now so sophisticated that, if there is any minuscule alteration in the rotation of the earth, leading to the shortening or lengthening of the day by even a millionth of a second, our observatories will at once detect it. The sensitivity of modern apparatus is such that, if just two words are added to a thirty-volume encyclopaedia, the increase in weight of the added ink will be exactly recorded. How great and how wonderful are the advances of man in the discovery of physical laws. But as far as social laws are concerned, he has not advanced so much as one inch.

It is not that man has not strained every fibre of his being to do so; he has, in fact, made as many herculean attempts to discover viable social laws as he has to discover the secrets of the universe. The truth is that, hard as he may try to find a just basis for the laws governing his society, this will always elude him, for it is something which is beyond him to find. The limitations of the human mind prevent it from grappling successfully with the infinitude of facts which it would be necessary to apprehend and systematise if truly just and equitable laws were to be enacted. We are forced to come back to the tenet that there must be a Mind vastly superior to the human mind, which is the origin of all truth. We must likewise come back to the fact that revealed law is unsurpassable in the permanence of its justice.

## Notes

1. G.W. Paton, *A Textbook of Jurisprudence*.
2. W. Friedmann, *Legal Theory*, p. 18.
3. *The Muslim*, Islamabad, December 29, 1984.
4. *A Textbook of Jurisprudence*, p. 104.
5. *Early Law and Custom*, p. 5.
6. *Legal Theory*, p. 450.
7. Quran, 4:34.
8. *Time*, March 20, 1972, p. 28.
9. *Reader's Digest*, December 1957.
10. *The Hindustan Times*, 12 September, 1960.

11. See *A Textbook of Jurisprudence*, p. 15.
12. Sir Alfred Denning, *The Changing Law*, p. 103.
13. *Ibid*, pp. 117-18.

# The Life We Seek

Friedrich Engels (1820-1895), a close associate of Karl Marx, was known to the world as an atheist and a socialist. He held that 'first of all, man needs clothes to cover his body, food to fill his stomach; only then can he put his mind to philosophical and political matters.' Nowhere in this supposedly all-embracing dictum is God mentioned. But Engel's atheism was a late development in his life, a reaction to an early, unfavourable environment. As he grew older and more mature in intellect, he became more and more sceptical of the traditional forms of religion he had known in his youth. To a friend he wrote, "Every day I pray that the truth should be made plain to me. Ever since doubts have arisen within me, this prayer is perennially on my lips. I cannot accept your faith. As I am writing these lines, my heart is heavy and my eyes laden with tears; yet I feel that I have not been turned away from the gate. Hopefully, I will find God. Heart and soul, I yearn for a vision of Him. And, by my soul, do you know what this longing—this intense love—of mine amounts to? It is a manifestation of the holy spirit. Even if the Bible refutes my words a thousand times over, still I cannot accept its refutation."

Such was the longing for truth which welled up in Engels when he was young; yet he was unable to find fulfilment; disillusioned with conventional Christian religion, he became lost in economic and political philosophies. But, in truth, man has a much more fundamental need than these. First and foremost, he needs to know his own nature and the nature of the world he lives in, how he came into this world and what will happen to him after death. More than anything else, it is man's nature to seek answers to these questions. The world in which he lives is lacking in nothing; it lacks only the answers he seeks. The sun provides him with heat and light, but he does not know the sun's true nature, or why it has been put to his service. The wind is a source of life for man, but he is not able to stop the wind in its course and ask it what it is, and why it acts as it does. Man's own being stares him in the face, but he remains in the dark as to what he is, and why he has come into this world for. It is beyond the human mind to work out answers to these questions. Yet answers he must have. Not everyone puts these questions into words, but still they linger in the human soul, causing untold anguish and something welling up with such force that they lead to insanity.

What this longing stems from is an instinctive human consciousness of a Lord and Creator. Ingrained in the subconscious of every human being lies the thought: "God is my Lord; I am His servant." Everyone tacitly makes this covenant on coming into the world. The idea of a Lord and Creator—one who watches over and sustains creation—runs in the veins of every human being. Until he has found his Lord, man feels himself lost in a vacuum. William James (1842-1910), an American philosopher who was one of the founders of pragmatism, said that "faith is one of the forces by which men live, and the total absence of it means collapse."[1]

Subconsciously being aware of God, man wants more than anything to reach God. Above all else, he desires to hold firm to the Lord he knows in his heart he cannot do without. But the God he instinctively is aware of, has yet to appear before him. Only by entering into spiritual communion with God can this longing be truly satisfied. As for those who fail to find Him, they give expression to their emotions before some other false god. Every human being needs someone to turn to, someone to whom he can dedicate the finest feelings he has to offer.

On August 15, 1947, the Union Jack was lowered from Indian government buildings and the national flag hoisted in its place. On this occasion, the eyes of Indian nationalists were filled with tears. This was the moment of freedom they had longed for. In reality, they were doing obeisance to freedom; for that was what they had made their god. Now that they had attained freedom; it was as though they had actually found God. Their joy knew no bounds, for they had devoted the better part of their lives to the achievement of this end. The pattern is similar when national leaders visit the tomb of the 'father of the nation' and bow their heads in veneration. They imitate the actions of a man of religion when he bows low, then prostrates himself before his Lord. No different is the communist who slows his pace and lifts his hat in salute to Lenin as he passes by his Mausoleum. There is no one in this world who does not need to make someone his lord and master, even if he be only a figurehead. There has to be someone to whom he can dedicate himself and the very best that he has to offer.

But if one makes this offering to anyone other than God, one is indulging in polytheism and in the words of the Quran, one is doing a "great wrong." This paying of homage to false gods is what the Quran calls *zulm*. The word *zulm* actually means putting

something in the wrong place, somewhere that it is not meant to be. It would be like taking the lid of a vessel and attempting to use it as a cap. Turning, therefore, to anyone other than God to fill the psychological vacuum that every normal human being feels is also an instance of *zulm*. This is putting a right feeling in a wrong place; giving to others what should be given to God. To seek to lay everything one has at someone's feet is a natural instinct in man, and, initially, it finds expression in a natural way. To begin with, people turn to their true Lord and Master to satisfy their spiritual hunger, but then, under the influence of irreligious circumstances and environment, they begin to fill the inner vacuum from wrong sources.

In his early youth, philosopher Betrand Russell was fervently religious and regularly used to pray. In those days, his grandfather once asked him what his favourite prayer was. "I am tired of life and succumbing under the yoke of my sins," was young Russell's reply.

At that time, Russell worshipped God. But when he reached the age of twelve he gave up this practice. The company he kept, being predominantly antipathetic towards religious traditions and age-old values, turned Russell's mind away from these things. He died an atheist, having devoted the latter part of his life to mathematics and philosophy. In 1959, Russell was interviewed on the BBC by John Freeman, who asked him whether his enthusiasm for mathematics and philosophy had proved a satisfactory substitute for religious sentiments. "Yes indeed," Russell replied. "By the time I was forty, I have reached the stage of fulfilment which, according to Plato, one is able to receive from mathematics. The world I lived in was an eternal one, free from the restrictions of time. I received a contentment (peace) not unlike that associated with religion."

This great English thinker may have turned away from the worship of God, but he could not do without an object of worship. So he had to assign to mathematics and philosophy the place in his life that had previously been occupied by religion. Not only that, but he was forced to attribute to them qualities—

freedom from the restrictions of time and space, which can only be inherent in God. For, without these things, he could not have received the quasi-religious contentment, which he instinctively sought.

If an article were to appear in a newspaper proclaiming that the late Prime Minister of India, Jawaharlal Nehru, had been seen bowing down in worship as Muslims do in prayer, no one would believe it. Yet, on the last page of *The Hindustan Times* of October 3, 1963, there was a picture which showed Nehru doing just that. Here was Nehru with head inclined and hands on knees, in the very posture that Muslims adopt *ruku* during their regular prayers. The occasion was Mahatma Gandhi's birth anniversary, and the Indian Prime Minister was ritually paying homage to the father of the nation at the Gandhi Samadhi on the banks of the River Jamuna in Delhi.

Such things happen every day, all over the world. Millions of people, who do not believe in God or attach any weight to religion, can be seen bowing down before gods of their own making. In this way, they satisfy their inner urge to submit to somebody. Such events show conclusively that man has an innate need for an object of worship. No further proof of the existence of God is required: the very fact that man needs God proves that He exists. If man does not bow down before the real God, he has to bow down before other gods instead, for without a god there is no way the central vacuum of his nature can be filled.

But the matter does not end there. Those who take some thing or person other than God as their object of worship cannot ever find true fulfilment. They are just like a childless woman who cradles a plastic doll in her arms, trying to derive emotional satisfaction from it. However successful atheists may be, there come times in their lives when they are forced to reflect that there is more to life than they have ever been able to discover.

In 1935, twelve years before India's independence, Jawaharlal Nehru completed his autobiography while in prison. In the concluding chapter he wrote: "I have a feeling that a chapter of my life is over and another chapter will begin. What this is going to be I cannot clearly guess. The leaves of the book of life are closed."[2]

When the pages of the book of Nehru's life were reopened, it was his destiny to become the Prime Minister of the third largest country in the world. For nearly twenty years, he exercised power over a sixth of the world's population. But this accomplishment did not bring him satisfaction. At the very pinnacle of his career, he still felt that there were some pages of his life which were yet to be opened. The very questions that are rooted in the human intellect when one first comes into the world were still revolving in Nehru's mind when his life's story was nearing its close. In January 1964 a conference of orientalists, attended by 1200 delegates from India and abroad, was held in New Delhi. In the course of his address to them, Pandit Nehru said that being a politician, he found little time to think about life. Still, sometimes he was forced to wonder: what is this world? what is its purpose? what are we, and what are we doing here? He said that he felt convinced that there were powers that forged our destiny.[3]

Disillusionment of this nature is rooted in the souls of all those who have denied God. From time to time they become so involved in their worldly activities and temporal interests that they feel they are on the verge of fulfilment; but once they are extracted from their artificial environment, Truth begins to surge within them, reminding them of how far they are from true fulfilment and peace of mind.

Hearts which have not found God are bound to experience unease in this world. But their affliction does not stop there. Far from being confined to the short period of their lives on earth, it will remain with them forever. The world which awaits them is one of unending darkness, great waves of which strike at them here in this ephemeral world. In that world they will have absolutely nothing to fall back on; in this world they already feel something of that helplessness, as a warning of what is to come. In the life after death, terrible ordeals await those who have denied God. In this world mental unease gives them an inkling of those ordeals. The doubts which beset them on earth are like puffs of smoke from the Fire of Hell, which all those who denied God or worshipped false gods will enter after death. If they heed the warning, they will be able to save themselves from that awful doom. Imagine that a person's house catches fire while he lies asleep. A whiff of the smoke reaches him while the fire is in its early stages. If he is roused then, well and good; he will be able to save himself. But it will do him no good to become alert to the danger when the fire has already engulfed him, for then he is bound to perish. If only his senses had been sharper, he could have avoided the impending danger! Now that it has descended on him, there is nothing he can do to escape it. Will no one awaken while there is still time?

McGill University's Professor Michael Brecher has written a political biography of Jawaharlal Nehru. While preparing this book, he met Nehru several times. One of these meetings took place on June 13, 1956, during which he put to India's late Prime Minister the following question:

What constitutes a good society and the good life?

Nehru replied:

I believe in certain standards. Call them moral standards, call them what you like, spiritual standards. They are important in any individual and in any social group. And if they fade away, I think that all the material advancement you may have will lead to nothing worthwhile. How to maintain them I don't know; I mean to say, there is the religious approach. It seems to me rather a narrow approach with its forms and all kinds of ceremonials. And yet, I am not prepared to deny that approach... I think it's silly for a man to worship a stone but if a man is comforted by worshipping a stone why should I come in his way... so while I attach every considerable value to moral and spiritual standards, apart from religion as such, I don't quite know how one maintains them in modern life. It's a problem.[4]

Here we find an indication of a second predicament by

which modern man is surely afflicted. There has to be a certain standard of honesty in society if any civilized order is to be maintained. But once man has abandoned God, he is left baffled as to how the code of ethics so necessary to the smooth running of society is to be established. For hundreds of years, man has searched for an answer to this question and he has yet to find an answer. There are, of course, innumerable examples of well-intentioned attempts to bring moral upliftment to society. For instance, in an endeavour to improve relations between government officials and the public, one week of the year has been declared 'Courtesy week' and is supposedly observed. But when civil servants persist in their officious and high-handed demeanour, the ineffectiveness of this method becomes clear: obviously mere exhortations to be courteous are not sufficient actually to make people change their ways. With commendable moral rectitude, posters in railway stations all over the country proclaim that "Ticketless Travel is a Social Evil." There is a certain naive enthusiasm about railway authorities who hope to reverse their heavy losses through a poster campaign of this type, for posters really do nothing to prevent ticketless travel. If there is to be an end to such dishonesty, the impetus has to come from the public itself. Merely labelling ticketless travel a "social evil" will not set in motion any great measure of reform. Similar campaigns in the news media tell us that "Crime Does Not Pay." Yet crime figures all over the world continue their upward spiral. Clearly, worldly punishment is not enough to wean people away from criminal habits. Again, with great naivety, the walls of government buildings are pasted all over with posters which are meant to impress upon government employees the evils of corruption. "To Bribe and to Take Bribes is an Evil," they preach in a variety of languages. But inside the very walls proclaiming this message, bribery continues unabated. One is forced to the conclusion that government propaganda is in no way effective. Corruption continues to spread even as more and more posters are stuck on the walls. In railway compartments too we read: "The railways are national property. Damage to the Railways is

damage to the entire nation." This admonition is there for all to see, but that does not prevent people from running off with toilet mirrors and bulbs from compartments. Evidently the consideration of 'national' interests is not compelling enough to restrain people from the dogged pursuit of their own selfish interests. Those who wield power are no less offenders than the general public. On the one hand it is announced that the "use of public resources for private profit is a betrayal of the nation," while, on the other hand, we hear of massive national projects having to be abandoned because the funds meant to finance it are being siphoned off by those in positions of responsibility. Intensive efforts have been made to improve the morals of society, but the majority of these have been an abysmal failure, and national life has remained bereft of the ethical standards that are a prerequisite for true progress.

All this testifies to the drastic effect the denial of God had on human civilization. Placing this denial in scientific perspective, Fred Hoyle, in his book *The Intelligent Universe*, writes:

> The modern point of view that survival is all, has its roots in Darwin's theory of biological evolution through natural selection. Harsh as it may seem, this is an open charter for any form of opportunistic behaviour. Whenever it can be shown with reasonable plausibility that even cheating and murder would aid survival either of ourselves personally or

the community in which we happen to live, then orthodox logic enjoins us to adopt these practices, just because there is no morality except survival... Frankly, I am haunted by a conviction that the nihilistic philosophy which so-called educated opinion chose to adopt following the publication of *The Origin of Species* committed mankind to a course of automatic self-destruction. A Doomsday machine was then set ticking whether this situation is still retrievable, whether the machine can be stopped in some way is unclear (Foreword).

Without God to guide it, the wagon of humanity has gone off course and is stranded in a quagmire of its own making. Only by turning to God can it extricate itself from this sorry predicament. The true importance of religion must be acknowledged; only then can society build itself anew. On any other foundation, its walls are sure to crumble and fall.

Chester Bowles, former American Ambassador to India observes:

> In planning and promoting industrial growth, developing countries are confronted by a dual problem, both aspects of which are perplexing.
>
> "The first half of the problem is how to encourage the most efficient use of capital, raw materials, and skills which are immediately available. What are the needs? What are the priorities?
>
> "The second perplexing aspect of industrial development involved its impact on people and institutions. While industry must be stimulated to grow as fast as possible, we must be sure that it does not generate more evils than it eliminates. In Gandhiji's words, scientific truths and discoveries should cease to be the mere instruments of greed. The supreme consideration is man."[5]

We can sum up his ideas in these words: the masses constitute the actual environment which is necessary for the development programmes to be implemented. The necessary tools of progress—investment and technical expertise, etc.—cannot function effectively in a political and cultural vacuum.

Modern thinkers have found no solution to the problems of how this vacuum is to be

filled and how an environment is to be built up in which the public and government officials can work together to build society. Personal views clash with social concepts, and if God is left out of the picture, all attempts at human progress are doomed to failure, because they fall a prey to self-engendered contradictions. On a social level, the aim of the people is to build a peaceful, prosperous community, but at the same time they are unable to suppress the desire to seek material prosperity on a purely individual basis. Now if everyone is so inclined, society cannot prosper as a whole; no society can survive the stresses and strains of clashing personal interests. Far from working together in the interests of the community at large, self-seekers are at each other's throats, hot in pursuit of their own selfish ends.

Materialistic philosophies which propound one theory for society and quite another for the individual will inevitably render ineffective any attempts to improve society.

When the accepted aim of life is the attainment of material prosperity, people feel free to satisfy their desires as they please. But the world we live in is a finite one, full of limitations. Here it is impossible for each and every individual to satisfy his or her own urges without this having an adverse effect upon others. In consequence, when self-centered people set out ruthlessly to fulfil their desires, they become a source of trouble, even danger, to others. People who are obliged to live on low incomes frequently feel deprived vis-à-vis others and, therefore, deeply frustrated. All too often, they then take to satisfying their desires by dishonest means—theft, fraud, bribery and so on. In so doing, they may materially compensate for their low incomes, but they then place society in that very predicament in which they had initially found themselves. The ideal of personal happiness has a catastrophic effect upon the happiness of society as a whole.

In modern times, human society has been affected by a novel, and extremely alarming malaise—juvenile delinquency. We must ask ourselves how a child becomes a delinquent. Since this problem is peculiar to modern society, we must attribute it to circumstances which did not in the past exist. And if such circumstances now exist, it is because of present day preoccupation with material happiness to the detriment of law and order. Matrimony too is no longer the respected institution that it was. It all too often happens that newly-weds, after exhausting the initial pleasures of married bliss, become tired of seeing the same face and making the same physical contacts and, in order the better to satisfy their sexual desires, go out in search of other partners. Eventually, whatever survives of the material relationship deteriorates to the point where divorce becomes an ugly necessity. Society has to pay for such separations, for the children then are no better off than orphans. They are alone in the world. With neither father nor mother to turn to, such children are unable to take their true place in society. They grow up embittered and unchecked,—in effect, discarded by society. There is rarely any alternative for them but a life of crime. In his book, *The Changing Law*, Alfred Denning has laid the blame for child and adolescent crime fairly and squarely at the door of broken homes (p. 111). One infamous product of a broken home, who has recently aroused the morbid fascination of the public, is the notorious international criminal, Charles Sobhraj.

The root cause of the majority of the ills of modern life lies in personal philosophies and social aims being so often diametrically opposed to each other. What we call crime, corruption and all the other attendant evils are nothing other than the results of any given society's members setting their sights on material happiness. Whether individuals, groups or nations are concerned, the moment the goal in life becomes individual prosperity, the seeds of destruction are sown for the rest of humanity.

The insatiable lust for self-fulfilment leads to innumerable social evils: fornication, robbery, looting, fraudulence, kidnapping, treachery, terrorism, murder and, ultimately war. All these are the result of people pursuing their own happiness, come what may—and, inevitably, it is society that pays the price.

The only solution to this problem is for humanity to turn to its true purpose in life. The fact that materialism has given rise to such conflict between individual aims and social purpose clearly indicates that man's true goal in life is quite other. Rather than aim at worldly satisfactions, he should set himself to earning the approbation of his Creator in the life after death, for this is what man's purpose in life truly is. If he were to adopt this course, the individual and society would be able to progress in harmony with one another, for there would then be no confrontation between the two; the individuals who constitute society would then be working towards ends which did not clash with those of society as a whole, but which contributed positively to the general good. Making eternity one's goal results in harmony. The pursuit of false objectives can bring nothing but discord.

In modern times, amazing advances have been made in the fields of medicine and surgery, claims having been made that science is able to control all diseases, with perhaps the single exception of cancer. Yet as science discovers cures for ancient diseases, new and often more terrible diseases appear which have to be contended with. The latest scourge, AIDS (Acquired Immune Deficiency Syndrome) has so far defied all medical attempts to quell it. People who contract this disease are often dead within just a few weeks, and its spread has begun to strike terror into the hearts of western civilization. Because of its origins in the kind of unnatural homosexual practices which are abhorred and specifically prohibited by religion, people have begun to think of it as a form of divine retribution which spares no one.

"Be that as it may, there are other areas of physical and mental affliction for which science likewise cannot claim to have a cure. These fall under the broad heading of nervous ailments. What are these, and what is their origin? They, too, are essentially products of contradictions in modern societies. While all man's efforts have been concentrated on the care and healing of the part of the human body which is made up of salts, gases and minerals, scant attention has been paid to the part which consists of consciousness, will-power and desire. This science has failed to cultivate. So we have a situation in which the material part of man has outwardly flourished while, inwardly, the real human part of him has been allowed to fall into neglect.

Authorities in the U.S.A. estimate that in big cities, 80% of medical patients are those whose illnesses can be put down to psychic causation. Psychologists who have investigated the nature of these causes have found crime, depression, paranoia, jealousy, indecision, stress, greed, tension and boredom to be predominant among them. When one thinks about it, all these afflictions come from man's forsaking of God. When a person believes in God, he puts his trust in God; it is to God he turns in times of difficulty. He is able to overlook minor problems in life, because he is seeking the highest goal there is, and that is God. When he believes in God, man has the best motivation for doing good, and a sound basis for a strong moral character. "A great moving force," is what Sir William Osler called the force that comes from faith. So great it is, that it cannot be weighed on any apparatus or examined in any laboratory. A mind nourished by this force is a treasure-house of well-being and equilibrium, while ignorance of, or lack of access to this source of psychic strength can only lead to derangement. Psychologists have shown great intellectual prowess in investigating the cause of mental disease; but unfortunately for the afflicted millions, they have failed miserably in prescribing any cure. According to one Christian intellectual: "All that psychiatrists have done is show us, in minute detail, the ins and outs of the locks which close to us the gates of good health."

Modern society in its functioning is at cross purposes with itself. On the one hand, it does the maximum it can to provide man with the material comforts he requires in life. Yet, on the other hand, it has neglected man's spiritual needs, with the result that man has become little better than a tormented soul. With one hand it doles out medicine, while with the other it administers poison. An excerpt from an essay on God in Medical Practice, by the American physician and surgeon, Paul Earnest Adolph, provides us with interesting evidence in this regard:

> "Back in my medical school days I learned a basic materialistic concept of the changes which take place in body tissues as the result of injury. Studying sections of tissue under the microscope I perceived that, as a result of the various favourable influences which are brought to bear upon the tissues, satisfactory repair takes place. When I subsequently entered upon my career of hospital intern it was with a degree of confidence that I did so—confident that I understood injury and the healing process to the extent that I could be sure of a favourable outcome when the appropriate mechanical and medicinal factors for the promotion of healing were brought into play. I was soon to find out, however, that I had neglected to integrate into my concepts of medical science the most important element of all—GOD.
>
> One of my patients in the hospital during my internship was a grandmother in her early seventies with a fractured hip. I had seen her tissues respond favourably as I had compared the serial X-ray pictures. Indeed I had congratulated her on exceptionally rapid healing. She had now advanced through the wheel-chair stage into the use of crutches. The surgeon in charge of her case had indicated to me that she should be discharged from the hospital in twenty four hours to go back home, since he was fully satisfied with her prospects of early and complete recovery.
>
> It was Sunday. Her daughter came to the hospital to see her on her routine weekly visit, at which time I told her that she

could come the next day to take her mother home, for now she could walk with crutches. The daughter said nothing to me about her plans but went to talk to her mother. She told her mother that she had conferred with her husband and it had been decided that she could not be taken back into their home. Doubtless, arrangements could be made for her to go into an old people's home.

A few hours later, when I was called to the old lady's side as the intern on her case, she was showing general physical deterioration. Inside of twenty-four hours she died—not of her broken hip but of a broken heart, although in desperation we had utilized all emergency medical measures that might conceivably restore her to health.

Her broken hip bone had healed without a snag, but her broken heart had not. Despite all the favourable influences in vitamins, minerals and immobilization of the fracture that we had brought to bear upon her condition, she did not recover. To be sure, the bone ends had united and she had a strong hip, but she had not recovered. Why? The most important element needed in her recovery was not the vitamin, not the minerals, nor the splinting of her fracture. It was HOPE. When hope was gone, recovery failed.

This made a deep impression upon me, since it was accompanied by the conviction that this would never have been the outcome if this lady had known the God of hope the way I, as an earnest Christian knew Him."

From this incident, we can form an idea of the deep-rooted malaise of modern society. Although science and technology are progressing by leaps and bounds and are contributing magnificently to the physical well-being of man, there is a disastrously negative aspect to them in that they deny the existence of God.

In fact, the entire educational system has been geared to ridding people's minds of all thoughts of their Maker. While man's body receives more and more nourishment, his soul is gradually being killed. Materially, he is pampered; spiritually, he is starved.

The result of this is only too tragically evident in episodes such as the one related above. At the very moment that the surgeons had successfully joined together broken bones, the heart had broken for a lack of healing faith. Physical health may be restored, but spiritual death can carry one off to the grave.

It is this dichotomy that has proved to be the undoing of modern man. The image he projects is one of brazen flamboyance, but this is only an outer shell which masks his internal anguish. Outwardly, he struts peacock-like, preening himself in glamorous clothes, but inwardly he is bereft of peace and contentment. Luxurious mansions shelter his body, but

that pampered body of his, conceals a heart which is torn with misery. The lights of his cities twinkle and shine, but its streets are dark with crime and affliction. Rulers surround themselves with material splendour, but it is this very preoccupation with material gain that makes their governments hotbeds of intrigue and mistrust. We see grand projects conceived only to collapse because those charged with their execution are more concerned with self-aggrandisement than with the success of the task in hand. The Lord has provided man with an abundant spring of spiritual energy. But man has failed to nourish himself from it. Human life, inspite of all its material advances, lies consequently in ruins.

It is spiritual starvation which has reduced man to his present state of mental turmoil in which he constantly seeks to satisfy his desires. Man is in conflict with himself, and the resulting disasters are plain for all to see. Scholars with great expertise in this field are the first to admit that man's psychological ills stem from his abandonment of God. Carl Gustav Jung (1875-1960), the eminent Swiss psychiatrist, has this to say:

> During the past thirty years, people from all the civilized countries of the earth have consulted me. I have treated many hundreds of patients. Among all my patients in the second half of life—that is to say, over thirty five—there has not been one whose problem in the last resort was not that of finding a religious outlook on life. It is safe to say that every one of them fell ill because he had lost that which the living religions of every age have given to their followers, and none of them has been really healed who did not regain his religious outlook.[6]

Jung's verdict is conclusively reinforced by the words of the former president of the New York Academy of Science, A. Cressy Morrison:

> The richness of religious experience finds the soul of man and lifts him, step by step, until he feels the Divine presence. The instinctive cry of man, "God help me," is natural, and the crudest prayer lifts one closer to his Creator.

Reverence, generosity, nobility of character, morality, inspiration, and what may be called the Divine attributes, do not arise from atheism or negation, a surprising form of self-conceit which puts man in the place of God. Without faith, civilization would become bankrupt, order would become disorder, restraint and control would be lost, and evil would prevail. Let us then hold fast to our belief in a Supreme Intelligence, the love of God and the brotherhood of man, lifting ourselves closer to Him by doing His will as we know it and accepting the responsibility of believing we are, as His creation, worthy of His care."[7]

## Notes

1. Quoted by Dale Carnegie in his book, *How to Stop Worrying and Start Living*.
2. Nehru: *Autobiography*, New Delhi, p. 597.
3. *National Herald*, January 6, 1964.
4. *Nehru: A Political Biography*, London 1959, pp. 607-08.
5. *The Making of a Just Society*, pp. 68-69.
6. Quoted by C.A. Coulson in *Science and Christian Belief*, p. 110.
7. *Man Does Not Stand Alone*, p. 106.

# A Final Word

It is the force of gravity which keeps human beings standing upon the surface of the earth as opposed to flying up into outer space, likewise keeping our oceans in their massive troughs, keeping our life-sustaining atmosphere safely around us and, at the cosmic level, keeping such mighty objects as the earth and planets in their proper orbit around the sun. Yet, imagine what would happen if this force were to be shut off, just like a sudden power failure in a factory which brings all machinery to an unexpected halt. The earth would then be dragged through space towards the sun at a speed of 6,000 miles an hour. It would only be a matter of weeks before the earth would become a ball of all-consuming fire and not a trace of today's beautiful world would be left. There would be not the smallest vestige of life to be seen—not even so much as a speck of ash from all the multifarious forms of civilization that have taken so many centuries to evolve on earth. There would be no sign that even a planet of the size and nature of Mother Earth had once existed in the solar system. Imagine how utterly panic-stricken the human race would be if it were known that any such cataclysm were about to take place!

But there are events actually taking place in this world about which we should be in not just a state of anxiety, but of utter panic: every minute, at least one hundred deaths occur in this, our world. This means that, in one single day and night, no less than 150,000 people are leaving the world, never to return. Imagine—mortality rate of 150,000 per 24 hours! Yet no one seems stunned by this information, which becomes all the more disturbing when we consider that no one actually knows for certain who these hundred and fifty thousand souls will be. No one can say with certainty that he or she will not be on that list of those who are destined to leave this world the very next day. There is no one on this earth who is not living under the shadow of death. At any moment, the Hand of Fate may light upon one and sweep one away, irrevocably, from this life.

And where do they go—all these hosts of people who leave the world? In the preceding pages, an attempt has been made to provide an answer to this question: they are brought before the Lord of Creation, to be judged according to their deeds on earth. Death brings an end to their life on earth in order that their eternal life may commence. Whether their life after death is good or bad will depend upon how they have conducted themselves in this life. It will be their lot either to dwell in a state of total felicity, or to be afflicted forever by unspeakable torments. That time must inevitably come. There is absolutely nothing we can do to avert it. The best we can do is strive to avoid bringing down upon ourselves untold and everlasting agony.

What, then, is mankind waiting for? Isn't death's inevitability enough to jolt people out of their moral lethargy and bring them finally to their senses? Do people need any further incentive to mend their ways? Does not the thought that if they do not do so, they will be condemned to burn in Hellfire forever, have any impact upon their depravity? Think of it. When you die, and your loved ones come to place flowers on your grave, you yourself may already be suffering the severest and most agonizing punishment for your contumacy. Ponder over this. Is not this something to be feared?

What a day the Day of Judgement will be! The heavens and the earth will be turned upside down, and a new world will be formed in which truth will appear as truth, and falsehood as falsehood. No one will be allowed to remain in a state of self-delusion, nor will it be possible to delude others. All will be brought low before God: no one besides Him will have any power whatsoever. All matters will be judged on the basis of truth and no intercession will enable people to escape the outcome of their actions. All the fine phrases devised by man to distort the truth will be scattered to the winds. All the philosophies contrived by him to bolster his falsehood will be shown as hollow and without foundation. All his specious hopes will be exposed as empty and illusory. The power he wielded on earth will not help him there. The idols he bowed down to, will fail to respond. How utterly bereft of support will man be on that day. How totally destitute will he be, just when he needs something or someone to hold on to more than ever.

Now is the time for man to take heed, for, when the Hour comes, it will be too late to repent. Now is the time for him to contemplate his life as it actually is, for, on the Day of Reckoning, it will be too late to make amends. The path to the Lord is open before him, and he must free himself from the shackles of selfish desire in order to stride fearlessly along it. The Quran and the Hadith are there to guide his every footstep and he can do no better than follow the pattern set by God's Prophet.

If he is to prepare for the Last Day, now is the time. It is in this that his true success lies: in this lies the good life, the life that he seeks.

# Index

## A

Abraham, 33, 202
Abu Huraira, 178
Abu Jahal, 164
Abul Fazal, M., 165
Abu Sufyan, 164
Abu Talib, 162
Abu Umayyah, 162
Achilles, 116
Adam, 204
Adams, A.C., 102
Adolph, Paul Earnest, 271
Africa, 155, 156, 157, 169
Aisha, 166
Alexander, 174, 186
Ali, 162, 163
Ali, Abdullah Yusuf, 34
Allahabad, 210
Allen, Frank, 87, 107
America, 37, 75, 145, 174, 219
An Essay on the Principle of Population as it Affects the Future Improvement of Society, 175
Animal Biology, 62
Antioch, 181
Arab, 34, 155, 209
Arabia, 170, 177, 179, 180, 184, 189
Arabian peninsula, 180
Arabia, Saudi, 221
Arabic, 189, 193, 213
Arab world, 209
Arakan, 210
Arberry, Professor, 193
Arcadius, 185
Aristarchus of Samos, 207
Aristotle, 208
Armenia, 186
Asia, 183, 235, 236
Asia Minor, 182, 186
Asimov, Isaac, 93
Assam, 117
Augustine, Saint, 192
Austin, John, 232, 237
Australia, 97
Avars, 186

## B

Badr, 168

*Index* • 281

Baibakov, Nikoli, 236
Bangladesh, 210
Battle of Waterloo, 174
Beccaria, Cesare, 247
Beck, Dr. Bodog, 223
Bentley, 67
Berkeley, 190
Berman, Edgar, 245
Berthold, Prof. Fred, 239
Bible, 7, 139, 188, 190, 191, 192, 209, 213, 221, 224, 227, 229
Bible, the Quran and Science, 191, 213, 221, 224
Blacket, P.M., 220
Black Sea, 155, 156, 180, 186
Blake, 134
Blount, George Herbert, 46
Bohr Theory, 26, 78
Bonaparte, Napolean, 174
Book of Exodus, 188
Bowles, Chester, 266
Bracton, 253
Brahmaputra, 118
Breasted, James Henry, 31
Brecher, Michael, 263
Britain, 37, 127, 174, 233
British Museum, 104, 201
Broad, C.D., 146
Brown University, 147
Bucaille, Dr. Maurice, 191, 209, 213, 221, 224
Bukhari, 171
Bulgaria, 156
Burma, 210
Byzantine, 180, 185

## C

Cabades, 187
Caesar, 174, 185
Cairo, 188
Calendar, lunar, 32
Cambridge University, 227
Canada, 220
Capitalism, 39, 134
Carrel, Dr. Alexis, 54, 116, 153, 159, 240, 245
Carthage, 183
Caspian, 156
Caucasus, 156
Cave of Hira, 162
Chambers Encyclopaedia, 231
Chambers, Whittacker, 45
Changing Law, 256, 268
Chatagam, 210
Chaucer, Geoffrey, 189
China, 37, 117, 238
Chinese, 190
Chosroes II, 181, 183, 186, 187
Christianity, 16, 133, 170, 180, 182, 190
Christ, Jesus, 7, 202
Citizen, The, 220
Clearer Thinking, 55
Coke, Lord, 253
Colorado Agricultural College, 223
Columbus, 155
Communism, 18
Communist Manifesto, 18, 174
Comte, Auguste, 10
Conklin, Prof. Edwin, 105
Constantine, 180, 187
Constantinople, 182, 185, 187
Copernican theory, 45
Copernicus, 207
Cordoza, Justice, 247
Cornwall, 99
Crete, 156

Crookes, Sir William, 147
Crusades, 243

## D

Darwin, Charles, 12, 60, 141, 142, 241, 265
Darwinian theory, 195
Darwinism, 26, 63, 194
Das Kapital, 134
Dastgard, 186
David, 202
Davis, George Earl, 112
Decline and Fall of the Roman Empire, 180
Delaware, 248
Delhi, 261, 262
Democracy, 37, 174, 197, 199
Denning, Alfred, 268
Descartes, 69
Dihyah ibn Khalifah al Kalbi, 164
Dirac, Paul, 226
Ducasse, C.J., 145, 147
Duke of Wellington, 174
Dwyer, Gwynne, 176

## E

Eddington, Sir Arthur, 64, 241, 242
Egypt, 37, 156, 182, 186, 188, 205, 206, 250
Einstein, A., 226, 240
Einsteinian universe, 109
Empire State Building, 134
Encyclopaedia Britannica, 60, 197, 203, 214, 217
Encyclopaedia of Ignorance, 196
Engel, O.R. Von, 219
Engels, Friedrich, 18, 257
England, 97, 108, 144, 201, 227, 252, 253
Entropy, law of, 72, 73
Eudocia, 185
Euphrates, 180, 181
Europe, 117, 145, 156, 157, 169, 223, 234

## F

F.A.O., 176
Flammarion, Camille, 147
Fort Collins, 223
France, 37, 157
Freeman, John, 260
Freud, 15, 123, 124, 144
Friedmann, W., 233, 242
Fuller, L.L., 231

## G

Galbraith, John, 203
Gandhi, Mahatma, 261
Gandhi Samadhi, 261
Ganges, 210
Gaulle, General de, 37
Geography of the Flowering Plants, 219
Georgia, 235, 236
Germany, 174
Gibbon, Edward, 180, 182, 184, 185, 187
Goethe, 132
Good, Prof. Ronald, 219
Greece, 156
Growth of Law, the, 247
Gulf of Mexico, 211
Gupta, Samudra, 41
Guye, Charles Eugene, 107

## H

Haeckel, 111

Haegel, 137
Haldane, 62
Hales, Mathew, 139
Hamann, Cecil Boyce, 23, 24
Hannibal, 185
Hardy, 137
Harvard University, 245
Hathaway, Claude M., 51
Hebrew, 15
Heisenberg, 226
Heraclius, 181, 182, 183, 185, 187
Hijrah, 187
Hijri era, 32
Hilliard, Marion, 246
Hindustan Times, The, 128, 175, 261
Hira, 162
History of Western Philosophy, 201
Hitler, Adolf, 177
Hodgson, Dr. Richard, 147
Holland, 174
Homs, 164
Hoyle, Fred, 36, 105, 107, 195, 196, 265
Human Destiny, 108
Human Personality and its Survival of Bodily Death, 145
Hume, 10, 13, 226
Huxley, Julian, 9, 11, 13, 17
Hyksos, 206
Hyslop, Prof., 147

# I

Iberian Peninsula, 157
Ibn Abi Muayt, Uqbah, 165
Ibn-al Muqaffa, 172
Ibn Harith, Nadhr, 163
Ibn Hisham, 163
Ibn Rabia, Utba, 166
Ibn Rabiyah, Labid, 172
Ideal Prophet, The, 163
Idrisi, al, 155
Impact of Science on Society, 208
Imperial College, 220
Inayatullah Mashriqi, 227, 228
India, 37, 41, 155, 220, 254, 261, 262, 266
Indian Constitution, 254
Intelligent Universe, 105, 195, 265
Interpretation of Legal History, 247
Iraq, 182
Isaiah, 89
Islam and its Founder, 179
Italy, 157
Ivy, Dr. Andrew Conway, 111

# J

James I, King, 253
James, Lady, 227
James, William, 258
Jamuna, 210, 261
Jeans, Sir James, 45, 87, 106, 121, 142, 227, 228
Jeddah, 221
Jerusalem, 164, 181, 183
Joseph, 202, 205, 206, 207
Judaism, 16, 206
Jung, Carl Gustav, 274

# K

Kabah, 162, 165, 172
Kagan, Prof. Jerome, 245
Kamaluddin, Khwaja, 163
Kant, Immanuel, 139
Karakeram, 156
Keith, Sir Arthur, 46, 63

Kelvin, Lord, 132
Keningham, 130
Kessel, Edward Luther, 72
Khadija, 162, 168
King Abdul Aziz University, 221
Knovalov, Dr. Vladimir, 205
Kohler, 237
Kolet, Ezra, 206
Koran, 221
Krutch, Joseph Wood, 239

## L

Lane, E.W., 167
Lane-Poole, Stanley, 167
Langley Field, 51
Laplace, 12
Latin America, 250
Law in Quest of Itself, the, 231
law of entropy, 73
law of Entropy, 72
Leathes, Prof. J.B., 107
Lebanon, 156
Leitner, Dt., 165
Lenin, 18, 159, 259
Leverrier, U., 102
Life of Mahomet, the, 180
Life of Muhammad, the, 163
Limitations of Science, the, 66, 159
Linton, Ralph, 15
Lisbon, 117
Lodge, Sir Oliver, 147
Lombrozo, Ceasare, 147
London, 131, 196, 220
Loret, Prof., 188
Lull, R.S., 60, 201

## M

Madinah, 166, 168, 169, 178, 184
Mahomet, 187
Maine, Sir Henry, 238
Makkah, 160, 162, 163, 166, 167, 168
Malthus, Robert, 175, 176, 177
Man and the Universe, 60, 113
Mander, A.E., 55
Man Does Not Stand Alone, 47, 87, 106, 191
Man in the Modern World, 35
Man, Piltdown, 201
Man the Unknown, 240
Mark, 202
Marxism, 40
Marx, Karl, 40, 134, 174, 203, 257
Mary, 202
Mathematical Analysis of the Evolution Theory, 111
Matthew, 202
Maurice, 180, 181, 183
Mauz bin Jabal, 238
Maxwell, 132
McGill University, 263
Mediterranean, 155, 156, 211
Mendeleev, 99
Merneptah, 188
Mesopotamia, 186
Messiah, 202
Miles, T.R., 11, 35, 49, 119
Milky way, 77
Mill, John Stuart, 59, 71
Mississippi, 211
Missouri, 145
Modern Temper, the, 239
More, Dr. Keith, 220
Morrison, Cressy, 87, 97, 106
Moscow, 235, 236
Moscow University, 86
Moses, 188, 190, 205, 207
Mother Earth, 277

Mount Everest, 118
Mount Palomar, 75
Mount Safa, 163
Mughirah al Makhzum, 162
Muhammad, 160, 161, 162, 164, 166, 167, 170
Muhammad, His Life and Doctrines, 173
Muharram, 33, 34
Muir, Sir William, 168, 179
Mummies, the Royal, 188
Munich, 153, 177
Muslim Calendar, 32
Myers, F.W.H., 145, 147
Mysterious Universe, the, 45, 228, 239

## N

Naike, Bandara, 248
Napolean, 174
Napoleon, 136
National Advisory Committee on Aeronautics, 51
Necropolis, Tomb of the, 188
Nehru, Jawaharlal, 261, 263
Neptune, 102
New Delhi, 128, 175, 205, 206, 220
New Testament, 191, 202
Newton, Sir Issac, 92, 102, 225
New York, 10, 59, 128, 134, 274
Nile Valley, 181
Nineveh, 186
Noah, 7, 39
Nobel Prize, 116
North Pole, 93
Nouy, Le Comte Du, 108

## O

Organic Evolution, 201
Origin of Species, the, 60
Osler, Sir William, 270

## P

Pacific, 95
Page, Robert Morris, 50
Pakistan, 37
Palestine, 156
Panama, 250
Paris, 174
Park, Thomas David, 45, 98
Pasteur, 12
Patau, Professor, 194
Paton, G.W., 232, 237
Patriarch, 182, 183
Pauling, Dr. Carl Linus, 114
Pentateuch, 192
Persia, 181, 182, 184, 186, 187
Persian Gulf, 180
Peru, 238
Pharaoh, 188, 206
Philosophy of Law, the, 237
Phocas, Captain, 181, 183
Plato, 199, 234, 260
Plato's Apology, 130
Pluto, 76
Portugal, 117
Pound, Roscoe, 247
Princeton University, 105
Proletariat, 18, 134

## Q

Questions of Economy, 235
Quran, 238, 242, 243
Quraysh, 162, 164, 166, 167, 168
Qutb Minar, 41

Qutbuddin Abek, 41

# R

Radburch, Gustav, 233
Radio Munich, 153
Rajab, 33
Rameses II, 188
Reade, Winwood, 131, 132
Red Sea, 180, 188
Religion and the Scientific
   Outlook, 49
Renaissance, 244
Rex, Earl Chester, 45
Rome, 181, 183, 185, 234
Rosenberg, 133
Rousseau, 132, 197
Roxburgh, Ian, 226
Russell, Bertrand, 10, 134, 201,
   208, 240, 260
Russia, 40, 235

# S

Sackett, Dr. W.G., 223
Safar, 34, 35
Sain, 183
Sale, George, 34
Sassan, 186
Satan, 123
Saudi Arabia, 221
Science of Life, 59
Scipio, 185
Selection from the Quran, 167
Shakespeare, William, 189
Shaw, G.B., 137
Shensi, 117
Sicily, 157
Sidgwick, Mrs. Henry, 147
Simpson, G.G., 60
Sinai Peninsula, 205
Siroes, 186
Skinner, Prof. B.F., 244
Smith, Bosworth, 170
Smith, Elliot, 188
Smith, John Maynard, 196
Sobhraj, Charles, 268
Social Contract, 197
Society for Psychical Research,
   144
Solar Calendar, 32
Solar System, 26, 44, 45, 76, 77, 78,
   99, 102, 119, 216, 226, 241, 277
Solon, 234
South America, 219
Southern Atlantic, 174
South Pole, 93, 220
Soviet Union, 40, 235
Spain, 157
Spencer, Herbert, 136
Spinoza, 197
Sri Lanka, 248
Stalin, Joseph, 40, 235, 236
Stanford Research Institute, 45
St. Helena, Island of, 174
St. Louis, 145
Stobart, J.W.H., 179
Stoner, Peter W., 190
Strait of Gibraltar, 157, 211
Strobel, Fronter, 153
St. Sophia, 183
Suez, 156
Sullivan, J.W.N., 44, 66, 110, 132,
   159
Sun, 76, 77, 88, 90, 93
Syria, 156, 164, 182, 186

# T

Taif, 166
Taj Mahal, 75

Tauris, 187
Thaqif, 166
Thebes, 188
Tigris, River, 180, 186
Times of India, The, 205, 220
Toronto University, 220
Trebizond, 185
Turkey, 156

## U

Ukaz, 172
Umar, 169
Union Jack, 259
University of California, 190
U.N.O., 250
Uqba, 168
Urwah, 169
U.S.A., 96, 127, 145, 245, 255, 270
U.S. National Advisory Committee on Aeronautics, 51
U.S.S.R., 40, 235

## V

Vishnu, Lord, 41
Voltaire, 12, 136, 140

## W

Wallace, Alfred Russel, 147
Wegener, Alfred, 219
Well, H.G., 201
West Africa, 157
West Asia, 32
Whitehead, Alfred North, 92, 241
White, Morton, 96
Witness, 45
Wollaston, 173

## Y

Yahveh, 15
Yemen, 238

## Z

Zachariah, 182